ANCIENT INDIA AND ANCIENT CHINA
TRADE AND RELIGIOUS EXCHANGES
AD 1–600

Ancient India and Ancient China

Trade and Religious Exchanges

AD 1–600

Xinru Liu

DELHI
OXFORD UNIVERSITY PRESS
BOMBAY CALCUTTA MADRAS
1994

Oxford University Press, Walton Street, Oxford OX2 6DP

OXFORD NEW YORK
ATHENS AUCKLAND BANGKOK BOMBAY
CALCUTTA CAPE TOWN DAR ES SALAAM DELHI
FLORENCE HONG KONG ISTANBUL KARACHI
KUALA LUMPUR MADRAS MADRID MELBOURNE
MEXICO CITY NAIROBI PARIS SINGAPORE
TAIPEI TOKYO TORONTO
and associates in
BERLIN IBADAN

First published 1988
Oxford India Paperbacks 1994

ISBN 0 19 563587 6

Printed at Rekha Printers Pvt. Ltd., New Delhi 110020
and published by Neil O'Brien, Oxford University Press
YMCA Library Building, Jai Singh Road, New Delhi 110001

For my dear mother
and
my motherland

FOREWORD

This is a study of trans-continental trade during the first half of the first millennium A.D. The trade under discussion links commercial centres from the Mediterranean across India and central Asia to China, although the focus is on Sino-Indian trade. The items exchanged were essentially luxury goods, the predominant products being Chinese silk and Indian precious stones. This might in part explain why this trade has often been more romanticized than factually analysed, involving as it did the rather inaccessible oasis cities of central Asia.

Xinru Liu attempts to integrate various aspects of this trade such as the routes, the commercial centres, the items, the people involved in the exchange and their religious expression and observes the trade from the two foci of Indian and Chinese interests. The expansion of Buddhism from India through central Asia to China coincided with the growth of this trade. Inevitably therefore any historical study of this trade has to examine the possible links between the nature of Buddhist institutions and ritual and the broader commercial activity of the times. This examination is a major focus of the study.

This study is important both in itself, in terms of the analysis made by the author, as also because it is among the first few studies relating to early Indian history made by Chinese historians in recent decades. Access to both the Indian and the Chinese data enriches the quality of the research and one hopes that this effort at integrating data from two different cultural traditions will be continued in future studies.

New Delhi 1987   Romila Thapar

CONTENTS

Part III

MAPS (between pp. 106 and 107)

FIGURES (between pp. 106 and 107)

ACKNOWLEDGEMENTS

My first thanks are due to Dr Ludo Rocher and Dr Nathan Sivin for encouragement and intellectual guidance which prepared me to deal with two important ancient civilizations, and for their patient reading and critical comments of my first draft.

Dr Romila Thapar suggested focusing on trade as the key to exploring the connection between India and China. Her courses at the University of Pennsylvania during the spring of 1983 provided me with an entirely new perspective on ancient Indian history. In the last few years she has continually helped me, quickly answered my questions, and suggested new methods and approaches to the topic. Her warm encouragement and strict supervision made this work possible.

I am grateful for the help given by many other scholars. Dr Wilhelm Halbfass provided an incisive critique of the chapters dealing with Buddhist theology. Professor Chen Hongjin first guided me towards the field of Indian history. Dr Elfriede R. Knauer helped me with the western classical sources. I owe thanks also to Dr David Ludden, who, in addition to reading and criticizing my work, invited me to participate in the seminar for graduate students in South Asian history. Dr Victor Mair's vast knowledge of Sino-Indian relations equipped me with much specific information for this study. His comments have helped me avoid many detours. Dr Michael Meister kindly read one draft and provided me with the perspective of an art historian. Dr A. K. Narain also made many useful comments on the same draft. Dr Heather Peters helped me with the sections dealing with Chinese archaeology. Dr Gregory Possehl guided me through South Asian archaeological sources for this study and generously let me use his library. Dr Shereen Ratnagar from the Jawaharlal Nehru University guided my research on theoretical aspects of ancient trade. Dr Himanshu Ray from the same university read my draft and discussed many details with me. Dr David Utz pointed out important sources on Central Asian history. Professor Wang Ning-sheng provided important information on archaeological work in China. I thank them all.

I am deeply indebted to the whole faculty of the Oriental Studies Department, University of Pennsylvania, for admitting me as one of their first graduate students from the People's Republic of China and for supporting me financially. I owe particular thanks to Dr Allyn Rickett, who introduced me to the faculty and has always been concerned with my well-being in the US, and Dr Rosane Rocher, whose guidance and care helped me to overcome many difficulties.

During research in India many scholars helped me to use facilities there. Unable to name all of them, I shall mention only a few. Dr Chhaya Haesner from the National Museum, New Delhi, enabled me to examine textile samples from Central Asia. Miss P. Iyer, Director of the Central Antiquary Collection section of Purana Qila, and her assistant Mr B. S. Negi, as well as many of their assistants, not only helped me to examine pottery samples but also taught me much about Indian ceramics. In the Mathura State Museum the Director, Dr A. K. Srivastava, the Assistant Director, Ms Pushpa, and the Guide Lecturer, Mr Rajan Shukla, all spent a lot of time helping me with my research.

In the process of writing my dissertation I received warm encouragement and help from many of my fellow students, most of whom were busy finishing their own work. Special thanks are due to Christina Gilmartin who carefully proof-read and corrected mistakes in the draft. My friend Valerie Hansen shared her opinion with me at every step of the work and spent a tremendous amount of time in helping me to improve my writing. James Heitzman provided a serious critique of my work and kindly lent me the original copy of a map from his own work. Thanks are also due to Nancy Orton who generously let me use her unpublished paper on Red Polished Ware and provided detailed information about South Asian pottery; also to Angela Sheng who shared her knowledge of ancient Chinese textiles.

I also owe thanks to the American Association of University Women, the PEO International Scholarship Foundation, and the United Board of Christian Higher Education in Asia for financial aid—for my trip to the US and in the course of study at the University of Pennsylvania—and the American Institute of Indian Studies who sponsored my trip and research in India.

Note on Romanization

The orthography of proper names and concepts which originate in the Sanskrit, Pali and Prakrit languages follows the normal conventions of romanization without diacritical marks, except for italicized words, which are direct quotations from texts or inscriptions. The romanization of Chinese words follows Wade-Giles.

An Hsüan 安玄

An Shih-kao 安世高

Chang-che 長者

Chang Ch'ien 張騫

Chang Chün 張駿

Ch'ang-ma 長馬

Chao-hsüan 昭玄

Chieh-ch'a 羯又

Chien-fu-ts'ao 監福曹

chih 智

Chih Lou-chia-ch'ien 支婁迦讖

Chih-meng 智猛

Ch'in-shih-huang 秦始皇

Chu Fa-hu 竺法護

Ch'ü-hsien 朐縣

chü-shih 居士

Chung-kuo 中國

Empress Dowager Hu 胡太后

Emperor Hsiao-chuang 孝莊帝

Emperor Hsiao-wen 孝文帝

Emperor Hsiao-wu 孝武帝

Emperor Hsien-wen 獻文帝

Emperor Hsüan-wu	宣武帝
Emperor Kao-tsu	漢高祖
Emperor Ming of the Later Han	漢明帝
Emperor Ming of Wei	魏明帝
Emperor T'ai-wu	太武帝
Emperor Tao-wu	道武帝
Emperor Wen-ch'eng	文成帝
Emperor Wen of Wei	魏文帝
Emperor Wu of Chin	晉武帝
Emperor Wu of Han	漢武帝
Er-chu Chao	爾朱兆
Er-chu Jung	爾朱榮
Er-chu Shih-lung	爾朱世隆
Fa-hsien	法顯
Fa-hu	法護
Fa-kuo	法果
Fa-ta	法達
Fan Yeh	范曄
Feng Su-fu	馮素弗
Fo-t'o-yeh-she	佛陀耶舍
Fo-t'u-teng	佛圖澄
fu-t'u-hu	浮圖戶
Hsi-yu-tu-hu	西域都護
hsin	信

Names and Words Recorded in Chinese

Hsü Miao	徐嫩色	
	仁二	*jen*
Hsüan-tsang	玄奘	
	日逐	Jih-chu
hsün-lu	熏陸	
	高肇	Kao Chao
Hu-han-yeh	呼韓邪	
	葛洪	Ke Hung
hu-nu	胡奴	
	耿秉	Keng Chung
Hu-t'ung Monastery	胡統寺	
	怪其詭異	*kuai-ch'i-kuei-i*
Hui-shen	慧深	
	觀音	Kuan-yin
i	義	
	孔奮	K'ung Fen
i-i	邑我	
	孔望山	K'ung-wang-shan
i-chu	邑主	
	過所	*kuo-so*
i-lao	邑老	
	示坚	*li*
i-shih	邑師	
	李皓	Li Hao

liu-li	琉璃
Liu Pao	劉豹
Loyang Ch'ieh-lan Chi	洛陽伽藍記
Lü Kuang	呂光
ma-nao	瑪瑙
Ma-t'i Monastery	馬蹄寺
Man-i-ti	蠻夷邸
min	民
nung	農
Pan ch'ao	班超
Pan Ku	班固
Pan Yung	班勇
Ping-ling Monastery	炳靈寺
Prince Ying of Ch'u	楚王英
P'u-t'i-liu-chih	菩提流支
Seng-cheng	僧正
Seng-chih-hu	僧祇戶
Seng-chin-lü	僧祇律
Seng-chih-su	僧祇粟
Seng-ts'ao	僧曹
Sha-men-t'ung	沙門統
Shan-yü	單于
shih	市
shih-lou	市樓

NAMES AND WORDS RECORDED IN CHINESE

Romanization	Chinese	Romanization	Chinese
Shih Ch'ung	石崇	T'i-wei Po-li Ching	提謂波利經
Shih-hsien	師賢	t'ieh-chuan	鐵券
Shih Le	石勒	To-pao-fo	多寶佛
Shih-li-fang	室利房	Tou Hsien	竇憲
shui-ching	水精	Tou Ku	竇固
Ssu-i-kuan	四夷館	Ts'ang Tz'u	倉慈
su-ho	蘇合	Ts'ao Ts'ao	曹操
Sung Yün	宋雲	Tso Ssu	左思
T'an-ching	曇靖	Ts'ui Hao	崔浩
T'an-tu	曇度	Ts'ui Kuang	崔光
T'an-yao	曇曜	Tu Wei-na	都維那
Tao-cheng	道整	Tung-hai-miao	東海廟
Tao-jen-t'ung	道人統	Tz'u-shih	刺史

五行　　　　　*wu-hsing*

瑤光寺　　　　Yao-kuang Monastery

焉耆　　　　　Yen-ch'i

嚴佛調　　　　Yen Fo-t'iao

閻立本　　　　Yen Li-pen

陰陽　　　　　*yin-yang*

永寧寺　　　　Yung-ning Ssu

元琛　　　　　Yüan Chen

元顥　　　　　Yüan Hao

元暹　　　　　Yüan Hsien

元懌　　　　　Yüan I

願民　　　　　*yüan-min*

永明寺　　　　Yung-ming Monastery

王濟　　　　　Wang Chi

王充　　　　　Wang Ch'ung

王符　　　　　Wang Fu

王愷　　　　　Wang K'ai

王莽　　　　　Wang Mang

王肅　　　　　Wang Su

魏略　　　　　*Wei-lueh*

維摩詰　　　　Wei-mo-chieh

維那　　　　　*Wei-na*

魏收　　　　　Wei Shou

魏書　　　　　*Wei-shu*

文殊山　　　　Wen-shu-shan

五銖　　　　　*wu-chu*

Introduction

Ancient commercial traffic between India and China along the famous trans-Eurasian Silk Route, especially during the period before the sixth century AD, has not hitherto attracted sufficient attention. The relative paucity of material evidence on Sino-Indian trade, when compared to that on trade between the Mediterranean world and the East, may account for this neglect. Recent archaeological findings in South Asia, Central Asia and China have supplemented the body of available evidence, but not dramatically. Even though the volume of this exchange may not have been impressive its possible connection with another great change, the transmission of Buddhism from India to China, grants it great significance.

Since the last century scholars have constructed different models of Asian society; one of the most well-known is that of 'oriental despotism' based on the Asiatic Mode of Production (Wittfogel 1957). All such models, however, underestimate the role of urban centres in Asian civilization. Although the urban population in most parts of ancient India and China never exceeded a small proportion of the whole, and although most urban residents—e.g. merchants, artisans, servants and entertainers—generally made up a low social strata because they lacked the prestige linked to land, urban people had a significance which cannot be overlooked. They lived in proximity to political power, supplied the needs of the ruling élite, provided links to rural areas and foreign countries through handicraft and trade, and thus often controlled large amounts of wealth. Their importance in ancient societies far exceeded their number.

Commerce was one of the most important ancient urban activities. The word 'commerce' here, however, encompasses more than its modern denotation of a supply-and-demand market system. It includes various forms of transactions. Economic anthropologists have long debated whether or not the rules of classical economics based on the modern market system account for the patterns material transactions take in traditional societies.[1] Starting with Malinowski (1922), anthropologists have shown that ritual, religious and social considerations often outweighed material motives. In primitive societies the exchange of goods between people of different tribes, and in more advanced societies between élite families at times of weddings and funerals, illustrates this clearly. Other scholars have pointed out that ritual and religious activities also facilitated the production and distribution of property (e.g. Thapar 1978: 105ff.). Examining both commercial and religious transactions thus offers a new perspective on the study of ancient urban society.

Because Buddhism was the most active religion in the Kushan state (first–third centuries AD) and became the dominant religion in China in the period under study (first–sixth centuries AD), and because the transmission of Buddhism from India to China paralleled an active trade between the two countries, it would be logical to expect some connection, be it limited or extensive, between these two developments. To explore this connection I will examine the nature of Sino-Indian trade by analysing its environment and the commodities exchanged. I will then investigate the Buddhist role in encouraging this specific trade by surveying doctrinal and institutional developments in north India and north China during this period. It seems sensible to begin with the general political and economic conditions in north India and north China in the first and second centuries, when commercial contact between the two countries intensified.

The Kushan State and Roman Trade

The Kushan state extended across northern India and Central Asia, encompassing various ethnic and cultural groups of different lifestyles and subsisting at different levels of production. This unusual unification facilitated commercial, cultural and ideological trans-

---

[1] For the controversy between the Formalists and the Substantivists among economic anthropologists see Le Clair *et al.*, 1968: *Economic Anthropology*. The Formalists accept that economic theories are, partially or totally, applicable to non-Western, pre-modern societies, while the Substantivists insist that classical economic theories are products of the modern market system, applicable only to that system.

mission through a vast region, extending from East Asia to the borders of Europe. As a result, the Kushans attained a high level of achievement in handicraft manufacture and commerce.

Historians have debated several fundamental issues regarding this state, especially its chronology, the ethnic background of its rulers and its territorial extent. The chronological problem concerns the dating of the reign of Kanishka, the most famous Kushan king. Kanishka's reign provides a useful point of reference to ascertain the chronological changes of Kushan territory and the state's relations with other sovereignties, in particular the Shaka Kshatrapas in west India. At the first conference concerning the dating of Kanishka's reign held in London in 1913, scholars were divided between assigning 58 BC or AD 78 as the first year of Kanishka's rule (Whitehead 1968: 1–2). At the second conference held in London in 1960, which was attended by historians, archaeologists and art historians from Europe, South Asia and the US, opinions were divided between AD 78 and some fifty years later. In the words of A. L. Basham: 'It seems that it will never be finally elucidated unless some startling new evidence appears, and such may ultimately come to light, whether in Central Asia, Afghanistan, Pakistan or India.' (1968: xi). Although further discussion of the problem took place at the International Conference on the History, Archaeology and Culture of Central Asia in the Kushan period held in Dushanbe, USSR, in 1968, no solution was reached.

Also unresolved is the question of the Kushan national origin. It is generally accepted that the Kushan state was built by the Yüeh-chih people who were driven westwards out of Chinese Turkistan by the nomadic Hsiung-nu. Based on linguistic, literary and numismatic evidence, some scholars believe the ethnic background of the Yüeh-chih to be Turkish, while other scholars argue it was Mongolian or Iranian (Puri 1977: 2–3). Recently, authorities have begun to agree that the Yüeh-chih were Tocharian in Western accounts, Tushara or Tukhara in Indian accounts. Linguistically they were the eastern-most Indo-European speakers (Chattopadhyay 1975: 8–12; Narain 1981: 252).

As for the problem of territory, in *A Historical Atlas of South Asia* (1978) Schwartzberg cites the Kushan period as a particularly vexatious example of problems in mapping ancient states and introduces ten views of the Kushan territory (xxix, xxxiii). Using inscriptions, finds of coins and different literary sources, scholars continue to debate the extent of Kushan political power.

Fortunately, my objective here is to evaluate the Kushan role in unifying different cultures, especially in linking the Chinese and Indian civilizations, and not to resolve problems of political history. For my purpose it is sufficient to know that the Kushan state existed around the first to the third centuries AD in a vast area from the western part of Central Asia—Soviet Central Asia and Afghanistan—to north India, with its area of major dominance extending from Gandhara to Mathura (see Map 1).

Determining the methods adopted by Kushan rulers to control such a diverse region has proved difficult. Unlike the *Arthaśāstra* of the previous Mauryan period (321–181 BC), no work tells us about the administration of this period. Inscriptions have yielded skimpy pieces of information, such as the existence of *Kṣatrapa* and *Mahākṣatrapa* under the king. *Ksatrapa* was a title used by the Shakas, a people who entered north India before the Kushans. Under Kushan rule this might have been a designation of provincial governors (Chattopadhyay 1975: 115; Narain 1981: 265). Other titles were *Daṇḍanāyaka* and *Mahādaṇḍanāyaka*, to which scholars assign military, judicial or police functions, or define them as titles of feudatory chiefs. Narain (1981: 265) suggests that the *Ksatrapas* and *Daṇḍanāyakas* were officials in two parallel hierarchies of civil and military administration.

The lack of information concerning Kushan administration suggests that its state machinery was not as centralized as that of the Mauryan empire. The Kushans, however, inherited an important legacy from the Mauryas: the trunk routes built for administrative and commercial purposes across north India. The routes from Taxila to Pataliputra continued to be used throughout the post-Mauryan period and formed part of the commercial arteries of the Kushan state. Cities flourished along these trade routes. Architectural remains and coin deposits testify not only to a prosperous urban life but also to cultural and commercial links with outside regions, extending from the Mediterranean to China. In addition to collecting land revenue, the Kushan rulers' major administrative task was to control trade routes and commercial activities. Abundant standardized gold and silver coins provide solid evidence of the rulers' commercial endeavours (Narain 1981: 262).

There is no direct evidence concerning the revenue system of the Kushan government. Its control over the urban economy seems to have been based on handicraft and trade guilds. Guilds (*śreni, seni*) appear in Indian literature as early as the time of the Buddha, but information about their function in that period remains sketchy. During the early centuries AD many guilds appear in votive inscriptions as patrons of Buddhism and Jainism. More than sixty occupations are mentioned in the *Milindapañha* and *Mahāvastu*. The *Mahāvastu* shows that in important ceremonies, such as royal weddings, the king summoned his priets, his tutor, townsmen with their leaders at their head (*śreṣṭhipramukho naigamo*), the community of tradesmen with the caravan leader at their head (*sārthavāha pramukho vanijagrāmo*), and all the eighteen guilds (III, 161, 442). Contemporary literature, especially the law books, attests to the guilds' political and economic influence. The famous law-maker Manu advocates that the king should protect the guilds by punishing those who break their rules (VIII, 219). Guilds seem to be important social institutions with which the kings had to deal (Das 1925: 112; Adhya 1966: 86).

Religion was another important institution in regulating social life. The development of the Mahayana school in the early Christian era enlarged the number of Buddhist lay adherents. Jainism also attracted numerous disciples. Traders and guilds supported monasteries financially. An urban culture born in a community of merchants, artisans and Buddhist monasteries crystallized in the boom of Buddhist art and architecture during the Kushan period. Guilds and monasteries thus formed the most important institutions in Kushan cities.

Numismatic collections of this period underscore the cultural cosmopolitanism of the Kushan empire. Kujula Kadphises cast an image of the Buddha on his coins. His son, Wima Kadphises, preferred Siva instead. Both of them used bilingual legends in Greek and Prakrit. Although Kanishka used only the Greek script, his coins show deities of various religions and cultures: Siva, the Buddha, the Persian gods Oado and Atash, and the Sumerian goddess Nana (Sircar 1951: 147).[2] His successor Huvishka followed

---

[2] Scholars differ on the origin of Nana. K. Chakraberti agrees with Sircar in assigning Nana as the Sumero-Babylonian goddess Ishtar (1981: 46). Bhaskar Chattopadhyay considers her a rendition of the Persian goddess of creation (1967: 62).

the same practice, but Vasudeva limited the deities on his coins to Siva and Nana (Puri 1968: 136). Gold and copper coins with different legends and motifs circulated within and outside Kushan territory. The kings' coins both embodied state authority over the economy as well as performed their usual function as media of exchange. This diversity in motifs and legends suggests that the Kushan rulers adopted a liberal attitude towards religion in order to facilitate commercial exchange in their culturally diverse country and trade with other countries.[3] Under the early Kushan kings Kujula Kadphises and Wima Kadphises Kushan coins appear to have circulated only in the regions dominated by Buddhism or Brahmanism. As the Kushan territory and influence expanded, Kanishka's coins indicate that trade extended to regions of variegated cultures. The motifs and legends on Kanishka's coins testify not only to the king's religious tolerance but also to the wide circulation of his coins. Similarly, the reduction in the variety of coins after Huvishka may represent a contraction in circulation, and the quality of the coinage deteriorated simultaneously.

Despite the government's open-mindedness towards the depiction of various religious motifs on its coins, Buddhist monuments dominate urban centres and Buddhist Sanskrit literature dominates extant works from that period.

The Brahmanical tradition did not favour urban life even when cities started to flourish in the Ganges valley in the middle of the first millennium BC. By the early centuries AD the authors of *dharma* works exhibited more tolerance. Yet Manu still advised the king to regulate urban life by banishing bad elements, including 'men living by showing their proficiency in arts, and clever harlots', and 'those non-Aryans who disguise themselves as Aryans' (IX, 259). In Kushan cities alien rulers patronized both heterodox sects as well as Brahmans, and this surely could not have pleased the orthodox Brahmans. In contrast, Buddhist writers always made their homes in the cities. The *Milindapañha* praises a prostitute who shocked King Ashoka by making the Ganges flow backwards. She attained merit by treating all customers equally, despite their different caste origins (I, 183).

Both the Central Asian territory and north India experienced a

[3] The locations of coin finds are not indications of the extent of political control of a state because coins can spread through commercial channels.

period of urban prosperity under the Kushans. Excavations conducted by Soviet scholars reveal numerous town sites. Not only did cities flourish on the upper course of the Oxus, such as Termez and Samarkand, but also on the lower Oxus (Frumkin 1970: 90, 108–27). In north and central India many ancient cities developed further or expanded. Buddhist sculptures in the Gandhara region and Mathura city reflect many aspects of social and economic living. The clothing, toilet and human poses all represent a highly developed urban life. Literary sources corroborate this sophistication by mentioning many specific kinds of textiles, toilet items and precious stones. This life-style required a trade in luxury goods. Commercial activities in their turn provided further impetus for urbanization.

The Kushan empire certainly stimulated the inland trade in north India from Taxila to Varanasi. Meanwhile, Eurasian trade— with the Roman world, and from Central Asia to China—was more vital to its treasury than to those of previous Indian dynasties. The significance of the trade may be one of the reasons why, in spite of its cultural ties to India, the political centre of the Kushan empire remained within the north-west and the west Ganges area, and also why the political centre of the earlier Mauryan kingdom on the middle Ganges plain fell into relative oblivion during this period.

Trade between the Roman world and South Asia was carried on long before the Christian era, mainly through Arabian middlemen. Regular trade started in the reign of Augustus (27 BC–AD 15), when envoys from various states of India visited the Roman emperor (Warmington 1928: 36). The beginning of frequent direct exchanges between Rome and India stemmed from the discovery of the monsoon on the Arabian Sea by Hippalus in the first century AD. Whether Hippalus 'discovered' the monsoon or learned about it from the Arabs is unknown, as are his exact dates. For our purposes, however, the early first century AD is an accurate enough date to correlate the heightened Roman trade with urban development in north and central India.

Following the dissemination of knowledge of the monsoon, Egyptian-Greek ships crossed the Arabian Sea after leaving the Red Sea, then reached the seaports along the coast of India, from the mouth of the Indus to the Malabar coast. Port Barbaricon on the mouth of the Indus was connected with Punjab and Gandhara through the routes along the Indus. Barygaza, the most important port for Roman trade, was linked via Ujjain with Mathura, which controlled the trade on the Ganges plain and north-west India, and with the Deccan via the ancient routes passing through Sopara and Kaliyana along the coast, and which led south-east along the Godavari and Bhima valleys. From ports along the Malabar coast Roman ships often departed for South-East Asia.

To the two north-Indian ports of Barbaricon and Barygaza Roman traders brought gold and silver coins, silver wares, coral, wine, sweet clover and perhaps some more or less expensive perfume from Italy and other Mediterranean countries; glass, clothing and styrax from Egypt and other eastern provinces; more wine, chrysoliths (or topaz?), dates, antimony,[4] red orpiment[5] and frankincense from the Persian Gulf and Red Sea; and slaves and colourful girdles of no specific origin (Warmington 1928: 261–72; Schoff 1912: 167; *Periplus*: 28, 39, 49; Pliny: xxxii, 11).

Among the Roman exports sweet clover was the only one that, after being manufactured into chaplets in India, was traded back into the Roman empire (Warmington 1928: 266). Other products circulated in India at varying distances. Colourful girdles were probably for a local tribal people near Barygaza (Schoff 1912: 190). At Barbaricon, 'all cargoes are carried up the [Indus] river for the king.' (*Periplus*: 39). Expensive silver plates, slave musicians or pretty girls, the best quality wine, the finest cloth and choice perfume were sent to 'the king' from Barygaza (*Periplus*: 49). Gold and silver coins were exchanged at a profit for the local currency (*Periplus*: 49). Other commodities also reached Indian markets from Barygaza. Some commodities brought by Roman traders went north-west into China. Coral and glass were highly valued foreign goods in China in the first few centuries AD, although it is debatable how many genuine Roman glass vessels reached China. Two fragrances, frankincense and styrax, were available in China through Central Asia probably in the second and the third centuries AD.[6]

---

[4] An ingredient for ointment and eye tincture.

[5] A red sulphide of arsenic which was used as a cosmetic.

[6] *Hsün-lu*, recorded in *Wei-lüeh* as a product of Ta-ch'in (Roman empire), was frankincense (*SKC*: xxx, 861: Hirth 1885: 266ff.; *Chung-yao Ta-tz'u-tien* 1977:

From Barbaricon and Barygaza Roman traders carried away indigenous north- and west-Indian products such as indigo, ivory, cloth, onyx stones, myrrh and long pepper (Pliny: xxxvii, 23; Warmington 1928: 200; Watt 1908: 891; Schoff 1912: 73, 192; *Periplus*: 39, 48, 49). Other products came from the 'upper land': bdellium, cloth, lycium and spikenard native to the Himalayas, costus from Kashmir, turquoise from the Hindu Kush and lapis lazuli from Badakhshan (*Periplus*: 39, 48, 49; Miller 1969: 69, 84, 88; Schoff 1912: 168–70; Warmington 1928: 201, 255; Bernard 1978: 49).

Also shipped out of these two ports were Indian imports from Central Asia and China. 'Chinese skins', classified by Pliny as the most expensive animal hides, were very likely Central Asian products (Pliny: xxxiv, 41; xxxvii, 78). Silk yarn and silk cloth were mainly from China.

However, the heavy traffic along the coast and inland routes to the north-west did not leave as much material evidence of Roman trade as scholars had expected. Surprisingly few Roman coins have been discovered in the north-west, while hoards of Roman coins and vessels have been found in the south. This phenomenon has puzzled many historians. Wheeler proposes that the trade with the south was terminal; thus many items were deposited there. Because trade with the north linked a larger area, and because goods passed through this region to their destinations further north, little evidence of the trade remains. Wheeler supports this hypothesis with evidence from Begram—the royal city of the Kushan king Kadphises and the so-called 'summer palace' of later kings. Whereas excavations at Sirkap, the site occupied by the early Kushans who were contemporary with the *Periplus*, yielded few Roman items, phase II of Begram, assigned to Kanishka, produced a collection of exotic wares from the Mediterranean, India and China. Wheeler (1954: 163) suggests this collection represented a royal treasury that accumulated over 150 years. Those items were collected from traders passing through the region as a form of toll. Wheeler further supports his argument by pointing out that goods exported from the Indus were seldom indigenous (154).

Wheeler's hypothesis is plausible but not conclusive. Another

1379). Styrax was called *su-ho* in the *Hou-Han Shu* and *Wei-Lüeh* as products of Ta-ch'in—the Roman empire (*SKC*: xxx, 861; *HHS*: LXXXVIII, 2919; Hirth 1885: 263; Needham 1954: v, pt 2, 137).

argument is that Roman gold and silver coins became a highly valued currency in western and south India and thus survived as archaeological artifacts. B. D. Chattopadhyaya (1977: 104) suggests that the *suvarṇas* mentioned in a Nasik inscription of the period of Nahapaṅa (*c.* AD 119–24) referred to Roman gold coins. The inscription gives the relative value of the gold coins against the local silver coins (*kārṣāpaṇas*) as 35:1 (*EI*, viii: 82–3). Chattopadhyaya argues that the Roman coins imported through Barygaza were used as currency reserves and capital deposits because south India and western India under the Satavahanas did not have indigenous gold coinage (113–17). If Chattopadhyaya is right in asserting that Roman gold and silver coins were imported as currency, they could have easily flowed to the north along with other commodities imported through western India. Once they entered the domain of the monetary system in the north, where the standard of coinage reached unprecedented uniformity, the Kushan kings most likely melted down the foreign currency to make their own coins. In the south, where there was no gold coinage and where silver coins were rare, Roman coins came to supplement the local currency.

Other archaeological evidence, however limited, confirms a relationship between the Eurasian trade and urban prosperity in north-west India. The Taxila site, Sirkap, covered only a short phase of the Kushan occupation, but Marshall's excavations revealed rapid urban development in the century preceding the Kushan era. As B. N. Mukherjee (1970: 16) has suggested, the lucrative Eurasian trade motivated Wima to invade this region and enrich the Kushan state. During Kushan rule conflicts between Rome and Parthia, especially under the reign of Trajan (AD 98–117), made the route through the Indus and seaports of the west coast essential for Roman trade to Central and East Asia (Warmington 1928: 94–5). Also during the Kushan period, Indian kings cast for the first time gold coins according to the standard weight of the Roman aureus, perhaps in order to establish a gold standard for use in the Eurasian trade (Chattopadhyay 1975: 132; Dani 1969: 6).

However, difficulties stemming from the uncertainty of Kushan chronology and territory blur this harmonious picture of extensive trade routes. If Kanishka was a contemporary of Rudradaman, a Shaka Kshatrapa who occupied Gujarat and its vicinity in the first and second centuries and carried on a flourishing sea trade, then it is debatable how much control the Kushan kings had over the seaports. It is possible that the western Shakas became subordinated to Kushan kings (Puri 1965: 21–6). If so, the trade between the west coast and north-west India was unimpeded. However, this chronological problem may not be insurmountable. Indian exports from Barbaricon and Barygaza were mostly products of the 'high lands' which were all under the control of the Kushans. Both botanical products such as bdellium, spikenard and costus, native to the Himalayas or to Kashmir, and minerals such as turquoise and lapis lazuli, were only available from the core Kushan territory. Also under the control of the Kushans were Indian imports from Central Asia and China such as animal hides and silk products. As long as they controlled the rich resources eagerly sought by Roman traders, the Kushans could easily have obtained commodities brought in by Roman ships and could have benefited from the trade passing through their territory even if they did not have direct political control over the seaports.

With commodities passing through north-west India from three directions, the west, South Asia, and the Far East, and yet leaving few material traces in the region, how can we best assess the fundamental influence of the exchange? Wheeler (1954: 165) points out the clear western influence on Gandharan art. But here I want to emphasize the role of trade as a vanguard of religious transmission, of the propagation of Buddhism to China.

THE CHINESE PRESENCE IN CENTRAL ASIA

Chinese political influence had extended to Central Asia since the era of Emperor Wu of the Former Han dynasty, who sent Chang Ch'ien in 138 BC as an envoy to the Great Yüeh-chih to make an alliance against the Hsiung-nu. Although Chang Ch'ien failed to convince the Great Yüeh-chih to join the Han empire to fight the Hsiung-nu, he brought back much information about Central Asia and his trip initiated Chinese official activities in Central Asia. During the whole Former Han period (206 BC–AD 9) the government's struggle with the Hsiung-nu decided whether its policies towards Central Asian countries would be peaceful or confrontational.

Hsiung-nu conflicts with China dated to much earlier than the Han dynasty. Wang Kuo-wei identifies the Hsiung-nu as a people located in northern or north-western China. They had contact with Chinese civilization as early as the Shang and Chou dynasties (*c.* 1000 BC) and from then on continuously plundered the Chinese frontier (1959: 13/1a–12b). Around 200 BC, when the Han dynasty was just established, the Hsiung-nu were so rampant along the frontier that they surrounded the Emperor Kaŏ-tsu in P'ing-ch'eng (modern Ta-t'ung, Shansi) for seven days (*SC*: VII, 385). Yü Ying-shih explains these incessant raids of the Hsiung-nu as determined by their economic dependence on sedentary Chinese agricultural society; food and clothing constituted most of the payment they extracted from the Han government (1967: 41–2). Thomas J. Barfield suggests that the structure of the Hsiung-nu polity led to this economic dependence. As the head of a confederacy a *shan-yü* of the Hsiung-nu built his authority on wars against sedentary societies.[7] Gifts and bonuses from successful wars brought him prestige, and even failure in the battlefield gave him the power to command the otherwise quite autonomous tribes during the common endeavour. Barfield points out that the major items supplied by the Chinese—wine, grain and silk—were only enough to keep a *shan-yü's* court in style and not sufficient to meet the needs of the general populace (1981: 530). Thus the Chinese supply failed to transform the Hsiung-nu into a sedentary agricultural society. The Hsiung-nu harassed the frontier to press the Han court to supply goods, but these activities never led to large-scale invasion or occupation. Emperor Wu's ascent to the throne (140 BC) signalled a change from defence to offense in the Chinese attitude towards the Hsiung-nu.

The motivations for this change were multiple. Barfield argues that the rise of a Sinocentric ideology in the court prompted the emperor to undertake an aggressive policy, just as the policy of ensuring peace through bribery had stabilized the frontier (1981: 57). However, a Sinocentric ideology had always prevailed at the Han court, and the Hsiung-nu never ceased to attack the Han frontier even when the peace treaty was in effect. Barfield himself mentions that the Hsiung-nu incessantly plundered the frontier to demand more supplies. In fact Emperor Wu began his campaign just after a series of destructive invasions by the Hsiung-nu along Tai-chün and Yen-men (*HS*: VI, 170–6). It was not that earlier emperors of

---

[7] More precisely, a *shan-yü* built his authority by conducting wars against both sedentary and other nomadic tribes.

the Han dynasty did not want to get rid of the Hsiung-nu—they were simply unable to do so. By the time of Emperor Wu the Han empire had fully recovered from the post-Ch'in devastation. Hence the war against the Hsiung-nu was economically possible and even beneficial. Gradually accumulating greater wealth and military strength, the Han court was more and more enraged by increasing Hsiung-nu demands.

The Han war with the nomadic peoples quickly spread to Chinese Turkistan. Chang Ch'ien's information about Central Asia stimulated not only the emperor's ambition but also the court's curiosity. However, the war proved to be much more exhausting than Emperor Wu and his ministers had anticipated. It lasted almost through the whole reign of Emperor Wu (140–87 BC) up to the end of the Former Han, and resumed in AD 73 in the Later Han. It changed from what initially had been a confrontation of the Hsiung-nu with the Chinese army along the Han frontier to what became competition over the control of eastern Central Asia.

The Han empire never subjugated the Hsiung-nu. Whenever defeated in battle the pastoral tribes simply moved to another area and never considered retreat a failure. Even their final withdrawal to the north-west was due to a natural disaster rather than military defeat. But the Han generals did achieve some military gains in the war. First of all they extended the Han frontier from the Great Wall of Ch'in Shin-huang to Yü-men (Jade Gate, in modern Kansu). The colonization of new prefectures—Chang-yeh, Chiu-ch'üan, Tunhuang—sinicized the corridor running between the territory of the Hsiung-nu and the Ch'iang, a nomadic people based in the area of modern Ch'ing-hai, and paved the route to Central Asia. Secondly, with the acquisition of this new territory the Han empire became the dominant political force in the eastern part of Central Asia.

The shift from the Hsiung-nu to the Han dominance of Central Asia occurred during the expedition to Ferghana (101 BC). Ferghana was located at the very far western end of the 'Western Region' which fell within the area of the Han government's influence. The ostensible reason for this expedition was to gain a kind of divine horse for the Han emperor. Whether the blood-sweating horses had any practical use for the Han emperor is debatable. But because the horse held a religious significance (Waley: 1955) it became a symbol for Han influence in the Western Region. After the defeat of Ferghana the oasis states along the route all showed their respect to the Han by sending princes as hostages to the Han court (*HS*: XCVI, 3873). From then on the relationship between the Han and Central Asian states gradually changed from one-way gifts to the Hsiung-nu to a two-way exchange between the Chinese and the Hsiung-nu. But only after the disintegration of the Hsiung-nu, together with the surrender of the tribal chiefs Jih-chu (60 BC) and Hu-han-yeh (52 BC) was Han dominance over the Western Region established. From 60 BC the Western Region was under the rule of an administrative officer sent from the Han court—the Protector-General of the Western Frontier Regions (Hsi-Yü tu-hu).

During this protracted warfare in Central Asia, material exchanges between the Han and the Hsiung-nu and between the Han and the oasis states in Central Asia occurred constantly. The forms of exchange with the Hsiung-nu included supplying the goods stipulated in the peace treaty, opening border markets and smuggling. Border markets had existed long before the Han dynasty. The Hsiung-nu exchanged their pastoral surplus of horses and furs for agricultural products and luxury goods, mainly silk. They also smuggled some items forbidden by the Han government, such as iron and weapons.

Before the Han established dominance in Chinese Turkistan, envoys such as Chang Ch'ien journeyed to the oasis states carrying many gifts, such as cattle, sheep, gold, and silk worth a hundred billion cash (*SC*: 3168). Because of the dangers involved in the task, most envoys were from poor families; they often became rich after their missions (*SC*: CXXIII, 3171). Except for gold, silk was the most popular currency; envoys sometimes had to pay for their food in silk (3173). As the influence of the Han empire increased the oasis states had to provide free food and lodging to the Chinese envoys and to send tribute, including delicacies such as raisins, as well as precious stones, furs and other Central Asian specialities. But the Han emperors did reward them with silk and other Chinese goods as gifts.

In short, material exchanges with Central Asia in the Former Han dynasty were always subject to political pressures. The Former Han government was notorious for its suppression of merchants. It is true that emperors sometimes were enticed by the profit of trade. When Emperor Wu once heard from Chang Ch'ien about a possible short-cut to India through south-west China, he sent an expedition to open the route to obtain access to Indian rarities. But whenever there were financial difficulties the Han policy-makers blamed the merchants first. For example, those who advocated monopolizing salt and iron, a policy disadvantageous to merchants, based one of their arguments on the fiscal difficulties caused by the war with the Hsiung-nu (*Yent'ieh Lun*: 1/1a-b). However, once the routes were open the attractions of material and cultural exchange seemed irresistible.

The Han empire lost its dominance over the Central Asian oasis states during the civil war at the end of the Former Han dynasty. The Hsiung-nu immediately regained their influence over the Western Region. Even after the establishment of the Later Han (AD 25), China could not afford to interfere in the affairs in the region for about half a century. During this period, however, a serious drought on the Mongolian steppe caused the Hsiung-nu tribes to disintegrate. In AD 48 the Hsiung-nu split into two polities, the Northern and Southern Hsiung-nu. The Southern Hsiung-nu surrendered to the Han and became one of the minorities within the Han territory. They settled down and were gradually sinicized. Their relations with the Han government were not always peaceful, but differed from those of nomads who lived by raiding the sedentary society. Meanwhile, the Northern Hsiung-nu retreated northwest to the T'ien-shan range north of the Takla Makan desert.

With the Northern Hsiung-nu so far from the Han frontier, their conflicts with the Han empire were no longer a matter of plundering Chinese settlements and extracting gifts from the Han court. The Northern Hsiung-nu and the Chinese now fought for control of the Western Region. Trade or other forms of material exchange with the agricultural society continued to be necessary for the survival of the Hsiung-nu. Even after they had retreated to the north-west they sent envoys with tributes to negotiate a peace with the Han court (*HHS*: LXXXIX, 2945–8). In order to keep the Southern Hsiung-nu leaders' loyalty the Han court had to turn down these proposals. Denied this source of supply the Northern Hsiung-nu desperately vied with the Han empire to extort wealth from the oasis states.

Later Han campaigns in Central Asia began in AD 73, when the generals Tou Ku and Keng Chung routed the Northern Hsiung-nu, and when Pan Ch'ao first went to Central Asia as an envoy. Later Han military action in Central Asia was based on the territory colonized under the Former Han. From Wu-wei to Yü-men the Jade Gate, the corridor leading to the Western Region, was well-guarded and no longer threatened by Hsiung-nu raids. The military campaigns were much smaller in scope than those of the Former Han. The main interest of the Later Han in Central Asia was to keep the route to the Western Region and beyond clear. Actually no substantial new territory was added to the Han empire as a result of Central Asian warfare during the entire Later Han.

Here one must deviate briefly from the topic of Central Asian trade in order to discuss the Later Han empire's attitude towards commerce, because this attitude influenced its Central Asian policies. Unlike the Former Han government the Later Han rulers were lenient with merchants. As trade with Central Asia increased, the demand for special goods from the west developed among the ruling élite and the urban population. No doubt most of these goods such as coral, pearls, precious stones, exotic animals and fragrances, whether indigenous Central Asian products or imported from West or South Asia, ended up as tribute to the court during the Han; but various furs and woollen textiles reached markets of both high social levels and the common peple.

As early as the Former Han merchants in the capital, Ch'ang-an, sold all kinds of furs from Central Asia in their stores (*HS*: XCI, 3687; An Tso-chang 1979: 124). Merchants in the Later Han were anxious to acquire goods from Central Asia, so that when Pan Ch'ao attacked Yen Ch'i merchants comprised substantial parts of his force (*HHS*: XLVII, 1581). Pan Ch'ao's elder brother, the historian Pan Ku, asked Ch'ao to buy him some wool blankets and rugs. He also mentioned that Tou Hsien, an influential minister in the court, had purchased wool blankets, horses and styrax from the Western Region. They all paid with bolts of white silk (*Ch'üan Hou-Han Wen*: 25/4a). That the border markets continued to function even during the war suggests that there was a regular trade with Central Asians along the border (*SC*: CX, 2905). Even soldiers guarding the watch towers along the frontier engaged in trade (Yü Ying-shih 1967: 95). But these marginal commercial activities were inadequate to meet the needs of interior cities. The desire for western products

provided an important impetus for the Later Han's military involvement in Central Asia.

While the Han empire's interests in Central Asia were growing,
the oasis states scattered around the Takla Makan desert were caught
between the nomadic Hsiung-nu and the sedentary Han. In addition
to agriculture these oasis settlers also engaged in pastoral production,
such as raising horses and sheep. Because of low precipitation they
depended on melting snow from the T'ien-shan and K'un-lun
mountains to irrigate their land.

The ecological and economic conditions of the various oases
were quite similar but the settlements were isolated from each
other. Their similar self-sufficient economies stimulated little interest
in mutual trade (Lattimore 1951). Subject to both Indian and Chinese
influence from very early times, the different oasis states had
developed high civilizations but never managed to consolidate
into one political entity because of their lack of common interests.
Located on the major routes of migration, the oasis people were
used to changes of rulers. According to contemporaneous Chinese
historians, under the Hsiung-nu dominance not only were agricultural products extorted from them but they also were subjected to
large-scale enslavement and forced migration (*HHS*: LXXXVIII,
2909, 2928, *HS*: XCVI, 3872).

According to Chinese documents alliances with the Han empire
protected these rulers from the Hsiung-nu and brought prestige to
them. They also desired Chinese goods, especially silk. The dilemma
of the small oasis states was that once the Han government took
over it also demanded heavy exactions. The Han empire did not
tax them but required that its envoys and garrisons be provided
with food. The envoys often led delegations of several hundred
members, many of whom were interested in making a fortune for
themselves through trade. These oasis states also had to send soldiers
to assist the Chinese forces, as Pan Ch'ao often used their troops to
attack a rebellious state. Whereas the Hsiung-nu plundered the
oases and seized their residents as slaves, the Later Han, mani-
pulating politics of the Western Region by establishing or over-
throwing local rulers, enslaved war captives and sent them back to
the interior. Pan Ch'ao captured 15,000 slaves at one time in the
war against Yen-ch'i (*HHS*: XLVII, 1582). No wonder *hu-nu* (foreign
slaves) appear in many art works and historical records of the

Later Han. These facts do not bear out the statement of the Han official historian that the states of the Western Region preferred Chinese protection.

In spite of the unpopularity of Han government, Pan Ch'ao and his son Pan Yung managed to control the situation in the Western Region with a small expeditionary force, and Han influence there lasted to the end of the dynasty. To explain this military feat one must look into the nature of Later Han interference in Central Asia. Han military achievements derived from individual heroism and diplomatic manoeuvring, which was totally dependent on accurate information about the political situation. That Pan Ch'ao could mobilize traders to take part in battles suggests that they were closely attached to the Chinese authority. These traders with vested interests in this region must also have supplied information to the Chinese army. Pan Ch'ao and his followers, as I have noted, also engaged in trade. Although the Han court did not levy taxes on the region, the foreign goods Pan Ch'ao sent to the court as his contribution (*HHS* XLVII, 1583) were certainly one of the factors that convinced the Han government the war was worthwhile.

In short, the oasis countries, the Chinese soldiers and other individuals engaged in Central Asian trade, as well as the Han court and urban residents in Han China, all shared common interests: to protect the trade route and ensure the safe passage of commodities passing through the region. Thus 'messengers come and go every season and month, foreign traders and merchants knock on the gates of the great wall every day' (*HHS*: LXXXVIII, 2931). These common interests made the Central Asian states prefer Han suzerainty to that of the Hsiung-nu, in spite of similar exploitation and oppression. They also enticed the Han military force to stay in the Western Region despite the Hsiung-nu threat on the frontier having disappeared, and despite the constant opposition of many government ministers to engaging in large-scale fighting on account of the financial problems they caused.

THE SILK ROUTE

Scholars of the Roman period believed that the Han people were not enterprising merchants. Even if this judgement were true it does not follow that Han China was inactive in world-wide commercial ventures in the first few centuries AD. In addition to the Chinese demand for western rarities the Roman demand for Chinese silk stimulated the traffic through Central Asia and the Indian Ocean. Although western and Chinese scholars have conducted an extensive search, there is no evidence of direct trade between these two empires. To the disappointment of the Chinese court even the so-called Roman envoy from the emperor 'An-tun' (Antonius) in AD 166 brought only a few gifts, such as rhinoceros horns and turtle shells, which were not Roman products. According to the *Periplus* (39, 49) Roman merchants could obtain a regular supply of silk and furs from Barbaricon and Barygaza. This fact suggests that the main path of the Silk Route during the first two centuries AD coursed through Central Asia to the Indus valley. Going directly to the sea coast along the Indus or detouring through Mathura, it connected with the Roman world by sea.

The merchandise had to travel long distances. The discovery of the monsoon made the sea route the easiest way to avoid Persian competition as well as to avoid the longer route which followed the coast closely. Navigation risks, extreme transportation difficulties and political turmoil in Central Asia must have added greatly to the cost of the silk. What did the West use to pay for it? Where did Roman coins and commodities go?

As I said earlier, the paucity of traces of Roman trade in north-west India has long puzzled archaeologists and historians. Recently M. G Raschke (1978: 632) tried to explain away the scarcity of Roman coins with the argument that urbanization in the Kushan territory provided a good market for Roman manufactured products. Neither Raschke's hypothesis nor the hypothesis that Roman coins went into circulation—as argued by Chattopadhyaya—account for the lack of other Roman commodities in north-Indian sites. As Wheeler pointed out, excavations at Taxila and other sites yielded few Roman products. The Begram hoard of precious goods from China, India, Central Asia and the Roman empire was more like a royal treasury than a storage of commodities available in the market place. Even if we were to grant Wheeler's hypothesis that the destination of the Roman commodities was further east and that the deposit in the Kushan empire was only as a toll paid to the royal family, there is almost no evidence proving that most of these commodities actually reached China.

Very few Roman items of the period have been excavated in China. There is only one piece of solid evidence of Roman trade with China, a vase from a grave in Honan province, and Raschke (1978: 629–30) after examining it carefully decided that it belongs to a much later period. As for the glassware Stein found at the oasis sites in Central Asia, Raschke rejects them as Roman goods on the grounds that their low quality and large quantity would not have justified shipping them the long distance from the Roman empire (625–9).

It is not the purpose of this study to solve this problem in the history of West-East trade, but the controversy over Sino-Roman trade has inspired several interesting findings relating to ancient Sino-Indian trade. Archaeological remains often provide concrete evidence for the existence of certain historical phenomena but hardly exclude other possibilities. Excavations have been limited to India, China and Central Asia. John Marshall's twenty-year excavation in Taxila barely touched the Kushan site, Sirsukh. Excavations on other Kushan sites are even less extensive. Aurel Stein's survey of archaeological sites in Central Asia has not resulted in systematic excavation, nor to the dating of many important sites.

The cultural preferences of ancient peoples often make it impossible for us to know much about their material life. The practice of cremation in India eliminated much information that can be found in other countries. As for the Chinese interior, most archaeological efforts have concentrated on tomb excavations. After the Later Han, burial patterns underwent a change. Instead of burying bronze, jade, silk and other precious objects treasured by the dead, people fashioned rather elaborate murals, terracotta figurines, carts, houses and animals. It seems they sought to recreate comfortable living conditions for the dead in the next world rather than to actually provide artifacts. It is unsound to conclude, based on the limited material evidence from the tombs, that there were no imported glass vessels from the Roman world in China in that period.

The biases of excavators or surveyors also limits the reliability of archaeological information. When historians were interested primarily in communication between the occidental and oriental worlds, archaeologists working in the East tried to identify objects from the West. But the Silk Route was not simply one route from east to west. Its different extensions passed through many civilizations. Its extension to South Asia not only affected Roman trade but also connected India to China. Objects rejected as Western imports by archaeologists might well have been the product of trade between the two Asian countries.

Even though the distance between India and China was much shorter than that between Rome and China, there were many physical difficulties and dangers since this trade had to pass through various peoples. Even more risks derived from changing political and economic situations in India, China, Central Asia and even the Roman empire. After the disintegration of the Kushan empire the north-Indian political centre shifted back to the Middle Ganges plain. During the Gupta period (*c.* AD 300–550) a system developed of granting land by kings to their subordinates or religious sects and individuals. Landed property gained value. Archaeological excavations of the period reveal that the urban economy showed signs of decline (Thakur 1981). Similarly, China suffered a long period of disturbance after the Later Han dynasty. Many cities were burnt down and rebuilt, and the monetary economy virtually broke down. Under these adverse conditions could the trade between the two countries continue to prosper? If so, how did it survive these political and economic vicissitudes? To seek answers to these questions it becomes necessary to examine the nature of the trade in relation to other aspects of civilization, especially in relation to the transmission of Buddhism.

In the first part of this book I shall analyse the effect of major historical events on trade by tracing shifts in trade routes and changes in urban life in north India and north China through the first five centuries AD. I will then examine the exchange of important items to verify that the trade was carried out through the period under study, and to ascertain the nature and strength of the trade. In the second part an analysis of certain theological and institutional developments within Buddhism, and of the relationship between Buddhist monasteries and the laity, will demonstrate the influence of intensive commercial activities on religious theory and practice in the Kushan period. Finally, a study of Buddhist institutional expansion and ritual activities in the Northern Wei (AD 386–534) will show the significant role of Buddhist conceptions and institutions in stimulating Sino-Indian trade. In short, four historical processes—long-distance trade, urbanization, developments in Buddhist theology, and the spread of Buddhism to China—will be shown to have overlapped and depended on each other. As we shall see, long-distance trade was one important factor in sustaining the urban economy, even during the declining phase of urbanization, in both north India and north China. This trade stimulated theological and institutional developments in Buddhism, and these new elements in Buddhism in their turn gave a new impetus to trade.

Part i

CHAPTER 1: TRADE ROUTES AND CENTRES FROM THE FIRST TO THE EARLY SIXTH CENTURIES

In order to analyse Sino-Indian trade during the first few centuries AD it is necessary to focus on the location of the Silk Route in China and South Asia. My goal is not to provide conclusive maps of these routes, but rather to trace the development and decline of a few important centres. This is done in order to suggest the possible connections of changes in these centres with those in trade patterns, and then, more generally, with economic and political developments from the first to the sixth centuries.

The many maps of the Silk Route differ slightly in detail but share the same overall outlines. For the route east of Tunhuang geographers normally draw a simple line passing through Ch'ang-an to Loyang, in spite of the fact that the two cities were deserted for long periods in history (see Table 2). The middle section, showing two main routes between Tunhuang and Kashgar, is more or less similar. From Tunhuang the Silk Route bifurcated into a northern and southern route. The northern route ran through the oases between the northern edge of the Takla Makan desert and the Tienshan mountains. The southern route ran along the southern edge of the desert and the Kunlun mountains (see Map 1). Although the locations of the cities of these oasis states shifted over time, the outline of the two routes did not change significantly because the almost impenetrable Takla Makan desert and the snow mountains narrowed the traversible routes into two corridors. The routes to South Asia from the Pamir plateau were less stable.

SHIFT OF TRADE ROUTES IN NORTH INDIA

After the northern route and the southern route along the edges of the Takla Makan desert met at Kashgar, the Silk Route again split into two branches. The northern branch was an extension of the northern route along the Takla Makan. It ran through Kokand and Samarkand in the countries of Ferghana and Sogdiana,[1] and then westward to the Caspian Sea. Sogdian merchants who left the letters found by Aurel Stein in Chinese watchtowers near Tunhuang might have frequented this route on their trips to China. The fact that Sassanian silver-coin deposits in Chinese Turkistan are only found on the northern route, namely in Kucha, Turfan and Ulugh Art (Hsia Nai 1974: 93), also suggests that this route was the main artery to Persia. The southern branch went through modern Bactria and met the northern branch at Merv in Margiana.[2]

Bactra, as Wheeler suggested (1954: 156), was the node for the international trade. From the city, which stretched seven miles in circumference, a route ran through Kapisi and the Kabul valley to the core region of the Kushan empire, namely Purushapura, Pushkaravati and Taxila. From Taxila the Mauryan highway connected the north-west to Mathura and the Ganges plain, or to Ujjain and the Deccan. From Kashgar another route leading to the Kushan core region and north India passed through Gilgit in Kashmir. Kharoshthi inscriptions along the route are dated from the first century BC (Dani 1983: 92), and this route gained significance in a later period.

There is little literary evidence concerning the route from Kashgar to Bactria up to the Kushan period. When the Han envoy Chang Ch'ien first visited Bactria on his mission to the tribal Yüeh-chih (138–126 BC), that country was still under Greek rule. Pan Ch'ao's expedition (AD 76) ended at the Kashgar region. The route to the 'Western Region' described by Fan Yeh (AD 398–445) in the Chinese annals of the Later Han history stopped at Kashgar. The author was aware that the northern route in Chinese Turkistan went through the countries of Ferghana and Sogdiana, and the southern route led to the country of the Great Yüeh-chih, i.e. to the Kushan state (*HHS*: LXXXVIII, 2914).

Archaeological evidence is more helpful in determining the route between Kashgar and Bactria. Excavations by the Soviet archaeologists reveal many Kushan sites upstream of the Amu Darya, presumably along the route leading from Kashgar to Bactria. Near the city of Termez in modern Uzbekistan the famous relief

[1] Modern Kirgiziya, north Tadzhikistan, and Uzbekistan of the Soviet Union.
[2] Modern Turkmenistan in the Soviet Union.

sculpture of Airtam in limestone shows Gandharan influences (Frumkin 1970: 110). In the same region the huge Buddhist monastery at the site of Karatepe, dated to the second–fourth centuries AD, was hewn out of rock in a style characteristically Indian though unique to Soviet Central Asia. Across the border in Afghanistan there is a similar rock monastery in Haibak of a slightly later period (111). Inscriptions in Brahmi and Kharoshthi scripts found in the monastery in Karatepe also resemble those of the Gandhara and Afghanistan sites (111–13). A little to the east, in the Kafirnigan valley, near its confluence with the Amu Darya, a typical Bactrian town next to modern Mikoyanabad contains ceramic ware that is analogous with Begram, the site of the city Kapisi (68). Further east in the Vakhsh valley, the Kushan site of Yavan yields seals and vessels of the Taxila type (63). These similarities in ceramic types demonstrate that consistent contact existed between these cities. On another site, the Kafyr-kala fortress, a document written in Brahmi script on birch bark appears among other Kushan remains (66). The fact that the Indian script was written on the typical Central Asian medium indicates the Brahmi script was commonly used in this region.

These sites, like many in Central Asia, were depopulated from the fourth to the fifth centuries AD (Frumkin 1970: 52). When the Chinese Buddhist monk Fa-hsien travelled to South Asia in the fifth century he took a short cut south through the Pamir plateau to the Gandhara region (857c–158a, see Map 6). This change of route suggests that the Bactria region might have temporarily lost its nodal function because of the pressure of Sassanians, and the subsequent damage done by the Hephthalites or White Huns.

The *Periplus* described the routes from Bactria to the south clearly: from the cities up in the north—Poclais (Pushkaravati), Gandarei (Gandhara), Cabolitic (Kabul)—merchants brought down the commodities sought by Roman traders to Ozene (Ujjain), the hinterland city of Barygaza (47, 48, 49). Excavations in Ujjain are too limited to demonstrate the city's role in the Roman trade, but remains of a bead industry there verify the existence of export trade to the West (*IAR* 1957–8: 34). A few excavations in Mathura have unearthed lapis lazuli which suggests contact with Central Asia (*IAR* 1954–5: 16). Because the only possible source of lapis lazuli was Badakhshan in north-east Afghanistan (Bernard 1978: 49), a trade network must have existed to bring the mineral to Mathura. An ivory comb found in Taxila is similar to one from Begram, and both were probably of Mathura origin (Ghosh: 1947–8: 80). Cultural contact between Begram and Mathura has been well established by Hackin's comparative study of the sculptures of the sites (1954: Figures 466–630). J.E. van Lohuizen-de Leeuw's recent work (1972) emphasizes Mathura's influence on Gandharan art. This unprecedented cultural assimilation was facilitated by frequent exchanges.

The *Periplus* does not give information on the connection between the upper Indus region and the Indus port of Barbaricon, but the exports from Barbaricon are revealing: lapis lazuli, Seric skins and silk yarn, among other commodities from the north-west. It is also worth noting that although the Chinese had only vague ideas about the Roman empire they knew that Roman merchants conducted a highly profitable trade with Persians and Indians through 'sea markets' (*HHS*: LXXXVIII, 29.19).

As I have mentioned in the introduction, the Kushan state might not have directly controlled the western coast but it controlled the major resources of the trade with the Roman world, i.e. the products from north-west India, Central Asia and China. Archaeological finds showing the distribution of Kushan coins also demonstrate the existence of an extensive commercial network in the Kushan state (see Map 2). The Kushans were the first rulers in Indian history to cast gold coins. Kushan coins, uniform in standard, have been found over a large continuous area from the Amu Darya to the east Ganges. However, few deposits appear along the trade routes connecting Mathura to the Gulf of Cambay and the lower Indus region, the area under the Shaka Kshatrapas. Given the fact that the Kushans exported many goods highly demanded in Roman markets it is not surprising that they did not spend much cash in western India. Curiously, large quantities of Kushan coins, including imitations, are found along the east coast in Orissa. At Sisupal Garh shards of Red Polished Ware (hereafter RPW) incised with marks of the *svastika* and graffiti are found along with Kushan coins (seen in the Central Antiquary Collection, Section Purana Qila, Delhi). As RPW originated from Gujarat it is possible that those incised wares and Kushan coins were brought via the sea route from the lower Indus region (see Map 2 and Map 4). The graffiti may be traders' marks. The distribution of Roman coins along the east coast from south India (Wheeler 1954: 138, Figure 16) also suggests that this region was connected with other parts of India through sea routes. The distribution of coins shows a commercial network not only encompassing the vast region from Central Asia to the western Gangetic plain but also extending beyond Kushan territory along international trade routes.

An analysis of the distribution of ceramic ware during the early Christian era can improve our understanding of the network of commercial activities within the Kushan state and with its neighbouring countries. Because ceramic ware provides an index of exchanges at basic levels involving migration and the trade of staple goods, the distribution of pottery supplies information about the economic framework underlying monetary exchange. Unlike the Mauryan period, when the major characteristic ceramic was Northern Black Polished Ware, there is no one uniform ceramic type for the Kushan period. Pottery deposits from the post-Mauryan period show great diversity in texture, typology and motifs. Some outstanding ceramics, such as the painted ware of Rang Mahal in modern Rajasthan, resembles only the ceramics in a few sites of Sind (Rydh 1959: 143–6). But in north India two trends are obvious: one is the typological influence of an élite pottery developed in the north-west (Sharma, G.R. 1968: 30–6), and the other is the spread of the Red Polished Ware that originated in Gujarat (Orton 1983). Both types have been found only in small quantities outside their original areas.

A distinguished typological tradition developed in the north-west in the early Christian era after absorbing influences from Greek, Roman and Parthian vessels (see Figure 1). But no uniformity of ceramic texture characterized the tradition. Some of the north-western types travelled to the Ganges and western India without altering the original texture of local pottery (see Map 3).

The Red Polished Ware, on the contrary, is much more uniform in texture (see Figure 2 for representative types). It is considered closely related to the Roman trade because it was distributed widely along the west and east coasts of India, and as far as the Persian Gulf (Whitehouse and Williamson 1973: 39). This pottery also extended to the Indus-Ganges divide and the Ganges plain (see Map 4).

Both the north-west tradition and the RPW reflect foreign influences on Indian ceramics. These met on the Ganges plain and the western coast of India. In many RPW sites the mutual influence of the two traditions is so overwhelming that it is hard to tell between the two.

If the spread of the Northern Black Polished Ware in the Mauryan period can be seen as the spread of a cultural pattern based on a certain level of technology following migration and the extension of administrative power, so too can the dispersion of ceramic types of the Kushan period be interpreted as an indication of commercial and cultural contact at higher social levels. For example, a very specific vessel type, the 'sprinkler', spread from western India to the Ganges plain and up to Akhnur, Jammu (see Figure 2 (a) and Map 5). This is a bottle with a spout and long neck; the mouth of the neck is perforated. Unable to conceive of any practical use for the bottles, scholars suspect that it has had some function in Buddhist ceremonies (Rydh 1959: 141). Traders and monks who travelled great distances might have transported this impractical pottery type. Of the pottery from Kushan levels, many of them, either coarse or fine, either gray or red, bear the impression of stamps. The motifs of these stamps are Buddhist symbols such as the *svastika* and *triratna*, or animals, trees and floral designs (Appendix III). The lack of uniformity of a basic ceramic pattern and the spread of a few luxurious types and symbols indicate that the commercial networks of the Kushan state did not organize the trade of staple goods necessary for daily life and production on an empire-wide scale. This network, instead, established a cultural contact through trade of luxury goods that were essential to urban culture and religious practices.

The cultural and commercial contact between the north-west region and western India, represented by the spread of the RPW and the north-western ceramic types, is also reflected in votive inscriptions. Kushan inscriptions in Sanchi verify the Kushan patronage of Buddhism there (Marshall 1940: 386). Sanchi's connection with Ujjain is obvious from the numerous Ujjaini votive inscriptions in Sanchi, and Ujjain's connection with the port of Barygaza is pointed out in the *Periplus*. Kushan inscriptions in the delta region of Sind also show that the power of the Kushans reached very close to the sea (Dani 1969: 14).

Did the links between the north-west region and western India continue after the Kushan period? From the third to the fourth centuries a series of political changes in Asia and Europe disturbed the trade network connecting China and the West through the western–north-western Indian routes. China remained divided for three centuries after the fall of the Han empire (AD 220), except over a short period of unification under the Chin (AD 280–316); the Byzantine empire broke away from Rome (AD 395); and the Kushan state fell prey to the Hephthalites (fourth century). The desertion of cities along the Amu Darya might have been a result of these political changes. Since these cities were located on the main trade route from China to India in the earlier period, their decline could have affected the trade passing through that region.

Despite the harmful impact of these political changes on communications, the Chinese improved their knowledge about the routes to the West at this time. *Wei-lüeh*, an outline of Wei history, mentions three great states that controlled the Southern Route: Shan-shan (Charklik), Khotan and Kushan. Kashmir, Bactria, Kabul and India were all under the control of the Kushan state (*SKC*: xxx, 859). *Wei-shu*, the official history of the Northern Wei dynasty (AD 386–557), describes the Southern Route as originating in Kashgar and extending south-westwards across the Pamir plateau to Bolor in Kashmir. The Chinese pilgrim Fa-hsien did not follow this route exactly in his trip (AD 404–14) (*WS*: CII, 2261, see Map 6). Instead, he passed through a city called Chieh-ch'a, which has not yet been identified, where a large Buddhist ceremony took place. Monks from many places went to this city on the Pamir plateau to participate in the ceremony; the king and his officials donated many precious goods to the monks (*FH*: 857c). Thus, this city must have been on the major route to Kashmir. From there Fa-hsien turned west to the old Kushan central region along the Indus. This short-cut, studied by A. K. Narain (1957: 135), has been verified by recent archaeological surveys. In the region, which is traversed by the modern Karakorum highway, many rock carvings and inscriptions in Kharoshthi, Brahmi and Chinese show that this was an artery of communication for centuries (Dani 1981, 1983). A Chinese inscription of an ambassador from the Great Wei might have been left by Sung Yün, the Northern Wei pilgrim (Dani 1981: 11).

Chih-meng, a pilgrim contemporary of Fa-hsien, went along

with his companions to India through Kashmir. According to Chih-meng monks in Kashmir often visited the Charchan river on the southern route in Chinese Turkistan (*KSC*: III 343b). It seems that by the fifth or the sixth century there were two routes into India from the southern route of Central Asia. One followed the Kashmir valley, the other passed through the later Kushan core region along the Indus river.

The accounts of Hsüan-tsang, the Chinese pilgrim who travelled in India in the seventh century, provide a reference to the change of route in the earlier centuries under study. Although he did not always follow the major routes, making many detours in order to visit all the important Buddhist holy places, his descriptions of the urban centres give a clue to the major trade routes of his time. His accounts of Afghanistan and north-west India correspond to the archaeological evidence: Taxila (Beal 1906: I, 137), Purushapura (I, 98) and Udayana (I, 120) were all in ruins. Bactra was strongly fortified but thinly populated (I, 43, 44). However, among the many not very cultivated peoples of this region a few cities had developed. Srinagari, the capital of Kashmir, prospered, confirming the traffic through Kashmir (I, 148).

These records suggest that although the Hephthalite invasions of the fourth and fifth centuries might have caused a decline in the urban centres in Bactria and along the Amu Darya, communications between India and China continued and might even have improved. The route may have deviated slightly from the earlier one along the Amu Darya. Even though the Hephthalites were blamed for the destruction of Kushan cities, their exact impact on communications in north-west India is not clear. For example, silver coins found in the monasteries of Taxila—Dharmarajika (Marshall 1951: I, 289), Bhamala (396) and Lalchak (388)—show that the white Huns may have encouraged trade.

If the white Huns did not cut off communications between India and China, did the division of the Roman empire and the rise of Gupta power change the trade routes of South Asia? The Indian literature of the Gupta period testifies to the prosperity of the Ujjain region and its connection with trade. Many plays have Ujjain as their setting. Kalidasa praises Ujjain as 'a brilliant portion of heaven, brought down by the surplus merit of those who had lived in heaven and came down because the fruit of their virtuous deeds had run short.' (*MD*: 30). Ujjain's prosperity enjoyed such a reputation in Kalidasa's time that it was considered better than any place on earth, only slightly worse than heaven. Vidisha was also a capital city famous throughout the world (24). In the *Mrcchakatika* Vidushaka, the companion of Ujjain's leading merchant Carudatta, amazed by the wealth in the house of Vasantasena the courtesan, asks her: 'Girl, have you any vessels going abroad?' (168–9). *Mrcchakatika* dates from the fifth to the eighth centuries. Excavations at Ujjain show the occupation of the city continued until the Muslims occupied this region (*IRA* 1956–7: 27). Ujjain was an important centre for mathematics, and probably other scientific thinking, as its location was the meridian for calculating astronomical positions in the Gupta period (Winter 1975: 153).

Inscriptions of the period show that the Gupta kings, Samudragupta, Chandragupta II and Skandagupta, were all interested in controlling the Saurashtra coast. Based on these inscriptions H. Chakraborti suggests that the region around Barygaza was still commercially active in Gupta times (1978: 101–3). Barygaza continued to be occupied until the seventh to the eighth centuries (*IAR* 1959–60: 19). According to Hsüan-tsang seaports on the west coast were still flourishing by the early seventh century. The cities of Kacha (Bharukaccha, Barygaza, Beal 1906: II, 266), Valabhi (II, 266), Surashtra (II, 277), and Kacheshvara on the Indus (II, 266), had many rich merchants and precious goods. Similarly, the hinterland cities of those ports flourished too. Ujjain (II, 270, 271) served as a link between the seaports and the Ganges and Deccan. Anadapura on the north-west of Valabhi (II: 270), Gujjara on the north of Valabhi (II: 270) and Mulasthanapura (Multan, II, 274) connected western India to the Indus. On the other side of the Indus the prosperity of Pitasila (II, 279), Ghazna (II, 284) and Kapisi, which attracted merchandise from all parts of the world (I, 54), suggest another route from the lower Indus to Central Asia.

While trade in western India during the Gupta age continued, the persistence of trade on the north Indian plain is less clear. Fa-hsien was the first Chinese pilgrim to reach the Ganges plain. He formed a favourable impression of the 'Middle Country', i.e. the west and middle Ganges plains, but could not help recording the depressing scenes of some of the cities on the middle Ganges plain that were famous in Buddhist literature. Shravasti, Kapilavastu, Kushinagara,

Gaya and old Rajagriha were all desolate. However, not all of the cities in north India were deserted. According to Fa-hsien Benares and Kaushambi were not in such terrible straits. Sankasya was even densely populated and flourishing. The most prosperous city in the region was Pataliputra, the Gupta capital (860b–663a).

Pataliputra's prosperity did not entirely depend on agriculture. It was the terminus of the northern routes leading from north India to Kashmir and Central Asia. In the other direction, further east on Fa-hsien's journey, there were two port cities in the regions that Fa-hsien called the 'Great state Champa' and the 'Tamralipti State' (864c). The commercial activities here serve as indicators of another important aspect of the Gupta economy—maritime trade. This trade lies outside the scope of my work. What I want to draw attention to is the fact that the traffic on the Indian Ocean may have had some impact on the markets and supplies of Indian seaports, thus affecting the continental trade to China.

While Fa-hsien did not travel extensively enough to present a full account of urban centres in the north Indian plain, Hsüan-tsang (AD 630–44 in India) provided supplementary information. Hsüan-tsang's impression of north Indian cities basically matches Fa-hsien's reports: many cities in the middle Ganges valley were wasted and desolated. Over this depressing picture of urban life he superimposes a series of rich cities and cities in fine condition (see Map 6). In Kashmir Parvata was densely populated (Beal 1906: II, 275); in Sakala although the old city was damaged a new and smaller town prospered on the site and people there even wore silk (I, 167); in Jalandhara people's dwellings were luxurious (I, 167); silk was also popular in Satedru (I, 178); Sthaneshvara's families were interested only in luxury goods and profit but not agriculture (I, 183–4); Mathura people wore very fine cotton fabric (I, 179); Kanyakubja was a beautiful city with woods and lakes, and full of valuable merchandise (I, 207); Kaushambi was famous for its productivity (I, 235); Varanasi's houses possessed many objects of special value (II, 44); Ghazipur was a small town east of Varanasi but very wealthy. Further east Fa-hsien's favourite city, Pataliputra, was deserted (II, 82) because it had lost its position as capital of north India to Kanyakubja. But the port cities that Fa-hsien had seen two centuries earlier continued to prosper.

Hsüan-tsang's visit in India was two centuries later than that of

Fa-hsien and another pilgrim, Chih-meng. Is the information from Hsüan-tsang applicable to the Gupta period? Hsüan-tsang's descriptions of cities in north-west and north India basically correspond with those of Fa-hsien and with the archaeological evidence of the Gupta levels of urban sites; when many cities in Bactria, Gandhara and north India declined, certain urban centres still endured, or even developed. More specifically, the flourishing cities mentioned by Hsüan-tsang formed a route connecting Kashmir with the Yamuna and the Ganga. Although Chih-meng did not give details of his journey, the few places he mentioned indicate he followed this route from Kashmir to the middle Ganges (see Map 6). Because the accounts of Fa-hsien and Chih-meng demonstrate that Hsüan-tsang's descriptions were at least partially valid for the Gupta age, it seems reasonable to conclude that even when north India suffered a general urban decline in the Gupta period, certain cities along the trade route from Kashmir to the north Indian plain prospered.

In summary, political changes in the post-Kushan period disturbed the Eurasian commercial network from the Roman empire to China but did not destroy it. A major shift took place in the north-west, where the route through Kashmir connecting India to Central Asia gained importance. As the seaports in western India continued to flourish the new Kashmir route brought both western India and the Ganges plain closer to China.

CITIES IN NORTH INDIA

North India during the Kushan period experienced a high degree of urbanization. Many urban centres came into being in the regions of Soviet Central Asia and Afghanistan. Urban wealth and markets stimulated further agricultural production based on massive irrigation systems (Frumkin 1970: 51). In the regions of modern north Pakistan cities developed along the route in the Peshawar valley, from Pushkalavati to Taxila. Dani claims that the urbanization even of modern Pakistan has not reached the stage it did in the Peshawar valley during the Kushan period (1969: 16). This urban growth spread to north and central India, but unfortunately many important sites such as Mathura and Ujjain have not been fully excavated. In those which have, Kushan levels have not been distinguished from those of other periods. G. R. Sharma, the excavator

at Kaushambi, noticed that the Kushan level is marked by great
building activity (1969: 41). Excavations at Ahicchatra show that
stratum IV, identified as the Kushan level, marked the most prosperous period of construction. If the third sub-period of period IV
at Hastinapura can be identified as the Kushan level, it too confirms the contention that north India during the Kushan period
experienced a high degree of urbanization (Ghosh 1975: 109). The
Kushan level of Rajghat, a site at Varanasi, was the most prosperous level in the history of this site (Narain: 1976–8: I, 28).
Kushan levels on the Ganges plain display a unified brick size over
a large area. The size of bricks in Ahicchatra is $18 \times 12 \times 2$ in.;
Kaushambi it is $17.5–18 \times 12 \times 2.5$ in.; in Kumrahar, a site at
Pataliputra, it is $18 \times 12 \times 2.5$ in. (Ghosh 1975: 109); in Rajghat it
is $16 \times 10 \times 2$ in. (Narain 1976–8: II, 12); in Sonkh, near Mathura,
it is $15 \times 9 \times 2$ in. (Hartel 1976: 75); in Broach, the site of ancient
Barygaza, it is $16 \times 11 \times 3$ in., or $13 \times 8 \times 2.5$ in. (*IAR* 1959–60:
19). The uniformity of brick size demonstrates that these cities
developed under similar economic conditions, and that frequent
contact prompted them to adopt the same construction techniques.

The sparse literary accounts of the urban life of this period
basically support the archaeological evidence of urban development. Manu, like other Brahmanical lawmakers, was hostile to
urban residents such as officials, physicians, artisans and prostitutes
(IX 259). He counselled the king to keep watch over these elements
and to exact punishment for crimes committed (IV 261–2). He
referred to many city facilities, such as assembly houses, brothels,
taverns, crossroads, playhouses and artisans' shops, as dangerous
places that the king should closely guard (IX 264–6). Regardless of
whether Manu approved or disapproved of urban life the king had
to deal with the problems it generated.

In Buddhist literature a rich country is supposed to contain
many cities. The *Mahāvastu* gives the conventional number of
60,000. Thriving commerce, of course, symbolized a good city
(*MV*: I, 272, p. 225; 283, p. 238; II, 177, p. 171). These cities were
beautiful and opulent, had well-laid out bazaars and gardens, and
possessed rest-houses along their roads (*SN*: I, 43, 49, 51). There
were specialized markets for flowers, perfume, fruits, medicine,
jewels and general products, etc. (*MP*: v, 5). The earth shook with
the hoofbeats of horses bringing wealth into these cities (BC: III,

25): there were lines of shops, parks, gardens and temples (*MP*: v, 4). The *Milindapañha* named seventy-five professions: makers of consumption goods, such as clothes and utensils; makers of luxury goods, such as perfume and jewelry; or musicians, artists and various kinds of entertainers (v, 4). According to this work the king should be the architect of a city (*MP*: v, 4) and attract people to the city by low taxes (*SN*: i, 56). More interesting still is the mention of a cosmopolitan feature of the ideal city for that period: it should contain people from all over north India as well as Scythia, Bactria and even China (*MP*, 5).

In spite of all these details our knowledge of urban administration is sketchy. The few lines from Manu previously mentioned indicate the importance of guilds to the king (viii 219). Kushan sites in north India yield many seals testifying to the existence of guilds and certain regulations for commercial activities. Several seals found at Bhita near Allahabad bear the legend in Kushan script of 'nigama', or 'nigamasa' (Marshall 1911–12: 56). If 'nigama' signified a 'township', as Maity has suggested, these seals represented the authority of some autonomous urban administration.[3] In Shaikhan Dheri the stamps of Kushan royal symbols on pottery have attracted the attention of archaeologists. Allchin has noticed several stamps on receiving vessels of distillation apparatuses. After examining a similar pottery type found in Taxila, Rang Mahal, and Charsada he concludes that these apparatuses were used to make alcohol, the receiving vessels used to store distilled alcohol, and that the stamps were licences which rulers gave to the manufacturers (1979: 766). The practice of impressing royal symbols on liquor containers, which began in the Kushan period (769), confirms that the Kushan kings were interested in regulating certain items of trade, such as liquor, and probably other valuable commodities.

Archaeological evidence indicates that the urban economy in north India declined after the Kushan period. The deterioration of cities in the Gupta and post-Gupta periods has been researched by V. K. Thakur (1981). Here I only want to mention a few important facts relevant to this study. In Soviet Central Asia, as I said earlier, many cities disappeared during the fourth and fifth centuries. Along the ancient routes of Pakistan large cities like Taxila, Pushkalavati and Peshawar, one after another, became desolate. In the Punjab

[3] For the controversy over the interpretation of 'nigama', see Maity 1957: 157.

and the Indus-Ganges divide, because the sites occupied through the Kushan period were abandoned in the post-Kushan or Gupta periods, Kushan deposits in many sites are followed directly by medieval ware (Thakur 1981: 261–91). Hastinapura and Atranjikhera were deserted after the Kushan period, and even Mathura showed signs of decline (275–6).

If Fa-hsien was not aware of the decline of cities in the Punjab and west Ganges it is because he had not seen them at their height under the Kushans. He was deeply impressed by the desolation of cities of the middle Ganges, even though he knew nothing of their past. Archaeological findings confirm his accounts about Sravasti (Thakur 1981: 278), Kailavastu (281) and Kushinagara (284) by showing that these sites were abandoned after the Kushan period. Rich material remains also confirm Fa-hsien's positive descriptions of east Indian cities. Pataliputra was not deserted until AD 500 (Sinha: 1970: 56). Champa was abandoned in the post-Gupta period (Thakur 1981: 287); Tamralipti did not decline until after the Gupta period (294). Many important sites in Bengal and Bihar, such as Nalanda and Vikramashila, flourished after the Gupta period (292).

To explain the general decline of urban centres in north India Thakur has advanced six reasons: natural disasters, political changes, foreign invasions, feudal wars and the sacking of cities, religious preference and changes in economic structure (1981: 295–6). Natural disasters, such as floods, could cause shifts in the locations of individual cities, but not the de-urbanization in the vast area from north-west to north India. The disintegration of the Kushan state and foreign invasions might have been fatal to many cities in Soviet Central Asia and north-west India. Meanwhile the rise of Gupta power was favourable to the political, religious and educational centres on the Ganges, with Pataliputra and Nalanda serving as the best examples.

The disintegration of the Kushan state signified more than a shift of political centres. The distribution of Kushan coins (Map 2) shows a strong commercial network extending over the whole north Indian plain. Once the north-west lost its leading economic position, and once luxury goods were no longer transported to the Kushan core region, the Punjab and the Indus-Ganges divide no longer benefited from the market of the north-west region. In contrast, maritime trade nurtured eastern ports like Tamralipti to meet the demand of Gupta political and cultural centres.

Even more important than changes in trade routes, the Gupta age signalled certain significant developments in north India. Following the resurrection of Brahmanism, more value was attached to landed property. The Ganges valley beccame more oriented towards agriculture. Inscriptions of land-grants replaced the votive ones which had been popular in the Kushan period. Officers, Brahmans and even Buddhist monasteries received more and more land-grants. This transition is the most significant factor in Thakur's analysis and sheds light on the vast urban decline in the post-Kushan period.

However, even in the Gupta period cities did not all decline. Cities near Pataliputra and on the east coast prospered, as did cities in western India and those on the trade routes from Kashmir to the middle Ganges. No wonder the literature of the Gupta period gives such a favourable picture of urban life. I have already mentioned Kalidasa's praise of Ujjain and Vadisha. Like Ashvaghosha, the cities he describes also had prosperous markets (*rddhapāna*), royal highways (*RA*: xiv 30) and beautiful city gardens (*nagaropavana*) (*RA*: viii 32).

Not only did urban centres in certain parts of India continue to flourish during the Gupta period, urban civilization apparently attained further maturity as well. The urban institution of 'nigama' (township) continued to exist in Bhita and other sites (Marshall 1911–12: 56). In Vaisali the long legend on the seals of nigama indicate the institution was more complex than it had been in the Kushan period. There were nigama of merchants (*śreṣṭhi*), of caravan traders (*sārthavāha*) and of artisans (*kulika*) (Maity 1957: 156–7). While Manu's code of law contained only vague references to guilds, the lawmakers Narada and Brihaspati give detailed regulations for the guilds. Guilds were full-fledged urban institutions; they functioned as banks, religious patrons, organizers of public works and charity (Maity 1957: 156–9). They recruited new members through strict apprenticeship (*Nārada*: v 16, 17). Apprentices who tried to leave before the end of their contracts were to receive corporal punishment and be confined (v 18, 19). Narada also devised regulations for partnerships between traders (iii 1–7). Brihaspati formulated detailed rules to enforce agreements in an association

(XVII'). For instance, an association should have two, three or five advisors (10), and those who neglected common agreements would be fined or punished (14).

Guilds, of course, were not the only authority in the city. Brihaspati stipulated that the king should restrain the heads of associations and regulate their actions (XVII 18–19). In *Sakuntalā* the king has to sit on the seat of judgement (*dharmasana*) every day to deal with citizens' disputes (VI 7). Maity suggests that the Gupta kings' control over the economy was looser than that of the Mauryan kings. One notices though that, as in earlier times, when a merchant died childless his property reverted to the king (*SK:* VI 20, 29).

The most salient feature of urban life during this period was the role of citizens or urban dwellers (*paura* or *nāgaraka*) in influencing politics. Urban people appear in many literary works, often within crucial scenes. In the *Raghuvaṁśa* rumours circulating in the city about Sita among *paura* force Rama to exile her (XIV 38). In Bhasa's drama *Pratimānāṭaka* Dasharatha announces the consecration of Rama in front of preceptors, ministers and urban people (I 5). Urban people beset the royal highway when they hear of the departure of Rama (I 26). When Bharata goes looking for Rama urban people follow him (IV 1); Bharata tells Rama that city people wait to see him and therefore he, Bharata, needs Rama's sandals to convince them of his honesty (IV 28). In the *Raghuvaṁśa* the urban populace applaud Aja's victory in Idumati's *svayamvara* and so insult the other kings present (VI 85). Urban people obviously had a voice in state politics.

Among these people big merchants composed the leading force in city politics because they controlled public opinion through charity and patronage, and because their rise or fall affected the livelihood of urban residents. The character Charudatta, who appears in both Bhasa's play of the same name and in the *Mrcchakaṭika*, may represent the archetype of this kind of merchant. After he becomes poor many people under his patronage lose their jobs. Even in his impoverished condition his opinion carries weight in politics because his charitable deeds have secured him a group of followers. These people augment their influence through marital links with each other. One leading merchant who engages in maritime trade marries the daughter of a guild head in the city of Ayodhya (*SK:* VI 20, 29).

These rich citizens and merchants developed a highly sophisticated urban culture, of which the flourishing Sanskrit literature of Gupta times was a result. Maity has noticed, from the sculptures of Bharhut and Sanchi to those of Ajanta, that the fashion in clothing became much more elaborate (1957: 115). Attention to one's toilet in the Gupta period also exceeded that of the Kushan period (Chandra 1940). The city provided entertainment and recreation for leisure-seeking people (*RA*: xiv 30). City women's sportive movement of their eyes and brows was contrasted with country women's igno-rance of the art of moving their brows (*MD*: 16, 49). These phenomena demonstrate the existence of a sophisticated life-style.

The *Kāmasūtra* summarized the leisurely life led by these rich citizens. They might belong to any of the four varnas, but they had to be residents of the city. The necessary qualifications consisted of being learned, wealthy, a householder and living in a city or town (i 4.1–2).[4] The public women, who certainly knew how to move their brows and who were accomplished in many other arts (i 3), were urban dwellers' companions in many social assemblies (i 4). These men had the leisure to rear birds, watch fights of quails, cocks and rams (i 4.21), and to play many kinds of games (i 4.47). They conversed neither in pure Sanskrit nor in pure regional dialects but in a hybrid of both. They joined clubs (*goṣṭhī*) whose sole purpose was pleasure (i 4.52). Rich city dwellers were a social group that based their status almost entirely on wealth.

Now, in order to resolve the problem of the discrepancies between the general decline of the urban economy and the development of a refined urban culture, it is necessary to recognize that this life-style of a few rich urban people and their dependants, such as entertainers and servants, created only a narrow demand for certain goods. In addition to the necessities of a small population, the pro-duction of various luxury items continued or improved. Cosmetics were well developed. The designs and fabric of textiles exhibited on sculptures reveal that the textile industry produced extremely fine cloth. Stone-carving was another industry which reached a high level in the Gupta period (Thakur 1981: 119). Sculpture was used largely in religious construction, which was an important aspect of urban life.

In summary, the highly sophisticated urban culture appears to

---

[4] *nagare pattane khārvate mahati vā*. They might be categories of urban centres, according to their size, from large to small.

have been limited to only a narrow social group who populated urban sites along the dynamic trade routes. This group's role in politics and economy, and its material demand, shaped an urban life-style quite different from that of earlier times. Although Maity questions the accuracy of Fa-hsien's account according to which the people in the Middle Country used cowries as a medium of exchange (1957: 68), Fa-hsien might have been right. While gold, silver and copper coins circulated among urban residents, rural people in the so-called Middle Country, which was probably the region most seriously deprived of urban centres in north India, would have been very likely to resort to the older manner of exchange. The cowries did not necessarily impede the Gupta style of urban economy.

SHIFTS OF TRADE ROUTES IN NORTH CHINA

The routes connecting Central Asia to the Chinese interior can be divided into three segments: routes through Chinese Turkistan, through the Ho-hsi region (i.e. the modern Kansu corridor) and through the interior of China. The three were subject to Chinese sovereignty or suzerainty for periods of varying length over the centuries under study.

In an account of the Chinese military achievements in Central Asia the author of the history of the Later Han comments:

From the Chien-wu Era (AD 25–57) to the Yen-kuang Era (AD 122–5), communications with the Western Region were obstructed three times, and re-established three times. Since the Yang-chia Era (AD 132–5) those states [in the Western Region] became arrogant and fought each other because our influence had decreased. (*HHS*: LXXXVIII, 2912).

The Han government's control over the Western Region was not constant, but private commercial activities always continued. Even during the periods of 'obstruction' such forms of communication as payment of tribute, pilgrimage and preaching took place. A culture heavily influenced by West Asia, South Asia and China came to be formed in Central Asia. In addition to using commodities from surrounding regions the people of Central Asia wrote Kharoshthi, Brahmi and Chinese scripts on wood-slips and paper. The practice in Khotan was typical. Coins with Chinese legends on one side and Kharoshthi legends on the other circulated in Khotan from the first to the third century AD (Hsia Nai 1962: 60–2).

After the Han dynasty, when China was consumed by civil war, much warfare and conquest took place in the Western Region. But communication along the Silk Route never stopped. Kharoshthi letters, which have been found in Central Asia dating from the middle of the third century AD according to a Chinese document from the same site, mention that traders from China, possibly Chinese, came to Shan-shan on the southern route (Burrow 1940: 1). Ancient Sogdian letters dating from the fourth century testify to trips by Sogdian merchants in Central Asia and their activities in the interior of China (Henning 1948). Fa-hsien's travels in the early fifth century and Sung Yun's travels in the early sixth century both indicate that the routes were viable. The existence of this traffic does not mean, however, that the routes in Central Asia were safe. A Kharoshthi letter concerning a lawsuit stipulated: 'At the time the road is safe, they are to be sent here under escort' (Burrow 1940: 110). Thus travellers must have had great courage to undertake the risks caused by warfare and to tackle the geographical obstacles.

Unlike Central Asia, the Ho-hsi region—consisting of the corridor between the Tibetan plateau and the steppe tribes in the north—was always subject to the rule of a Chinese or Sinicized authority. Table 1 shows the political shifts in the region from the Han.

Like other regions in north China, the Ho-hsi region became one state or several small states whenever the rest of north China fell into disunity. Once unification was realized, even if only in the few years under the Former Ch'in, this region was annexed by the larger territory. Except for some marginal areas this region was always a part of the Chinese polity. Although warfare occurred intermittently in north China, the governors and kings of the Ho-hsi region benefited from the trade passing through here. They attached importance to keeping the routes clear. In the beginning of the Later Han, when all of China was still in turmoil, only the Ho-hsi region was at peace. At that time a county administrator could make a fortune in a few months' tenure. The author of the Later Han history praised governor K'ung Fen for encouraging trade with foreigners to enrich this region and for not seeking to profit himself (*HHS*: xxxi, 1098). During the Three Kingdoms period (AD 220–80) Ts'ang Tz'u, the governor of Tunhuang, protected foreign traders from the attacks of local élites by issuing passes

TABLE 1: POLITICAL SHIFTS OF THE HO-HSI REGION,
FIRST TO SIXTH CENTURIES

Political Status of Ho-hsi Region	Unified Period of North China	Divided Period of North China
Liang Prefecture	Later Han[5] 25–220	
Liang Prefecture	Wei 220–65	
Liang Prefecture	Western Chin 265–316	
Former Liang 314–76		Sixteen Kingdoms Period 317–420
Liang Prefecture	Former Ch'in 376–83	
Later Liang 385–403		
Southern Liang 397–414		
Northern Liang 397–439		
Western Liang 400–21		
Liang Prefecture	Northern Wei 439–534	

and providing escorts on the road (*SKC*: XVI, 512). The Western Chin (AD 265–316) governor Hsü Miao traded in gold, silk, dogs and horses in order to supply the needs of the interior and protected foreign trade passing through this region (*CS*: XXVI, 785). The kings of this region, such as Chang Chün and Lü Kuang, also traded with foreigners (*Liang-chou-chi*: 1–2).

There were also greedy governors who sought only to enrich themselves. Yüan Hsien, the governor of the Ho-hsi region during the Northern Wei, killed many rich merchants in the Liang prefecture and confiscated their property (*WS*: XIX, 445).

Even in the most chaotic period, when this region was divided into three small states (AD 400–14), the governor of Chang-yeh generously offered hospitality to Fa-hsien when the routes were obstructed because of political troubles. Also, the governor of

---

[5] The italicized words indicate independent political entities.

Tunhuang provided an escort and provisions for Fa-hsien (*FH*: 857a). Numerous Chinese documents of the Wei-Chin period written on wooden slips or on paper have been found along the route from Lobnor via Niya to Khotan. Among them, emperor's edicts and official letters tell little about the actual administration of the governments in Central Asia. But many 'passes' (*kuo-so*) issued by Chinese authorities, which were found in Niya, one of them signed by the Tunhuang governor himself, prove that local government in the Western Region co-operated with the Chinese authorities in the Ho-hsi region at least to the extent of protecting travellers (Sinkiang Museum 1977: 23).

For governors and local kings the potential profits made Ho-hsi a special place to govern, no matter what the political situation in China was. When Li Hao was the king (AD 404–17) of the Western Liang, he explained to his son the advantageous conditions of his kingdom: 'This place was admired by people everywhere even when the whole country under heaven prospered. Nowadays it is really an outstanding place.' (*CS*: LXXXVII, 2262).

The situation in the Chinese interior differed. The shift of political centres often directly affected the destinations of commodities, especially foreign commodities. Through the Han period the political and economic core region was in the Yellow River valley (see Map 1). Owing to the shift from the Former Han (206–8 BC) to the Later Han (AD 25–220),when the capital moved from Ch'ang-an to Loyang, the economic centre also shifted from the Kuan-chung region to the Ho-nan region. After the ethnically orthodox Chinese Chin dynasty retreated to the south (AD 317), the Yangtze valley succeeded the north in urban development until the sixth century AD, when north and south were again unified. In the north a few big cities took turns serving as capitals of kingdoms. Once they became capitals, especially capitals of the kingdoms which unified north China, they prospered for a period and then were inevitably destroyed when captured by enemies. Table 2 gives an overview of the rise and fall of the four most important cities in the north.

Except for Ch'ang-an, which was a relatively large city before it was sacked in 313, these cities were either desolate or revived only briefly as capitals of small kingdoms in the years they did not serve as capitals. If the destruction of old cities was sudden, the construction of new cities was surprisingly quick. The twist was that the

TABLE 2: THE RISE AND FALL OF THE FOUR MAJOR CITIES IN
NORTH CHINA, THIRD–SIXTH CENTURIES

Cities	Ch'ang-an	Loyang	Yeh	P'ing-ch'eng
Historical period when the city was the capital of north China			Wei 204–20	
		Wei and Western Chin 220–313		
Former Ch'in AD	376–83			Northern Wei 386–493
		Northern Wei 493–534		
	Western Wei 535–57		Eastern Wei 534–50	

government forced city residents of the old capital to migrate to its new one. When Ts'ao Ts'ao established his capital in Yeh he managed to gather a population from other cities and from his followers' clans (T'ao 1935: 92–6). According to Tso Ssu, in a very short time Yeh became a beautiful city, full of neighbourhoods, offices, hotels, stores and markets (*San-tu-fu*: 13a–14b). Loyang was destroyed after the fall of the Han but recovered its former wealth during the Wei and Chin periods (*CS*: XXVI, 783). When the Former Ch'in reconstructed Ch'ang-an the government had to move the population of Yeh to occupy it (Li Chien-nung 1959: 89). The same thing happened to the Northern Wei capital P'ing-ch'eng; the government moved the population from the annexed state, Chung-shan, to the city (*WS*: CX, 2850). Later on this same population followed the government to Loyang. Loyang soon revived as a city with rich neighbourhoods, a big market place of eight *li* in circumference (YHC: IV, 202), and more than a thousand Buddhist monasteries (V, 349). When Loyang fell in 534 the population, including the monasteries, moved with the government to Yeh (Preface, 1).

Foreign merchants seemed also to follow the migrations. When Ch'ang-an was the capital of the Former Han there was a special residence for foreigners, *Man-i-ti*, on Kao street (*San-fu Huang-t'u*: 6/7a). During the Later Han a residence with the same name appeared in Loyang (*HHS*: LXXXVIII, 2928). In praising a Yeh street for its many hotels Tso Ssu compared it to the residence on the Kao street in old Ch'ang-an (*San-tu-fu*: 13b): this street in Yeh was probably similar to that of Ch'ang-an. In Northern Wei Loyang there was a residence for foreigners from all directions, *ssu-i-kuan*, and a market served this residence (YHC: III, 161).

These facts suggest that the destinations of foreign merchants and foreign commodities were subject to the shifts of political centres, but the trade routes in the peripheral region and the region periodically under Chinese control were relatively stable, although affected to some degree by great political changes. Surely natural conditions in Central Asia and the Ho-hsi corridor prevented major changes in the routes. Most important is the fact that the cities' destiny did not totally depend on political shifts, as was true of cities in the Chinese interior. The difference in stability between cities and routes in the Chinese interior and that of peripheral regions lies in the nature of Chinese polity and the social structure of Chinese cities in this period.

Cities in North China

It is widely accepted that the Han dynasty was a favourable period for urban development and that the post-Han period was not. During the Han urban centres spread from the Yellow River valley to the whole of north China.

At this time the growth of the urban economy was to some extent independent of political changes. Even the establishment of Loyang as the capital in the Later Han was not fatal to Ch'ang-an's prosperity. But in the post-Han period, shifting a capital to another city meant moving all residents, including artisans, merchants, religious institutions, and the entire state machinery as well. After studying the records of Northern Wei Loyang Jenner argues that 'for all its enormous size and prosperity, it was never a city' (1981: 125–6). However, Loyang's lack of predominant influence on the national economy, which for Jenner disqualifies it as a city, is related to the changing nature of urban centres in different historical periods.

Even if archaeologists have difficulty in identifying the urban centres of early civilizations, one can hardly deny that Northern Wei Loyang was a city, based on its half-million population (YHC: v, 349), well-designed neighbourhoods, large marketplaces, monuments and more than a thousand Buddhist monasteries. It was certainly short-lived, but so were all important cities in north China from the post-Han to the Sui (AD 220–581). To understand the urban phenomena from the Han to the Northern dynasties a comparison of urban life during the two periods is necessary.

There is not much information about the physical disposition of Han cities except that marketplaces were separated from other wards. There were nine marketplaces (*shih*) in Ch'ang-an; there, government officials on a watchtower (*shih-lou*) supervised market transactions (*San-fu Huang-t'u*: 2/la). There were separate marketplaces in the Later Han cities, including Loyang. The carved bricks of the time show that the Later Han marketplaces were similar to those of the Former Han, with a watchtower set in the middle of street intersections (Liu Chih-yüan 1973: 57).

In Northern Wei Loyang marketplaces were located outside the city wall but close to the merchants' residential neighbourhoods. Around the large market there were rich merchants and artisans' neighbourhoods, musicians' neighbourhoods, liquor makers' neighbourhoods and coffin makers' neighbourhoods (YHC: IV, 202–6). There was a special market near the 'foreign residence' which was actually a neighbourhood with ten thousand households (YHC: III, 160–1). Curiously, there was no watchtower in the markets. Even the bell in the watchtower that survived from the Western Chin was moved to the palace for use in the ceremony of Buddhist lecturing (YHC: II, 75). Northern Wei Loyang possessed a major trait absent in Han cities: numerous Buddhist monasteries. Their influence on urban life cannot be overlooked.

The changing physical components of the cities reflected the changing urban life. The dominant economic policy of the Later Han government forbade people to engage in two occupations simultaneously. The thrust of this policy was to stop merchants from owning land and farmers from trading (Li Chien-nung 1959: 288). This policy derived from the orthodox Confucian idea that whereas agriculture was the root of economy, commerce was the least important upper branch of economy. The resentful comments by the scholar Wang Fu (*c.* AD 85–162) on the situation in Loyang reveal that this policy was not effective: 'The people engaged in lesser occupations are ten times as many as the farmers; the people engaged in worthless occupations are ten times as many as the people engaged in lesser occupations.' (3/18b). Here 'lesser occupations' means non-agricultural engagements, including handicrafts and commerce; 'worthless occupations' were service and entertaining. However, these 'lesser occupations' and 'worthless occupations' were more profitable than agriculture. Pan Ku quoted a folk proverb: 'Among the means for obtaining wealth when you are poor, agriculture is not as good as handicrafts; handicrafts is not as good as trade; just as doing embroidery is not as good as leaning on the market gate.' (*HS*: xci, 3687).

The Han government's effort to restrain merchants was mainly designed to limit their acquisition of land and prevent their further squeezing into the rank of scholar-bureaucrats. No matter how much wealth they owned, merchants without landholdings held too low a status to become government officials. This policy of restraining merchants, however, did not check the development of trade. There are no records of the imposition of a direct tax or toll on trade in Han history (Li Chien-nung 1957: 199). The political élite demanded commodities , especially luxury goods. Pan Ku, who praised the Later Han policy of suppressing commerce in *Liang-tu-fu*, did not forget to ask his brother to send him high-quality rugs from Central Asia.

Although the status of merchants and other urban residents was low, they were not totally defenceless against the government policy, especially those living in the capital or other administrative centres. One way to express their criticism was to compose songs and ballads, and a traditional way to test public opinion was to collect children's ballads and folk songs. 'Observing ballads among the people to keep discipline of officials' (*CS*: xxvi, 779) was a means of controlling the bureaucratic system. Criticism found in these songs and ballads could lead to a government censor's investigation and even to the punishment of misbehaving officials. A more important use served by these ballads was the prediction of political change. Chinese rulers believed that ballads, like astrological signs and natural phenomena, were omens of future events. Because officials carefully recorded the ballads and tried to interpret them, most standard histories include ballads in the 'Five Elements' (*Wu-hsing*) section, the section listing omens.

Many sarcastic ballads criticized government and officials. But those giving detailed or accurate predictions were perhaps composed to influence the political situation, or were forged later on. Nevertheless, the importance of the ballads, collected from marketplaces, mostly from the capital, shows that urban residents were a force the rulers had to take into account.

Since many rulers were nervous about these ballads and tried to eradicate the effects of bad omens, ballads often affected decision-making. The best example in Han times is that when Wang Mang usurped the throne (AD 9–25) the ballad saying 'Yellow cattle having a white belly, the *wu-chu* coins should be circulated again' was popular. Later interpreters viewed the ballad as a prediction of Wang Mang's fall (*HHS*: CIII, 3281) because Wang's symbolic colour was yellow and *wu-chu* was the Han currency. Actually, the ballad voiced complaints about Wang's changing currency system which had caused confusion and inflation. This policy was indeed one of the factors that caused Wang Mang's downfall.

Wiser Han rulers were aware of the importance of keeping the citizens' loyalty in their policy-making. In discussing economic theory Pan Ku quoted a politician of the previous Warring States period: 'Too high a price for grain hurts the people (*min*), too low a price hurts farmers (*nung*). Hurting people causes dissidence, hurting farmers causes a national deficit' (*HS*: XXIV 1124). Here the satisfaction of the 'people', obviously city residents who had to pay for their grain, was more essential to the ruler.

There were many rich merchants in Loyang during the Northern dynasties, although warfare and large-scale forced migrations were not conducive to trade. The merchant Liu Pao had a house built in every provincial capital where he maintained messengers and horses to keep himself informed of price fluctuations. It is said his business expanded everywhere a ship and cart could reach, and every place a human could tread..His carriage and apparel were as extravagant as that of a prince (YHC: IV, 202–3). Northern Wei rulers seemed to tolerate and protect such merchants. The government did not collect taxes from marketplaces and stores until AD 526, when rebellions along the frontiers caused a deficit (*WS*: CX, 2861). Even during a political crisis after a coup, when there was no emperor in the capital (AD 530), the regent Erh-chu Shih-lung kept the trade routes from the city open for three months (YHC: II, 105).

Actually, artisans and merchants improved their status substantially during the Northern Wei rule. When the Northern Wei unified north China the government monopolized the production of all major handicrafts. A government department registered all households of artisans. Artisans making luxury goods such as gold, silverware and high-quality silk were subject to special restrictions. Their children had to follow them in their professions. Meanwhile teaching their skills to outsiders could bring severe punishment. From princes to commoners, whoever kept artisans in their homes exposed the whole family to the death sentence (Wang Chung-lo 1979 II: 536). Under this kind of control the status of artisans was not much higher than that of slaves. Merchants shared a similar status (537).

However, this situation quickly changed. In AD 472 an edict allowed artisans and merchants to purchase land and engage in agriculture (Wang Chung-lo 1979: 537). In a society where land was the symbol of status this edict admitted an improvement of these people's social standing. Soon the government loosened control over silk weavers and allowed private households to make and sell fine silk. Merchants took advantage of this opportunity to enlarge their business and increase their profit (537).

A telling anecdote reveals how much the merchants' and artisans' position had been strengthened since the Han. In the Shen-kuei era (AD 518–20), the government felt that merchants and artisans were too arrogant and revived a sumptuary law from the Han dynasty that forbade merchants and artisans to wear gold and silver ornaments and silk clothes. But this regulation could not be enforced (YHC: IV, 205). Compared with merchants in Han times, who could indirectly affect politics and policy-making through their influence on public opinion in urban areas, what force supported the Northern Wei traders when political instability disastrously affected their business? In other words, how could certain commercial activities prosper in a declining phase of urban development?

Both north India and north China experienced two phases of urbanization in the period under study. After the prosperity of the Kushan period many cities in north India shrank or disappeared. Similarly, cities in north China after the third century were much smaller and fewer than those of the former period. Yet both Gupta India and north China under the Northern dynasties made great cultural achievements based on an urban economy, including trade. The next chapter will show that Sino-Indian trade continued through the two phases. Although an analysis of this long-distance trade cannot totally account for commercial activities in general in either north India or north China, it will reveal a few specific factors that supported trade and traders during the two different phases.

Chapter ii: Trading Items

The kinds of commodities transported along the trade routes between India and China shaped the nature of the trade. Tracing these commodities will reveal various economic, cultural and social factors which created markets and facilitated the supply or trade of goods.

Chinese standard histories from the Han through the Northern dynasties (206 BC–AD 534) are the obvious places to look for information about trade. The official histories, as well as unofficial sources, record numerous instances of tribute from the Western Region, including India. The term 'tribute' in these books refers to either a foreign ruler's gift to a Chinese emperor as acknowledgement of submission and as token of goodwill, or to a merchant's payment to the emperor for permission to trade in China. Exotic animals, such as blood-sweating horses, peacocks and elephants, or rare commodities, like asbestos cloth, fragrance and incense, prevail in most of these lists. The donors stressed the uncommonness of these items in order to impress the emperor; the emperor received them as symbols of his extensive imperial influence. The best example of such unusual gifts is the blood-sweating horse of Ferghana, supposedly a divine species, which only emperors and their favourites could legitimately use. In fact, it seems that very few of these items ever went outside the palace to Chinese markets. This kind of gift-trade facilitated the political alliances and peaceful relationships which were necessary for trade in general. Their significance will be discussed in Chapter iii.

The lists of products from the sources of the Western Region resemble more closely merchants' inventories than do the lists of tribute. The *History of the Later Han* records that India possessed elephants, rhinoceros, tortoise shell, gold, silver, copper, iron, lead, tin, fine cloth, woollen textiles, various types of incense, crystal sugar, pepper, ginger and black salt, as well as precious things from the Roman empire, because it traded with the Romans (*HHS*, LXXXVIII, 2921). Most items in this list were not rare and valuable enough to be shipped all the way to China. As for the commodities China exported to India, information is even scarcer. Thus, the best way to examine trade items is to locate those which were in special demand in China and available only in India or through India, or vice versa, in literary sources, and then to verify this information with archaeological evidence whenever possible. Judging from these sources, coral, pearls, glass and certain kinds of fragrances appear to be the important items transported from or through India to China; silk was the major item transported from China to India.

COMMODITIES TRANSPORTED FROM INDIA TO CHINA

CORAL   Since the period of the Former Han dynasty coral had been an extremely valuable commodity. In eulogies describing the court's brilliance in Former Han times, Later Han writers such as Pan Ku mentioned 'coral trees', i.e. branch coral (*Liang-tu-fu*, 4a). In fiction written in a later period coral trees symbolize the extravagance of the Former Han court. It is said that Emperor Wu of the Former Han built a shrine with 'coral window lattice', and with 'coral trees' planted around it, where he searched for immortality in vain (Lu Hsün 1939: 347). This tradition of using coral continued after the Han.[1] It seems coral was the most precious and, hence, the ideal item of tribute. More specific records about the use of coral appear after the Han. During the Three Kingdoms period the Emperor Ming of the Wei state in north China used coral beads as decoration on his crown. The Chin dynasty continued this custom (*CS*: xxv, 766).

In Chin times coral gradually spread from the court to the houses of other members of the élite. Two aristocrats, Shih Ch'ung and Wang K'ai, vied with each other to display their wealth. Wang K'ai boasted to Shih that he had received a beautiful piece of branch coral two feet (*ch'ih*) tall from Emperor Wu of Chin. Shih broke it into pieces with an iron bar. This action angered Wang

---

[1] Even as late as the T'ang. In the famous picture by the T'ang artist Yen Li-pen: 'Foreign envoys coming with their tributes' (Schafer 1963), many envoys carry a piece of 'coral tree'.

who thought Shih envied his coral. Saying 'Never mind, I will make up the loss', Shih had numerous pieces of branch coral brought out. Six or seven of them were three or four feet in height and their splendour filled people's eyes. Even the small ones were as good as Wang K'ai's had been (*Shih-shuo-hsin-yü*: xxx, 661). Here coral symbolizes wealth and status. Shih successfully demonstrated his superiority through his possession of, yet indifference to, such valuable things. When the author of Chin history criticized corrupt living standards he also viewed coral as an example of extreme ostentation (*CS*: xxvi, 783). After the Chin period Chinese rulers of the small states continued to acquire coral. When the tomb of Chang Chün, the king of the Former Liang, was robbed, a whip made of coral was found along with many precious items (*CS*: cxxii, 3067). Coral beads were also found in a stone casket in the foundation of a Buddhist site of the Northern Wei (Hopei Bureau 1966: 253).

From where and on what route did coral—so highly valued by the Chinese—come to China? Red coral from the western Mediterranean and the Red Sea was one of the major items shipped to the East from the time of the *Periplus* (28, 39, 49). The histories of the Later Han (*HHS*: lxxxviii, 2919), the Three Kingdoms (*SKC*: xxx, 861) and the Chin (*CS*: xcvii, 2544) mention coral as a product of Ta-ch'in, i.e. the Roman empire.[2] A later Chinese account gives a detailed description of how coral was collected from the sea in Ta-ch'in: the Romans dropped iron nets on the coral reefs so that the yellowish young coral would grow on them. Three years later they came back to collect the coral once it had turned red (*Hsin T'ang-shu*: ccxxi, 6261).

Those records definitely refer to Mediterranean red coral. There were three possible routes to ship the coral to China. The most frequented route was the Southern Route to India. In the time of the *Periplus* the primary destination of coral in Roman cargo ships was India. Pliny mentions that coral was as highly treasured in India as pearls were in Rome (xxxii, 11). Coral beads along with beads of other precious materials have been found in north-Indian sites, for example, at Rajghat in the level of the pre-Kushan period

---

[2] Ta-ch'in also meant the Deccan or Dakshina of India, Syria and Alexandria. But in the context of the *Hou-Han-shu*, *Wei-lüeh* and *Wei-shu*, it indicates the. Roman empire.

(Narain 1976–8: II, 12). Coral continued to fetch high prices in the Gupta period. As in China, it appears in literature as a symbol of the luxurious life. In Bhasa's works, there were 'coral trees' in the Ashoka garden of Ravana, and a coral gate-house along with a gold-gate house in Ravana's palace (*Abhiṣekanāṭaka*: III 1; v 1; Woolner 1931: 157, 165). Coral was also one of the treasures in the house of the rich courtesan Vasantasena (*MK*: 164–5).

The second possible route was through the Northern Route of Central Asia. The Wei history describes coral as originating in Persia, probably because some coral was transported through Persia and the Northern Route into Central Asia. Ferghana's gift to the Chao state in 331 AD included coral (Wang Chung-lo 1979: 704).

The sea route from the Red Sea to South China was the third, and the most unlikely, way. Although there are some vague references to coral imported from southern ports during Han times (*Shu-i-chi*: 1/3a-b), most other Chinese sources call coral one of the commodities from the Western Region. Because coral was not one of the items the northern states tried to get from the south in the periods when China was divided (Li, Chien-nung 1959: 84–6), it must have been available in the north. It seems reasonable to conclude that coral entered China from India via Central Asia.

Although the Chinese were aware that coral came from the far west, Roman traders, and later Byzantine traders, were not necessarily aware that the Chinese desired coral as much as the Indians did. Since India was the major market for Roman coral, it follows that coral which arrived in China passed mainly through this region. Coral beads have been found in a stupa at Mirpur Khas, a site on the Indus in Sind dated to the early Christian era (Cousens 1909–10: 85). Coral beads found around many stupas and chapels[3] of the Dharmarajika monastery in Taxila prove that coral actually reached this region during the period from the Kushan empire to the invasion of the Huns (Marshall 1951: 249, 267, 273, 279, 280, 283, 295). Coral beads excavated from a Later Han tomb of Niya, a site on the Southern Route of Central Asia, suggest that coral was one of the commodities going from India to China (Sinkiang Museum 1960). In addition to the coral from the Red Sea, Maity suggests coral was transported to north India from south India in Kalidasa's

[3] Marshall's word for small halls with shrines in the courtyard of monasteries in Taxila.

time (Maity 1957: 124). But M. S. Shukla found almost no records of coral fishing and ornamental coral on the shores of south India (1972: 44). No matter where the coral originated, north India was probably the main supplier of trans-shipped coral to China before the T'ang dynasty.

PEARLS   Pearls, like coral, were highly valued in ancient China. In Pan Ku's poems praising the Han palace, pearls figure as importantly as coral. Unlike coral, pearls originated in south India and Ceylon. Pearls were one of India's important exports to the West during the early centuries AD (*Periplus*: 56, 59, 61). Fa-hsien also remarked on the advanced organization of the Ceylon pearl fishery. The king controlled the sources and took three-tenths of all the pearls that were harvested (864c). It was more convenient to ship these pearls to south China via the sea than overland to the north through Central Asia.

However, the *Periplus* mentions that pearls from Persia, although of lower quality than those of south India, were also exported to Barygaza (36). The tiny pearls excavated from Mirpur Khas might have come from Persia (Cousens 1909–10: 85). Considering the heavy traffic along the west coast, south-Indian pearls may have been exported to Barygaza also. A story about Kanishka suggests that pearls were available in north-west India along the trade routes from the western Indian coast to Central Asia. When the Chinese pilgrim Sung Yün travelled in the Gandhara region in the sixth century he saw a stupa which, according to local tradition, was built by Kanishka. People told him that when the stupa was first built the king covered it with a pearl net. Later he worried that the pearl net would be removed after his death. He then buried the net beside the stupa and left an inscription saying that, if the stupa became dilapidated in the future, the sages of that time should repair it with [money they made from selling] the pearls dug out from the site (YHC: v, 328). In Taxila, in addition to beads scattered around stupas, Marshall found a casket full of various kinds of beads, including pearls, inside a stupa (1951: I, 327). That casket, not necessarily the one mentioned by Sung Yün, verifies the association of pearls with Buddhist buildings. In north China pearls were also associated with Buddhist remains. A few hundred pearls were found in a casket under the foundation of a Northern Wei monastery in Hopei (Hopei Bureau 1966: 253), and also around the foundation of the famous Yung-ning stupa in the Northern Wei Loyang (Loyang Archaeological Team 1981: 224).

It is difficult to determine whether pearls in north China came by sea or via Central Asia. A Japanese team found pearls in a site along the Amu Darya in Afghanistan (*CAKP*: I, 179). The fact that pearls were among the jewels found in the tomb of Chang Chün in Liang-chou (*CS*: CXXII, 3067) proves that at least part of those in China came from India through Central Asia. The following anecdote in the Northern dynasties also suggests that pearls travelled the Northern Route: after the Northern Wei, when north China was again divided into two parts, the Northern Ch'i (AD 550–77) in the east tried to purchase pearls from their neighbours to the west, the Northern Chou. The Northern Chou controlled the route to the Western Region. The fact that the Northern Ch'i sought pearls from a hostile neighbour—and not from the South—suggests that pearls were more easily available in north than in south China.

GLASS VESSELS AND BEADS   Tracing the history of glass as a commodity in Chinese foreign trade poses several problems. Previously, scholars thought that China did not develop glass-making techniques until the fifth century AD. But since the 1930s, many glass samples have been found in tombs dating from the fifth century BC. Doris Dohrenwend recently summarized the history of Chinese glass comprehensively. She divides Chinese glass into two categories. The small opaque items pre-dating the third century AD are *liu-li*, and the transparent vessels from the T'ang dynasty onwards are *po-li*. Between the two phases during the Northern and Southern dynasties there was a 'glass mini-boom', as indicated by a series of glass vessels of doubtful provenance (Dohrenwend 1980: 426–46).

Today no one doubts that the Chinese made glass long before the Christian era. There is also clear evidence that China imported glass from foreign countries even up to the Ch'ing dynasty. The real question is: did the Chinese regard the ancient opaque items made by them or their ancestors as being the same thing as the transparent or colourful glass they imported at the same time? Obviously not. Both terms, *liu-li* and *po-li*, appeared in the Chinese vocabulary after contact with the Western Region, and both have Sanskrit origins.[4]

The Sanskrit word *vaidūrya*, which means lapis lazuli, beryl or cat's-eye gem, is the origin of *liu-li*. Before Buddhism spread to China, the Chinese name for lapis lazuli, a precious stone from the north-west, was *miu-lin*. From the Han to the Northern dynasties *miu-lin* and *liu-li* came to be interchangeable terms for a few kinds of blue or green precious stone (Chang Hung-chao 1921: 3–5). In early Buddhist texts *liu-li* also denoted blue or green precious stone, primarily lapis lazuli.[5] The Buddhist literature which was translated into Chinese in the fourth and early fifth centuries describes the enlightened Buddha showing his hair, as beautiful as *liu-li*, to his father; devotees who did not hurt others would be born with hair the colour of *liu-li*. From the earliest times up to now Buddhist artists always paint the hair of the Buddha, Bodhisattvas and even other heavenly beings, sky-blue (3–5). At least in the Buddhist context of the early centuries AD, *vaidūrya* in Sanskrit and *liu-li* in Chinese meant lapis lazuli. Probably because the *liu-li* sold to the Chinese included not only lapis lazuli and similar precious stones but also blue or green glass, the Chinese gradually, certainly by the fifth century, found out that certain kinds of *liu-li* could be made by melting different kinds of stones together (*WS*: CII, 2275).

The word *po-li* underwent the same kind of transition. The Sanskrit word *sphāṭika*, *phalika* in Pali, meaning crystal or quartz, is related to *po-li*. In the early Chinese Buddhist context *po-li* and crystal (*shui-ching*) were synonyms (Chang Hung-chao 1921: 43). However, imported fake crystal enabled a few Chinese to realize that both *po-li* and the so-called crystal were man-made materials. Ke Hung (AD 284–368) pointed out that the imported 'crystal vessels' were actually made by mixing five kinds of minerals. He also ridiculed the 'ignorant people' who believed that the 'crystal' was a kind of natural precious stone like jade (*Pao-p'u-tsu Nei-p'ien*: II, 21). Because, by the third and the fourth centuries, most buyers

[4] The Sanskrit origin of the Chinese words for glass was pointed out to me by Dr Victor Mair.

[5] The modern usage of liu-li for blue and green glaze on tiles also derives from the early Buddhist connotation of *liu-li*.

did not distinguish between *po-li* and crystal, the two terms came to mean either rock crystal or transparent glass.

During the period when the ancient Chinese imported *po-li* or *liu-li* they also continued to make their own glass, probably in order to imitate jade. The Later Han scholar Wang Ch'ung describes man-made jade thus: 'The jade made out of melted jade-like stones is as brilliant as real jade' (Yang Po-ta 1979: 77). The major characteristic of Chinese glass, as analysed by P. D. Ritchie, is the high proportion of lead, and in some samples, barium (1937). It contains much less silicon, the major element of modern glass, than does glass from Egypt and other ancient countries. The high lead content resulted in a lower melting point and the greater fragility of the glass. Barium and other elements made it opaque. Wang Ch'ung made his comments in the period when the Chinese had already become aware of something called *liu-li* from the West. Because the Chinese continued to make this opaque fragile glass long after they had seen the transparent glass vessels from foreign countries, they apparently did not understand that both their opaque material and the transparent glass shared similar chemical components and thus belonged to the same category of glass, at least as classified by modern glass experts. When the author of the history of the Northern Wei records that a merchant from Yüeh-chih[6] taught the Chinese how to make *liu-li* (*WS*: CII, 2275), he does not consider the jade-like materials long produced within China to be *liu-li*.

The distinction between *liu-li* and *po-li* is not always clear outside Buddhist literature. The category *liu-li* includes transparent or translucent glass, which was a treasure for the emperors and other élite. In the legends about the Former Han Emperor Wu, *liu-li* was one of the treasures in his 'Exotic Jewels Palace', and the screen of another palace was made of 'white *liu-li*'—which can mean either white or translucent glass (Lu Hsün 1939: 347–9). In the Chin period a minister, Wang Chi, who was considered extremely generous and extravagant, entertained Emperor Wu with *po-li* utensils (*CS*: XLII, 1206). An anecdote of Chin times records a comment on a *liu-li* vessel: 'Why is this empty vessel a jewel? Because it is clear and transparent' (*Shih-shuo-hsin-yü*: XXV, 595). What the owners actually

[6] Probably the small Kushan state in north-west India after the disintegration of the Kushan empire.

treasured was the transparency of a glass vessel, be it called *po-li*, *liu-li* or crystal.

Chinese élites were not alone in yearning for the transparent material. Pliny complains that crystal was a 'crazy addition as symbol of wealth and prestige' in Rome (XXXVII 10). He says that Indian crystal was the most preferred (XXXVII 9). When the Indians exported crystal to the Roman empire some genuine crystal was probably also transported to China. Pliny's time also saw a rapid development of glass-making in the West. He says that the glassware of his days closely resembles rock-crystal (XXXVII 10, XXXVI, 67). A few centuries later in China, the most extravagant prince Yüan Chen in the Northern Wei boasted of a few dozen crystal plates and bowls, glass (*liu-li*) vessels and red-jade cups. All of these vessels came from the Western Region (YHC: IV, 207). These 'crystal plates and bowls' were very likely transparent glass, as Ke Hung had pointed out two centuries earlier.

A series of glass vessels excavated from either tombs or Buddhist sites located in north China during this period verifies these literary records.[7] The common features of these vessels are their plain design, an azure or green colour, and transparency. Their plainness usually causes difficulty in determining their provenance, but associated artifacts in the tomb of Feng Su-Fu, a minister of the Northern Yen state (AD 407–36), provide some clues. A gold ornament with the Buddha's image suggests Afghanistan and the Gandhara region as the area where it was produced. Su Pai rightly identifies the 'duck-form' vessel with a sea-dolphin vessel in Begram, Afghanistan (Su Pai 1977a 45–46; Hackin 1954: Plate XVIII, Figure 41). More important than details of form, the glass-blowing technique, unknown in China at that time, betrays the vessel's foreign origin.

Glass beads were another treasure in China. Like coral beads,

[7] Glass bowls and other containers, including a 'duck-form' vessel, all sea-green and transparent, from tomb of Feng Su-fu of AD 415 in Liaoning (Li, Yao-po 1973: 6–7). One glass bowl and five bottles found in a stone casket of the Northern Wei monastery in Ting-hsien, Hopei province, all azure and transparent (Hopei Bureau 1966: 257–8). One glass bowl with trailed thread decoration and a plain bowl from a tomb of Northern Wei, Hopei (Dohrenwend 1980: 438). A pearl-shaped green translucent vessel in a tomb of the Northern Ch'i (Wang, Kelin 1976: 393).

pearls and beads of other kinds of precious stones, glass beads were associated with Buddhist remains. To identify the provenance of a glass bead is even more difficult than for a vessel. But when glass beads are found together with coral beads and pearls, as in the case of the stone casket in Ting-hsien, they are possibly also foreign.

From the Han period on the Chinese viewed both the Roman empire and India as producers of *liu-li*. The official history of the Former Han described *liu-li* as a product of Chi-pin in the Kashmir region (*HS*: XCVI, 3885). At that time *liu-li* still mainly denoted lapis lazuli, whose origin was not far from Kashmir. By the time that the Later Han history identified the Roman empire as the origin of *liu-li* (*HHS*: LXXXVIII, 2917) the word *liu-li* had come to mean glass. Later historians followed this tradition of viewing *liu-li* as of Roman origin until the Northern Wei History, when Yüeh-chih merchants, probably citizens of the small state surviving from the Kushan empire, are credited with the introduction of glass-making techniques.

Like China, India began to produce glass much later than Egypt and Mesopotamia, but unlike China it produced good-quality glass very early. Very few samples from Taxila, Nalanda, Ahicchatra, Arikamedu and other sites show traces of lead, and none of them show any barium (B. B. Lal 1952). This feature enabled Indian workers to make transparent and clear glassware. Pliny referred to glass from India as being of good quality (XXXVI, 66; Schoff 1912: 220). Moreover, Roman traders brought flint glass to Barygaza (*Periplus*: 49). Indian workers must have been familiar with the technology of processing glass. The early Christian era witnessed the best period of glass production in ancient Indian history (Dikshit 1969: 25). However, Indian workers in the Kushan period do not seem to have been familiar with glass-blowing techniques. Most glass vessels found in Taxila were foreign imports, the local products being limited to moulded objects such as seals and beads (Dikshit 1969: 81ff.) Glass tiles in Taxila reveal that Indians were skilful at moulding large pieces of glass (B. B. Lal 1952: 22).

The making of beads also started very early in India. Ujjain was famous from the time of the *Periplus*, and excavations prove it to be a bead producer (*IAR* 1957–8: 34). The important seaport Barygaza yielded a large number of beads (*IAR* 1957–8: 34). Beads were such popular ornaments that they are found in almost every archaeo-logical site from all periods. In all the sites glass beads often far outnumber other kinds of beads, except those made of terracotta.

As for the glass vessels found in Taxila, Begram and other sites of north-western India, most of them probably came from the Mediterranean (Dikshit 1969: 27ff.). Glass vessels which were imported through Barbaricon could easily reach those cities and go even further, to China. The samples found in China do not have designs as elaborate as those found in Begram, but they were good enough to satisfy the Chinese élite's desire for transparent glass. Thus they found their way into Chinese tombs and stupas.

Both the imported glass vessels or indigenous Indian items were often associated with Buddhist sites. The glass tiles from the Dharmarajika monastery, Taxila, were used to pave the sacred path around the stupa (Marshall 1951 I: 238). In Charsada, ancient Pushkalavati, glass bottles, beads and small artifacts were buried along with reliquaries under Buddhist stupas (Dikshit 1969: 36). Glass beads were scattered outside Buddhist stupas or hidden inside along with other beads. As mentioned earlier, the similar association in China of beads and stupas suggests that, because they had similar religious meaning to Buddhists, glass beads were exported from India to China together with other beads.

OTHER COMMODITIES FROM INDIA Coral, pearls and glass are among the Indian exports to China that are traceable in both literary and archaeological sources. Some items, such as incense, appear in literary sources as commodities from India but do not leave material traces. Perfume and incense traded in western Indian ports also appear in Chinese literature from the Later Han onwards. By the second or third century AD not only were items such as styrax and frankincense brought by Roman ships sold in China, but so too were many Indian products, which were also shipped to the Roman empire. Bdellium, native to the dry region of western India (Miller 1969: 69ff) was imported into China under the name of *an-hsi-hsiang*, i.e. fragrance from Arsaces or Persia (Needham 1954: v, pt 2, 137). Costus, a product from Kashmir (Schoff 1912: 168; Miller 1969: 84), was also mentioned as a Persian product in the official history of the Northern Wei (*WS*: CII, 2270, Needham 1954: v, pt 2, 137). Another Indian product, myrrh (Miller 1969: 104–5), was imported to China through Central Asian routes (Needham 1954: v, pt 2, 137). These Indian products were obviously desired by both Roman and Chinese markets.

After the third century the demand for Oriental fragrances decreased in the Roman empire due to the puritanical attitudes of the early Christians (Bowen 1958, *c.* 84–5). Meanwhile, the demand in China seemed to increase. Up until the third century only royal families and their close social circle seemed to enjoy these imported fragrances. Following the propagation of Buddhism, people of some of the lower social levels also came to use incense because incense-burning was essential to Buddhist rituals. The Buddhist preacher Fo-t'u-teng (AD 232–348) insisted on burning bdellium (*an-hsi-hsiang*) in his religious practices (*KSC:* IX, 384a, 385b).

Some precious stones found at Chinese archaeological sites may have been of foreign origin, but it is impossible to determine their provenance. For example, the Chinese word for agate or carnelian, *ma-naô*, derives from the Sanskrit word *aśmagarbha* and was introduced by Buddhist literature in the Later Han (Chang Hung-chao 1921: 36). Some of the agate and carnelian ornaments found in China might have been imported from Central Asia and India under the inspiration of Buddhism. However, since agate was indigenous to China one cannot tell which artifacts are foreign.

Like the fragrances, other imported goods in Han times were also enjoyed almost exclusively by the royal family. Later, a lower social strata began to use these commodities. By the period of the Northern dynasties Buddhists became major buyers of these foreign goods. This phenomenon will be examined in the following chapters. For the present I wish to raise another question: what did the Chinese trade do for these Indian goods?

COMMODITIES TRANSPORTED FROM CHINA TO INDIA

SILK Because silk was the only Chinese product which had reached the regions west of Central Asia before the T'ang in large quantities, and because much silk was transported to Roman markets through India in order to bypass the conflicts between the Roman empire and the Persians, silk is the most likely commodity that China exported to India. However, evidence pointing to a market for Chinese silk within India is not as clear. Since Indians primarily practised cremation in the period under study, and since the Indian climate eventually destroyed any textile exposed to it, no samples are available to enable us to evaluate the extent of the trade. All one can do is extract clues from contemporary literature and speculate on the basis of textile fragments from Central Asia. Using literary sources, I will first investigate the nature of both the Indian market for Chinese silk and the sources of supply within China, and then examine Central Asian archaeological remains of the types of silk that might have been exported to India.

At the time of the *Periplus* and Pliny, China was the main supplier of silk to the Mediterranean world. Roman traders obtained their supply from the seaports along the western Indian coast, where Indians acted as middlemen. In addition to the Red Sea, the Persian Gulf was also a major route for shipped silk and other Indian exports to the Mediterranean world. The inscription known as the 'Tariff of Palmyra' and other inscriptions of caravan leaders from the Palmyra region in Syria describe the organization of these large caravans. They carried Indian commodities from the Persian Gulf to Palmyra along the Tigris and the Euphrates (Starcky 1952: 70–84). Fragments of Han silk found in tombs at Palmyra (Boulnois 1966: 110) verify Palmyra's role in shipping Chinese silk from India to the West.

It would have been surprising if Indians, while acting as middlemen, did not keep some of this fabric for themselves. The *Buddhacarita* (IV, 49; VIII, 21) and the *Mahāvastu* (I, 149, p. 118; 217, p. 172; 231, p. 187; II, 175, p. 169; 190, p. 183; 422, p. 375; III, 141, p. 137) show that silk was used for fashion and decoration in kings' palaces and cities. A piece of silk found in a Buddhist relic casket dated to the early centuries AD in Nagara is an evidence of the role of silk in Buddhist rituals (Mehta 1966: 186), although there is no information about the origin of the silk. In fact the silk traffic with China might have stimulated the growth of the silk industry in India, including western India. By the time of the Gupta period literary sources reveal that silk enjoyed wide use (Maity 1957: 113). The Mandasor inscription recording a silk weavers' guild which patronized a temple shows the strength of an established organization engaging in a mature profession (Sircar 1965: 299–307).

By the Gupta period the Chinese had already lost their monopoly over the silk market. This market underwent a series of changes due to political factors. Marketing and the production network over the Eurasian continent became immensely complex. The division of the Roman empire (AD 364), and the subsequent invasions of the Goths (AD 410) and Attila the Hun (AD 451), severely affected Rome's oriental trade. The decline of the Roman market for silk might have slowed down silk export and production in India. For example, many historians have attributed the migration of the earlier mentioned silk-weavers' guild from the Narmada valley to Mandasor in west Malva in the early fifth century to these events. However, many other considerations, such as the supply of materials, or political and religious reasons, could have caused the migration of one guild. Actually, the rise of the Byzantine empire almost made up for the loss of the Roman trade. Along with many other luxury goods from Asia, silk became necessary for the Byzantine court and church.

Byzantium's demand for silk was so insatiable that it continuously competed with Sassanid Persia for the Indian trade. Procopius, the Byzantine historian, described the Byzantine emperor Justinian's struggle with Persia for silk. The emperor tried to get Ethiopian merchants to buy silk from India, but the Ethiopians could not reach the source since Persia monopolized both the silk coming overland from China and that coming by sea from India or China (*Procopius*: I, xx 9–12). The demand for Chinese silk in the Mediterranean world continued to be one of the factors keeping the routes from the western India ports to Central Asia alive. Procopius made it clear that the silk for which Byzantium and Persia competed was 'the silk of which they are accustomed to make the garments which of old the Greeks called Medic, but which the present time they name "seric" [namely, Chinese silk]' (*Procopius*: I, xx 9).

While the silk market in the Mediterranean world suffered and revived in response to these political changes, the sources of the silk supply also underwent a series of changes. On examining the demand from Byzantium more carefully one notices that its markets demanded more raw silk material and silk yarn than ready-made silk cloth. Justinian's law that the cost of one pound of silk should not exceed eight pieces of gold (*Procopius*: VI, xxv 17–22) seems to have been imposed on silk floss or yarn. It is illogical to calculate the price of silk fabric in terms of weight, an attribute which has little to do with the quality of the cloth. Silk floss, in contrast, can be sold by weight. Around the fifth century AD cities in the Byzantine empire wove good quality polychrome silk whose design suited the western market better than did Chinese silk. Products from the cities of Beirut and Tyre were sold in European countries (*Procopius*: VI, xxv 12–17). If silk fabric made within the Byzantine empire was available, it might have cut into the demand for Chinese textiles.

Here too the Persians competed with Byzantium in silk production. Their polychrome silk found its way to tombs in Egypt and other places of the Byzantine empire. The Persian designs appealed more to western taste than did Chinese designs, but Persian silk still retained some exotic Oriental flavour. This fact led Joan A. McDowell to suggest that Sassanian polychrome silk took over the European market for Chinese silk during China's civil wars in post-Han times (Lecture in the University Museum, University of Pennsylvania, 3 Nov. 1983).

Byzantine and Sassanian silk even penetrated into the Central Asian market. A record dated to the fourth century AD mentions women in the Hsi-ho region, namely the Ho-hsi corridor, wearing five-coloured silk made in a foreign country (*Hsi-ho-chi*: 1). In the later fourth century the king of Kucha was said to have honoured the monk Kumarajiva with a seat made of silk from Ta-ch'in (*KSC*: II, 331a).[8] A debenture dated around the end of the fifth century to the early sixth century AD mentions 'polychrome silk from Kucha' (Sinkiang Museum 1977: 33). Since Kucha was on the northern route to Persia, either Persian silk or silk from this part of Central Asia seems to have penetrated the Chinese domain.

It is hard to determine to what extent Sassanian silk replaced Chinese silk in Central Asia, but it did enter the Mediterranean market during this period as a powerful competitor. During the period when Chinese silk textiles lost at least part of the market in Byzantium, they may have gained more consumers in India. The routes from the western Indian coast to the Gandhara region were not the only ones between India and China on which trade occurred. As has been mentioned while discussing the routes in India, the routes connecting the Ganges valley to China through the Kashmir region gained importance after the mid fifth century. Along this

---

[8] Kumarajiva's (AD 344–411) biography was written in the Liang dynasty (AD 502–57). Ta-ch'in here indicates either the Roman empire or the Byzantine empire.

route Hsüan-tsang noticed that silk clothes were popular in the Takka region (in modern Punjab) (Beal 1906: I, 116) and Satadru (I, 178).

Silk consumption in India was closely related to the lives of privileged social groups, especially of the urban élite, and to religious practices. Silk clothes fit well with Vatsyayana's picture of 'nagaraka' leisure. The Mandasor inscription on the silk-weaving guild mentions that 'a woman will not go to meet her lover in secret until she has put on two silken garments' (Sircar 1965: 303; Basham 1983: 99). Similarly Uravashi, like many women described in Sanskrit literature, put on silk clothes before seeing her lover Vikrama (VU: III 9). Silk was also used for weddings. Kalidasa described weddings in *Kumārasambhava* and *Raghuvaṁśa* where both the bride and bridegroom have silk outfits (*KSA*: VII, 7, 26, 73; *RA*: VII, 18, 19).[9]

Silk banners were indispensable for Buddhist ceremonies. Fa-hsien observed silk banners hung over monks' seats at a grand Buddhist ceremony held in Chieh-ch'a in Kashmir (857c); silk banners were donated to the Buddha's garden near Sravasti (860b); and silk banners were also hung in the parade of the Buddha's image in Pataliputra (862b). It is not clear whether the custom of hanging silk banners originated from India, then spread to Central Asia and thence to China, or whether it spread from Central Asia to both India and China. One century later Sung Yün and Hui-sheng witnessed 'several ten thousands of silk banners hung over' a stupa in Uzuntati under Khotan rule, and more than half of these were from their home land, Northern Wei China. They recognized one banner as belonging to the time of the Later Ch'in (AD 384–417) (YHC: V, 266). These envoys carried with them 1000 banners of coloured silk which were 100 *ch'ih* in length, 500 silk bags for incense and 2000 smaller banners. They donated them to monasteries starting from Khotan, and their supply was almost exhausted after Gandhara (YHC: V, 329). As official delegations were rare, most of these banners were donated by traders passing by, or by

[9] *Dukūla*, which normally means fine fabric. Maity argues that *dukūla* in the two works of Kalidasa refers to silk garments, because the fabric was characterized by elaborate patterns which would not be worth applying to cheaper textiles (Maity 1957: 113, note 1).

people who bought these banners.[10]

Banners made of Chinese silk appear in the Sanskrit literature of Gupta times. Interestingly, during a wedding ceremony in the *Kumārasambhava* rows of flags made of Chinese silk (*cīnāmśuka*) decorated the city (VII 3). Chinese silk flags (*cīnāmśukam keto*) are also mentioned in the *Śakuntalā* (I 33). These silk flags may have been similar to those found in Central Asia. In short, the demand for Chinese silk banners was caused by both Buddhist ceremonies as well as Hindu ceremonies such as weddings.

Even though Gupta India was a silk producer it demanded Chinese silk, probably because Chinese silks differed from Indian ones in quality, in style and in processing. Even as late as the seventh century, when Hsüan-tsang visited Khotan, the local custom was that artisans did not unreel silk fibre before the moths had gnawed through their cocoons. This practice resulted in short fibre, and hence a different style of silk textile. There is no information about the technology of silk weaving during Gupta India, but it is possible that Gupta artisans adopted techniques different from the Chinese. Furthermore, much Indian silk was from different species of silk-worms. Silk technology spread from south-west China to India through Assam in the early Christian era. A few local varieties of silk-worm of that region were cultivated, probably inspired by the mulberry silk (Schoff 1912: 264). As long as there were differences between Chinese and Indian silks, expensive silk products from a long distance held special value and prestige for the Indian élite and religious groups.

In summarizing the state of the international market from the fourth to the sixth centuries, it seems that the rise of the silk-weaving industry in Byzantium and Persia reduced the need for Chinese textiles, not raw silk floss. But in India the demand for silk fabric, partially Chinese silk fabric, increased. It is time now, therefore, to examine the proposition that Chinese silk production declined with the post-Han political turmoil. Many people have assumed

[10]The British Museum collection of painted silk banners recovered from Central Asia by Stein has been published recently (Whitfield 1982). Although these belong to T'ang or later times, they may give some impression of the quality and quantity of earlier silk banners.

that political disunity discouraged investment and hindered the development of the division of labour necessary to produce high quality polychrome silk.

The practice of emperors in the Later Han who granted their ministers and tribal chiefs tens and hundreds of thousands of bolts of silk reveal China's enormous capacity for silk production (Fang Hao 1963: 134). During the periods of division after the Han the region producing the best silk, Shu, was separated from the north. Rulers in the north nevertheless made up for this loss by encouraging silk production. Emperor Wen of Wei once boasted that the 'middle lands' were the only place producing good quality goods, especially all kinds of textiles.[11] Even polychrome patterned silk from Shu could not compare with Wei products (T'ao Yüan-chen 1935: 103). It is hard to know what proportion of this statement represents Emperor Wen's boasting, but silk weaving in the north certainly developed rapidly in this period. By the early fourth century a modest total for silk stored in the capital, Loyang, was 4,000,000 bolts (CS: xxvi, 783). In the Northern Wei (AD 386–534) the silk in the state treasury became too much to store, so the Empress Dowager Hu granted her ministers as much silk as they could carry (YHC: iv, 208). These records suggest that a great quantity of silk was produced over the period.

Many factors contributed to continued silk production in the post-Han period despite unfavourable economic and political conditions for the silk industry. One factor was the corruption of the monetary system after the Han. A series of short-lived governments which circulated poor quality coins caused chaos in the monetary system. As China rarely issued gold or silver coins before modern times, the value of copper coins depended heavily on the authority of those who cast them. When political changes took place frequently, no authority could maintain a stable monetary system. The result was that silk gradually replaced coinage as a medium of exchange. From the time of the Three Kingdoms, northern governments collected tax in silk and in grain instead of in coins. Even the unified Chin dynasty calculated the value of its treasury in silk and jewels. This situation certainly encouraged silk production.

[11] *Chung-kuo*, the Yellow River valley.

Silk currency, although inconvenient for domestic trade, was well suited to international trade in relation to the Western Region; actually, the Central Asian people preferred silk to Chinese copper coins. The Central Asia Kharoshthi documents dated to the early fourth century AD show that silk and silk clothes, such as Chinese robes, were not only a form of property but were also used as payment in transactions (Burrow 1940: 27, no. 149). For example, the price of a woman was forty-one bolts of silk (1, no. 3). Or, a Buddhist monastery fined monks in silk:

whichever monk does not partake in the activities of the community of monks shall pay a fine of one bolt of silk... whichever monk strikes another monk, [in the case of] a light [blow] five bolts of silk, [in the case of] a moderate [blow], ten bolts of silk, [in the case of] an excessive [blow] fifteen bolts of silk ... (95, no. 489).

It is not surprising that Buddhist monks in Central Asia owned so much silk. Rulers of north China in the fourth and fifth centuries often granted silk to monks, including foreign monks, as rewards for their religious services. For example, the ruler of the Later Ch'in (AD 384–417) granted Fo-t'o-yeh-she, a monk from Kashmir, 10,000 bolts of silk for his work on translating Buddhist texts. Although Fo-t'o-yeh-she declined the offer, 500 monks, local and foreign, who worked with him, accepted a large amount of silk (KSC: II, 334b).

Let me remind the reader that no Chinese silk samples have been found in India. Did some of the silk circulating in Central Asia reach India? In addition to the sketchy literary sources about Chinese silk, silk fragments found in Central Asia may provide some clues.

Stein catalogued the silk fragments he found in Central Asia into three groups:

A. Silk fragments from the site of Lou-lan (Shan-shan), Han products.

B. Silk fragments from Astana cemetery in Turfan, early T'ang period.

C. Silk fragments from Ch'ien-fo-tung, Tunhuang, between the later T'ang and the early Sung (1928: I, 233).

No Stein samples are dated in the period between the Han and the T'ang. Silk samples discovered after Stein mainly fall into the same three periods as Stein's. For example, the silk found at Niya was Han polychrome patterned silk (Sinkiang Museum 1960). Exceptions are samples dated around the Northern dynasties, such as a silk embroidery of the Buddha in Ch'ien-fo-tung, Tunhuang; and fragments from Uzuntati, the site where Sung Yün and Hui-sheng saw several thousands of silk banners (Sinkiang Museum 1972: 3). The dating of Astana cemetery is also more accurate. The museum in Sinkiang Uighur Autonomous Region catalogued the forty-five tombs they excavated into three periods. The first group belongs to the period from Western Chin to the middle of the Northern dynasty (third to sixth century); the second is from the Northern dynasties to the early T'ang (early sixth to seventh century); the third belongs to the middle T'ang (seventh to eighth century) (Sinkiang Museum 1973). This dating fills a vacancy in textile history of Chinese silk in Central Asia, namely the period after the Han to the T'ang.

From Han to T'ang a dramatic change took place in the technique of silk weaving. Weft-faced weaving, the wool weaving technique in the west of Central Asia, replaced the typical warp-faced Han weaving in producing polychrome silk. A group of textile samples of 'Sassanian design' is associated with the new technique. The representative design in a pearl roundel—a ring formed by a string of small circles (see Figure 5) —enclosing animal motifs. The animal motifs of Persian design could be boars, deer or a pair of horses facing each other, with or without riders. They are stiff in style in contrast to the lively horses, birds or other animals on Han textiles. Having studied these samples carefully Hsia Nai attributes the technical change to influence from Central Asia and to a change in style to suit the Persian market (1963).

Falling between the typical Han silk and weft-faced silk of T'ang, some samples dated to the Northern dynasties and the Sui dynasty show a transitional technique, the 'twill' technique. 'Twill' means a basic warp-faced textile using weft to cross the two (or more) warps, thus forming some design. Pattern design also differs from both that of the Han and the T'ang silks. Chinese scholars who have studied those samples consider silk of this period as a technical and stylistic extension of the Han. However, just as the twill marked a transition to a new weaving technique, the motifs also changed substantially from the Han style. Here I want to draw attention to some atypical Sassanian roundels and some stripes or chess-board designs among this group in order to suggest their possible connection to the Indian market.

Before discussing the new elements in textile design of the post-Han period, I want to dispel a serious misunderstanding of the origin of an important design—the pearl roundel. Stein, in his survey of Central Asia, simply attributed all pearl-roundel designs to the Persian style. Joan Mcdowell, by exhibiting similar motifs in Persian art, has carefully built up the connection between the facing horses in pearl roundels on Persian textiles and their symbolic meaning combining divinity and kingship (Lecture in the University Museum, University of Pennsylvania, 3 November 1983). However, she assumes the pearl roundel was part of the design and did not explain its meaning.

Having examined a series of Chinese damasks and brocades Michael Meister points out that roundel designs using twill technique existed on damask as early as the Han; the roundel was a popular design on Gupta sculpture, especially the pearl roundel with the lotus inside (1970). Indeed this kind of roundel even appears in Kushan sculpture in Mathura, as in a decorative plaque (Rosenfield 1967: Text of Figure 3). It is not possible to trace the origin of the roundel here, but these examples suggest that the pearl roundel was a popular design circulating in Asian countries in the period of communication between those civilizations, and was not exclusively Persian in origin.

Some pearl-roundel designs carry motifs different from both the Han designs and the typical Sassanian ones. A sample found in Astana by Stein shows a row of confronting phoenixes and a row of 'Indian roundels', i.e. the roundels of lotuses (1928: Ast. ix, 303). Three samples showing confronting peacocks in pearl roundels are dated between the Northern dynasties and the Sui. One is in the Stein collection (Ast. v, 2.01) and two were found by Chinese archaeologists in Astana (Figure 5; Figure 6a). The one published by the Sinkiang Museum in 1972 (Figure 5) has a Chinese character in the design. The one from the Stein collection has roundels enclosing confronting lions in addition to those of confronting peacocks. The peacock was not among the fauna of north China, nor was it an auspicious motif in literature and art like the phoenix. Up to the time of the Northern dynasties only a few had been brought to the emperors' court from India. Chinese artists of the time had hardly any chance to see them. In contrast, the peacock was an auspicious animal from a very early period in Indian history. Various motifs involving peacocks appear on many works of art. The prototype for the silk designer was probably some carving found in Begram (see Figure 6b). If this kind of silk was designed for export, as the location of the samples indicates it might have been, I would suggest it was for the Indian market.

Another interesting pattern the silk of the Northern dynasties incorporates is a striped or chess-board design. The weaver used different-coloured warps to form narrow or wide stripes which provided a background for stylistic motifs. The entire textile was divided into coloured stripes. The use of different coloured wefts regularly spaced forms a chess-board design. Because this is the simplest method of making a textile design it is still used in hand weaving in many regions. But, as polychrome patterned silk was an expensive textile, the design must have been produced to suit consumers' tastes rather than to accommodate a simple technique. Actually, many samples of this design show a complicated weaving technique.

Han silk did not adopt this simple design. Elaborate motifs are displayed on a one-colour background. Looking at the Gupta frescoes in Ajanta one can see in almost every picture with clothed human beings that the cloth has stripes or a chess-board design. Most of these are narrow stripes without further elaboration, yet some are wide stripes, with other motifs on them (e.g. Yazdani 1930–55: vol. I: XXII, XXVI; vol. III: iii; vol. IV : xx). Wide stripes with motifs on them also appear on sculptures (A. Ghosh 1950: Plate. v, vi). The Mandasor silk guild describes the beautiful design of their silk product as 'varṇṇāntara-vibhāga-cittena' (Sircar 1965: 303). Basham translated this as 'with varied stripes of different colours' (1983: 99). Although it is hard to determine if the colourful design in the text referred to a design of stripes of different colours, Basham, when translating the inscription, must have had this kind of design in his mind. Striped cloth was clearly widespread in fourth- or fifth-century India.

Unlike the frescoes in Ajanta, human figures painted in the caves in Tunhuang dated around the same period do not wear this kind of striped cloth. If this design was not pupular in even this frontier region of China, might it not have been made for another country, most likely India?

Motifs on the textiles also betray South Asian influence. No. 23 of the Sinkiang Museum collection shows Bodhi trees, a religious symbol for Buddhism, on stripes (Figure 3). No. 27 is a chess-board design silk with three rows of animals on three different coloured stripes: buffalo, lion and elephant (Figure 4). The crude design of lion and elephant indicates that the designer was not familiar with these animals. Like the peacock, the lion and the elephant were only rarely seen in north China, and only when presented as gifts by foreign countries. Although the buffalo design looks similar to the water-buffalo common in south China, the water-buffalo did not enjoy a reputation as an auspicious animal in the fifth or sixth century in north China. Known auspicious animals of ancient Chinese art are the dragon, tiger, phoenix and deer. This design of foreign motifs seems to have a specific purpose, which, I again suggest, was their marketing in India. If silk textiles similar to the ones found in Central Asia ever reached Indian consumers, the few samples I have discussed above would have been likely candidates.

Chapter iii: The Structure of Trade

Although none of the items traded between India and China were necessary for human subsistence, the exchange of these goods persisted throughout the period under study. In order to analyse the underlying causes of the trade I want to first analyse the trade mechanisms—or transactions—by which these luxury goods were transferred, and then to examine the trade in luxury goods within the context of the contemporaneous urban economy in India and China. An analysis of trade mechanisms will reveal various actors in the process, and the motivations of their participation. The economic context of Sino-Indian trade will provide a frame of reference to assess the role of the long-distance trade of luxury goods.

Forms of Transaction

Trade between the two sophisticated ancient civilizations of China and India was not limited to the purely simple forms of transaction of primitive societies, such as barter, nor did it extend to the highly developed market system of modern societies. Different social groups carried out transactions that constituted the trade. Because the Substantivists, among economic anthropologists, have analysed material transactions functioning along lines other than those of modern western societies, I will borrow their theoretical framework to analyse the mechanisms of the ancient Sino-Indian trade.

Polanyi classifies material transactions into three main patterns: reciprocity, redistribution and exchange (Polanyi *et al.* 1957: 250). He associates the three forms with societies in different stages of development: 'Tribal societies practise reciprocity and redistribution while archaic societies are predominantly redistributive, though to some extent they may allow room for exchange' (256)

Modern western societies, of course, practise mainly exchange. The three patterns of trade are accordingly represented by gift trade, administered trade and market trade (263). The economists of the Substantive school further link the three patterns of transaction to three types of economy. While in a marketless economy people practise reciprocity and redistribution, in economies with peripheral markets supply and demand forces in marketplaces do not function as in a market system but are 'qualified by idiosyncratic social influences and controls' (Bohannan & Dalton 1962: 16). Only in a market economy is market exchange a full-grown institution.

Applying these categories to the ancient Sino-Indian trade one finds that all the three main forms of transactions co-existed. Even 'exchange' or 'market trade' appeared in the period under study, although social and cultural influences had some impact on the forces of demand and supply.

The gift trade prompted other transactions between China, India and Central Asian countries. Starting with Chang Ch'ien, who in the second century BC visited the Kushans to seek an alliance against the Hsiung-nu, envoys continuously carried gifts across the Central Asian routes. Even though the governments of these countries changed the gift exchanges never ceased during the period under study (Chang Hsing-lang 1930: vol. 5). As I said at the beginning of Chapter II, most of the gifts sent to Chinese rulers were rare objects or even strange things, often reserved for the use of royal families. Chinese emperors and kings mainly sent silk, gold and silver bullion, and copper coins. During the Han dynasty the gifts of the Chinese emperors served a political purpose—that of making alliances against the Hsiung-nu. But the strategy was not always successful. The Kushans were never a reliable ally of the Han. They even fought against the Han in AD 90, probably during the peak of their territorial expansion (*HHS*: LXXVII, 1580). However, in order to obtain Chinese goods for their Roman trade, the Kushans had at least to maintain neutrality between the Han and the Hsiung-nu. Whatever the initial purpose of the gift trade, it prompted the powers involved to recognize the potential for trade in general. It also demonstrated their goodwill, which provided certain security for further exchange.

Once the gift trade had opened the door for inter-cultural exchange, governments often organized trade on a larger scale. The

Polanyi school sees ports of trade as the major form of long-distance administered trade. In ancient Mesopotamia and the east Mediterranean, where markets for inter-cultural trade did not exist, agents of governments carried out trade at certain agreed places. These ports of trade were located in politically neutral regions, where the transactions took place in front of an altar in order to guarantee the safety of participants (Polanyi *et al.* 1957: 52, 61, 116, etc.). If the governments engaged in the ancient Sino-Indian trade also dealt through ports of trade, the oasis states of Central Asia may be seen as the ideal places geographically for the ports of trade.

However, these states were neither politically neutral nor safe for inter-cultural transactions. They served more as caravanserais where commodities changed hands between travelling and local merchants. If we do not insist on the political neutrality of the location, the foreign quarter in a capital of a north China state could well serve as the port of trade. The establishment of a special neighbourhood for foreigners in each of the capitals in north China during the first to the fifth centuries (see Chapter I, section 3, p. 47) indicates that the trading community and their markets were under government control and protection. On one occasion, when the Han military force defeated the Hsiung-nu in a battle in central Asia, the emperor ordered the head of the Hsiung-nu chief to be hung in the foreigners' quarters (*HHS*: LXXXVIII: 2928). These foreigners were likely to have been the envoys of their governments and could convey the desired political message home. In most cases the foreigners' area is only casually mentioned in literary sources. But the quarter in the Northern Wei capital, Loyang, was clearly described as located outside the walled city, across the Lo river. Attached to it was a special market for foreign goods. A royal stable nearby housed two imported animals—a white elephant from the king of Gandhara and a lion from Persia (YHC III 160). This was the only neighbourhood separated from the walled city by the river, although a bridge connected it to the main gate of the city.

No information concerning how the Northern Wei government dealt with the foreign merchants is available. But the government's monopoly on production of high-quality silk and other luxury items indicates that foreign merchants had to go through the government in order to obtain merchandise. The Northern Wei rulers made the control of artisans, especially those making luxury goods, a priority when they unified north China. They moved the artisans from the Northern Yen capital, Chung-shan, and the Hsia capital, Ch'ang-an, to their capital, P'ing-ch'eng. A government department registered the artisans according to their speciality and supervised their production. The government also sought out the families who escaped registration in order to evade taxation and forced them to specialize in silk weaving. These weavers wove the fanciest polychrome silk textiles, serving the court and foreign trade (Wang Chung-lo 1979: 536). Even though the government gradually relaxed the restrictions on artisans, the major sources of silk textiles and other luxury goods remained in the hands of the government. Because silk was the major form of tax through the post-Han period (third to sixth centuries AD), government treasuries often overflowed with silk bolts. In short, the links between traders and political authorities, the physical separation of the foreign marketplace from local markets, and the monopoly of the production of luxury artifacts—all indicate that these foreign neighbourhoods might have served as ports of administered trade.

On the way between India and the Roman empire some of the western Indian seaports probably also functioned as ports of trade. All foreign cargo arriving at Barbaricon was taken to the king via the Indus (*Periplus*: 39). At Barygaza the king posted pilot boats as far as Saurastra to guide foreign vessels to the ports (44). For this service traders had to bring a list of special goods for the king—silver vessels, singing boys, beautiful girls, fine wine, thin clothing and the best ointments (*Periplus*: 49).

During the period when both the Chinese government and the kings who controlled Barygaza and Barbaricon partially administered the trade, there is little information about the Kushan handling of the trade. Extrapolating from the fact that Kushan gold coins met the Roman standard and copper coins accorded with the Chinese practice of a base metal standard (Allchin & Hammond 1978: 274), the Kushans might have cast their coins to suit foreign trade.[1] The standard coinage was probably a means to administer their foreign trade. If the government could regulate the trade in alcohol it

---

[1] Kushan copper coins are thick, heavy and good in quality. At that time there were no gold and silver coins in China, and copper coins were the main currency.

might have also regulated other imports and exports. However, the votive inscriptions from Mathura and other cities do not suggest strict governmental control of trade. Instead, traders organized themselves into guilds which regulated commercial activities. The Kushan government's interference in trade was probably limited to providing facilities for foreign trade and taxing the traders. This practice did not change significantly during the Gupta period.

Even in north China and the few ports of western India where the governments administered part of the foreign trade, individual merchants carried on trade with other countries. Both rich merchants in the Han capital Ch'ang-an and the Northern Wei capital Loyang, and traders who helped Pan Ch'ao to fight the Hsiung-nu in Central Asia, did so. The Barygaza merchants who made donations in the Buddhist caves in western India (Burgess 1881: 49) probably also independently engaged in trade. If these merchants profited considerably from the trade, as shown in the records, they must have acted according to the rules of supply and demand. Even in the ports of trade prices were not immune from the forces of supply and demand. However, we are dealing with long-distance trade in luxury goods in ancient societies—archaic societies in Polanyi's terms—where the transmission of information and transportation of goods were slow. In this imperfect market system supply and demand followed the fluctuation of prices not on a daily basis, as in the modern world market, but over a longer term. For instance, when the technology of making coloured glass was transferred to China in the early fifth century AD, the price of coloured glass fell because of the increased supply (*WS* CII: 2275). In India the glass industry declined after the Kushan period, but the making of false gem stones out of glass continued during the Gupta period. After the Gupta period until the ninth century the history of glass in north India is almost blank (Dikshit 1969: 59ff.). The survival of a limited specialized production and the final dying out of the glass industry were probably partially the consequences of the changing demand of a major foreign market, the Chinese market.

In the context of the ancient long-distance trade in luxury goods, cultural values often shaped demand.[2] In exploring the changes of supply and demand in the early Sino-Indian trade I will place the trade in luxury goods against the background of trade in general and of the urban economy in India and China.

THE UNDERLYING CAUSES OF TRADE

During the Kushan period the trade of luxury goods differed from the trade of more staple goods by its bridging many different states and cultures. The diversity of pottery types of this period suggests that the Kushan state did not achieve the uniformity of the earlier Mauryan state. Economic exchanges of most staple goods were limited to regional circuits. The vast distribution of Kushan coins indicates that the trade at a less basic level extended over a wider geographical range. Not only were gold coins used in large transactions, even copper coins held considerable value. Although Kushan coins go no further than Khotan, luxury goods such as coral, pearls, glass vessels and beads, perfumes and incense reached major cities in China. They have value even outside the area where Kushan coins circulated.

As the commodities passed through the many states of Central Asia, many transactions took place. Each transaction must have correspondingly increased the price of the commodities involved. Thanks to the horses and camels of Central Asia, caravans could carry the commodities across the deserts and mountains. Due to the extreme physical difficulties of the mountainous and desert route the quantity of the cargo was not large. Coral, pearls and glass remained fabulous items in Han literature. Even in India, coral and pearl were limited mostly to Buddhist sites.

Who engaged in the trade and enjoyed these commodities?

---

[2] Actually, this trend is even more visible today. The preference for blue jeans among young people of developing countries is certainly a result of American cultural influence. Here the cultural values even encroach on the domain of subsistence goods—the food, clothing and shelter necessary to sustain life—because there is more choice for subsistence goods now than in ancient societies.

Most likely Kushan rulers and rich merchants. Their desire for rare commodities as symbols of prestige, the trade in Roman goods and the profit from the transactions would have encouraged them to invest in the risk-filled business of purchasing silk from China. However, the association of coral, glass and pearls with Buddhist sites indicates that, unless one imagines that only the élites made donations to Buddhist institutions, the lower social levels were probably also involved in these transactions.

The association of trade goods with Buddhist sites becomes more evident by the Gupta period. The Guptas did not act as middlemen between East Asia and the West, as had the Kushans. Although western India still benefited from the trade with Byzantium and China, the commercial contacts between the Ganges plain and China can be explained only by the demand from within these two countries, as the middle and west Ganges was not the passage linking East Asia and the West. The shifts of trade routes from Bactria to Kashmir shortened the length of routes on maps, but according to the descriptions of Chinese pilgrims the mountains and valleys were even more difficult to cross. Pilgrims, preachers and traders nevertheless persistently trod across them. Traders certainly made a profit from the luxury goods they transported, but their profit depended on the appreciation and demand for these specific goods. The acceleration of the propagation of Buddhism in China in this period might have shaped the urban demand for certain kinds of luxury goods. Since this problem concerns both India and China let us first review the increase in the Chinese demand for Indian goods.

The demand for foreign luxury goods underwent some changes during the period from the Han to the Northern dynasties. Since the expedition to Central Asia under Emperor Wu of the Former Han, the degree of Chinese control over this region reflected the prestige and strength of the empire. Tribute from the Western Region was not only the pride of the emperors but, even more so, of the capital cities. Pan Ku claimed that Loyang had received tribute from more regions than that of the Former Han capital Ch'ang-an (*Liang-tu-fu*: 79a).

Exotic items from foreign countries invariably affected the tastes of urban dwellers. An obviously forged legend has it that, at the time of Emperor Wu of the Former Han, India sent a set of horse-saddles as a gift to the emperor. The saddles were made of white jade, agate and white glass. Luxury saddles became fashionable in Ch'ang-an. The cost of the decoration for one horse rose to 100 catties of gold because of the expensive saddles (*Hsi-ching-tsa-chi*: 2/2b). In this legend both the words for agate (*ma-nao*) and glass (*liu-li*) appear. Yet both entered the Chinese language only after Buddhist translations from Sanskrit; the story could not be earlier than the end of the Later Han. Although the horse was not indigenous to India proper, it was a product of the Central Asian territory of the Kushan state. In the Chinese Buddhist tradition the early missionaries were associated with horses. The first monastery in China was the 'White Horse Monastery' in Loyang. It was said that a white horse carrying Buddhist texts from the Western Region arrived there. Perhaps some Kushan preachers who came from Central Asia did ride horses. Regardless of the veracity of the story, it suggests how exotic foreign goods, even in the form of gifts for emperors, could affect urban consumption patterns by guiding the taste of urban dwellers.

Consumption patterns in cities could spread to rural areas. A later Han adage runs:

If the fashionable hair style in the city was high buns, in other places the buns will be one foot high; if it is fashionable in the city to paint long brows, the brows of people in other places will cover half of the forehead; if city people like to wear long sleeves, the sleeves of other places will use a whole bolt of silk. (*Ku-chin Feng-yao*: 16)

After the Han the demand for luxury goods came primarily from urban residents. During the ensuing political chaos many military and political figures rose rapidly. Unlike the established great families, who had always maintained their high status in spite of political change, the military families' rapid rise caused them to seek wealth, especially exotic foreign items, in order to increase their prestige. The Northern Wei aristocrat Yüan Chen, the owner of much glassware and other unusual goods, once declared that if Shih Ch'ung of the Chin dynasty, who came from only a common family, could be extravagant, what prevented him, a prince of the great Wei empire, from being so (YHC: IV, 207). Prince or not, he was not recognized by the established Chinese aristocracy as their equal. In contrast, ministers from some famous families sometimes sought to demonstrate their indifference towards wealth. When Empress Dowager Hu granted silk to ministers, everyone took many bolts. It was said two ministers carried so much that they fell and hurt their ankles. But Ts'ui Kuang, who came from the famous Ts'ui family of the Ch'ing-ho county, symbolically took only two bolts (YHC: iv, 208).

Since the Indian aristocracy favoured Chinese silk because it was expensive and came from afar, the new Chinese élites' desire for foreign goods facilitated the flow of silk to India and the West. Silk was also more perishable than coins and its value decreased with time. Yet, for a long period after the Han, the rulers of north China collected taxes in the form of silk. Thus there was often an over-supply in the state treasuries. This excess explains the impatience of the empress dowager to get rid of the surplus in the state treasury. Chinese rulers were eager to spend the silk surplus in exchange for precious foreign goods.

At a lower social level Buddhist monasteries were another important consumer of luxury goods. Stupas in ancient India and China were not the bare stone structures that they are today. The descriptions of pilgrims and the precious items found scattered around stupas suggest that they were decorated with gold and with beads made of a variety of precious stones. Archaeological finds associated with Buddhist remains match Yang Hsüan-chih's descriptions of the Yung-ning stupa and other Buddhist constructions in Loyang as being decorated with gold, jade and all kinds of beads.

This fashion of decorating stupas seems to have originated in India and then spread to Central Asia. Fa-hsien comments that in the six states east of the Pamir plateau jewels were mainly used for worship and for decorating stupas. And stupas in Suvastu, Gandhara, Taxila and Nagarahara were all decorated with gold, silver, glass and other ornaments (858b-c). Beads found around stupas, cells and monastery courtyards in Taxila verify Fa-hsien's comments (Marshall 1951: i, 353, 356, 363, 367, 387, 389, 390).

India also witnessed a revival of Brahmanism after the Gupta period. By the time of Hsüan-tsang there were already many Hindu temples in Indian cities. Hsüan-tsang noticed that the Hindu temples were richly decorated (Beal 1906: ii, 277). The competition between Buddhism and Hinduism heightened the demand for luxury goods.

Since these goods were related to religion, they often held a sacred meaning for the believers. This is particularly true for Chinese converts to Buddhism. Their practice of seeking genuine jewels for use in worship encouraged them to pay a high price for commodities brought from far away. Buddhism thus increased prices for some specific commodities. For example, the term 'seven jewels' was an important expression in Buddhism. Once the emperor of the Northern Ch'i tried to buy genuine pearls to make a 'seven jewel chariot' to please his queen (*Pei-shih*: 128). Here he did not necessarily mean them for a Buddhist purpose, but the Buddhist concept affected his taste. Correspondingly, commodities demanded by élites as signs of wealth and status could also become religious treasure. Once the items had gained a sacred meaning for devotees, religious practice in turn encouraged further demand for such commodities. In India the use of Chinese silk banners for Buddhist stupas and ceremonies might have derived from weddings and other ceremonies. Religious belief provided an important motivation for trade, both through the direct investment in another world by devotees and through its effect on secular consumption patterns.

Part II

Chapter iv: Buddhist Ideology and the Commercial Ethos in Kushan India

The evolution and maturation of Mahayana Buddhism in the early centuries of the Christian era paved the way for the school's dominance in China later on. In the same period Buddhist institutions underwent a series of changes, and, as I have shown in the last chapter, Sino-Indian commercial ties were established. In order to suggest some connections among theological developments, changes in Buddhist institutions, and relationships between the Buddhist sangha and its laity, I will first analyse a few important documents composed in this period, namely the *Milindapañha* (Questions of King Milinda), the *Buddhacarita* (The Life of the Buddha), *Saundarānanda* (The Story of Sundarnanda), the *Mahāvastu* (The Great Event), the *Saddharmapuṇḍarika* (The Lotus Sutra) and the *Sukhāvatīvyūha* (The Land of Bliss). This list is merely a sample of the most important Buddhist works extant from the early centuries AD. As in the case of much ancient Indian literature, it is impossible to date these texts precisely. All we know is that they were written in the Kushan period, sometime during the first to third centuries. The sequence I have presented them in suggests an order that reflects certain trends in Buddhist theology. The oldest text contains the early seeds of certain new ideas, and the latest the most mature forms of those ideas. I do not assign these works to the Hinayana or Mahayana schools because some of them show transitional features, because the division of schools is a complicated phenomenon, and, most importantly, because such assignment is not pertinent to this study.

THE DIVINE BUDDHA AND THE EXPANSION OF BUDDHIST COSMOLOGY

The first text is the *Milindapañha* (Questions of King Milinda). Historically Milinda (Menander) was a Greek king who ruled in Bactria and parts of northern India during the later second century BC. It is commonly accepted that this work was compiled *circa* the early first century in Sanskrit or Prakrit.[1] Unfortunately it is extant only in its Pali form. Nevertheless, this linguistic transformation and the possible distortions related to it cannot disguise a striking feature of the work. It betrays a crisis in Buddhist belief. Permeating Buddhism at the time were a number of questions concerning the apparent contradictions between the Buddha's personality as recorded in Pali texts and his divinity. For instance, how could the Buddha be omniscient when it is said that he extracts his knowledge from reflection (IV 1, 19)? Why did he admit Devadatta to the Buddhist order if he knew in advance of the schism Devadatta would create in the sangha (IV 1, 28)? Why did the Buddha boast that he could live for a kalpa, yet die young (IV 1, 71)? And how could the Buddha suffer if he had committed no sins in his former existence and if one's well-being depends on one's merits and the sins of former lives (IV 1, 62)? In answering these questions the sage Nagasena strenuously tries to reconcile human mistakes with the supposed perfection of a god. Whether or not the real king Milinda asked these questions is unknown, but this work must have reflected the doubts in the minds of Buddhists when the book was composed. It might well have served as a manual for Buddhist priests in their preaching.

[1] There is no Chinese translation after Book III. Many scholars consider the part from Book IV or V on as slightly later than the first section (Winternitz 1920: 181–3). But the geographical conception of the later section indicates this part was also written in the north-west. Even though this section is later in date, it represents a continuation of the ideological development of the earlier part. Since I am not trying to date this work, but to point out the ideological trend represented by the work, I will not distinguish the two parts in my analysis.

[2] 4,320,000,000 years.

Accompanying the divinization of the Buddha was a belief in his supernatural power. In early Pali texts Buddhists were not interested in changing environmental factors through supernatural power. The goal of each Buddhist was to reach nirvana. Indulging in the lesser achievements of magic power (iddhi) would prevent one from reaching arhatship (*Cūlavagga* VII 4, 7; in *Vinaya Texts*: III, 263). But the *Milindapañha* amplifies the ancient conception that the truth (*dhamma*) could mobilize divine power. In this text the believers use the truth for specific and practical purposes: 'by it, true believers make the rain fall, and fire go out, and ward off the effects of poison, and accomplish many other things they want to do' (IV 1, 43). For example, the virtuous king Sivi gains a new pair of eyes from heaven by summoning truth (IV 1, 42).

These deviations from early Buddhist principles paralleled the popularity of stupa-construction in north India. If the Buddha was a god and Buddhist belief embodied supernatural power, so too worshipping relics as idols of the Buddha was thought to be efficacious. From the time of Ashoka (third century BC) the building and worship of stupas gained prominence among Buddhist activities. But at the time of the *Milindapañha* the Buddha's words forbidding worship of his remains were still too well remembered for Buddhists to ignore. Nagasena's solution to the contradiction between the rule forbidding worship of relics and that saying the Buddha encouraged worship of relics is far from convincing: he defends worship of relics, explaining that the Buddha forbade only monks to worship relics because they had more important things to do (IV 3, 24–6).

The worship of relics enlarged the scope of potential donations to Buddhist institutions. In addition to providing food and housing for monasteries, the laity had to pay for the construction of and decorations on stupas as well as the jewels buried along with the relics. The increase in demand from the sangha stimulated a change in the relationship between the Buddhist sangha and the laity. In early Pali texts Buddhist patrons, mostly merchants, do not expect any direct rewards from the Buddha. Buddhist ideology encouraged donations. Early Buddhist literature praised the rich merchants who patronized the sangha while admiring their fabulous wealth. This attitude suited the aspiration of merchants to accumulate wealth and granted traders higher social status than did the Brahmanical system. It provided sufficient incentive for rich merchants to supply food and lodging to the Buddhist sangha as the merchants pleased.

But the author of the *Milindapañha* debates whether there are rewards for a lay devotee, and, more specifically, whether a Buddhist lay adherent can achieve arhatship. At one point Nagasena claims a layman can achieve arhatship only on the condition that he either enters the sangha or dies on the same day, i.e. he cannot enjoy arhatship in this life. His being a layman makes it impossible for him to be an arhat (IV 7, 7–8). On another occasion Nagasena admits that a layman can gain nirvana in his next incarnation because of the merits he has achieved in his former lives. Since no one can achieve nirvana in one life, and if one has already accumulated sufficient merit in former lives to reach nirvana, it is justifiable to remain a lay person and enjoy sensual pleasure in one's last life before nirvana. The main advantage of joining the sangha is to hasten the accumulation of merit (VI 1–26). Nagasena's conflicting opinions about the religious status of lay adherents suggest a possible trend in which Buddhist believers hoped for increased recognition of their patronage in the form of the granting to them of personal merit. Yet, at this early stage, nothing suggests that by virtue of their donations laymen would share the greater merit gained by monks. A layman's achievement depended entirely on his own effort in all his lives.

The dual trend of divinizing the Buddha and the increasing effort to attract lay devotees emerges more clearly in Asvaghosha's works. The *Buddhacarita* (The Life of the Buddha) meets the need for a biography of the newly divinized Buddha. In early Pali texts, although heavenly forces intervened in the Buddha's enlightenment, he still behaved humanly when he was a prince. He even went to have a last look at his son and wife before he left town to lead an ascetic life (Warren 1922: 62). This was, of course, long before he became a Buddha. The Pali texts described the historical transition from a prince to a Buddha. But Asvaghosha's biography depicts a Buddha who, even from the earliest stage of his life, has no affection for anyone whatsoever. The young prince, with all the brilliance of a god, was determined to desert his family and unhesitatingly left his home.

This divine Buddha wields tremendous, miraculous power which he willingly displays in order to convince people of his enlightenment. He flies up into the air, divides himself into many forms, walks on water, penetrates the earth, rains in the sky and shines like the sun. Only after fully amazing the townspeople of Kapilavastu does he begin to preach (*SN*: III 26). Superseding the *Milindapañha*, where supernatural power was embodied in true belief, Ashvaghosha's Buddha commands this power personally.

Ashvaghosha responds to the laity's search for salvation more positively than does Nagasena, the sage in the *Milindapañha*. He introduces some alluring heavenly worlds in addition to the quiet, even rather dull, state of nirvana. However, Ashvaghosha's loyalty to Buddhists' final goal of achieving nirvana is strong enough to make him emphasize the transient nature of these heavenly worlds. For example, after the Buddha takes Nanda to Indra's heaven to encourage his aspiration to marry a beautiful apsara (*SN*: x 35ff), the Buddha then makes him understand that even a stay in paradise is temporary. After one has used up one's merit, one inevitably descends to lower worlds, even to hell (XI 39ff). In other words, Ashvaghosha does not go so far as to promise a goal other than the perfect state of nirvana.

The *Mahāvastu* (The Great Event) takes a great step forward from Ashvaghosha's works in divinizing the Buddha. Here the Buddha is not only a divine being but also one who enjoys eternal existence. Everything about the Buddha is transcendental. He may take a bath, consume medicine, drink or eat, but only in order to accommodate the customs of this world. He is immune from age, disease and external decay. He stays in this world not because he is under the control of karma, but of his own free will (I 132–4, pp. 168–70). The author of the *Mahāvastu* thus introduces the concept of the eternal Buddha. The historical Buddha is only one manifestation of the eternal Buddha. The idea that numerous Buddhas deriving from this eternal Buddha appear periodically in this world forms the basis of a rich Buddhist mythology.

SEVEN TREASURES: COMMODITIES AND RELIGIOUS SYMBOLS

According to the *Mahāvastu*, the worship and patronage of a Buddha appearing in this world offer tangible benefits. A king who builds a palace of precious materials for a Buddha has the full right to claim Buddhahood by virtue of this act of merit (I 49–50, pp. 41–2). Strikingly, the main items used in honouring a Buddha and other sacred figures in this religious context consist of just the merchandise we encountered in the last chapter. Pearls, coral, lapis lazuli (*vaiḍūrya*), silk and other precious substances were common religious gifts. The claim that it is not on the basis of the taels of pearls and coral that the monk becomes very rich but on the basis of the merit he obtains (II 358, p. 325) indicates that pearls and coral were forms of wealth, at least in monasteries. There is also an example of cartloads of pearls and lapis lazuli as gifts (II 180, p. 175). Coral, pearls and lapis lazuli were not only general forms of wealth but also partially comprised the seven treasures (*sapta-ratna*).

As I said earlier, the *sapta-ratna* was a traditional Buddhist concept. Both *sapta* and *ratna* may have derived from the conception of state machinery. The Mauryan theorist Kautiliya envisaged state machinery in terms of seven limbs (*saptāṅga*);[3] *ratnin*, the treasury-bearers in *Brāhmaṇa* literature, were state functionaries (Jayaswal 1943: 203). The seven treasures first comprised the Buddhist view of the main constituents of early state sovereignty. They included the wheel (*cakra*), which is a symbol of rule; an elephant (*hastin*) and horse (*aśva*), both symbols of the monarch's status; a gem (*mani*); a queen (*strī*); a householder (*gahapati*) who collects wealth for the king; and a minister (*pariṇāyaka*). It is not clear when, or for what reason, the *sapta-ratna* began to designate seven kinds of precious items.

The definite components of the collection did not take shape until the time of the *Mahāvastu*. Some Pali texts use *sapta-ratna* as a collective term to refer to a group of precious substances, such as gold, silver and jewels, but with no specific list in mind (*Buddhist Hybrid Sanskrit Dictionary*). The *Milindapañha* mentions a string of precious substances together with many kinds of flowers (v 17), but not as components of the *sapta-ratna*. The *Mahāvastu* repeats a specific list many times: *suvaṇa* (gold), *rūpya* (silver), *vaiḍūryā* (lapis lazuli), *sphāṭika* (crystal or quartz), *muktā* (pearl), *lohitikā* (a red precious stone, or red coral), *musāragalva* (ammonite, agate, or

[3] The king (*svāmi*), the minister (*amātya*), the territory (*janapada*), the capital (*durga*), the treasury (*kośa*), the coercive power (*daṇḍa*) and ally (*mitra*) R. S. Sharma (1959: 31–49).

coral) (I 49, p. 41; 63, p. 52; 194, pp. 152–3; 195, pp. 153–4; 249, pp. 204–5; III 226, p. 221; 227, p. 222; 323, p. 314). The composition of the *sapta-ratna* was thus fixed in the *Mahāvastu*, and subject to only slight changes in later Buddhist texts. In some texts, where the list omits *muktā* (pearl), the last three treasures are *rohitamukti* (red pearl, rubies, red coral beads, carnelian beads or other red precious stones), *aśmagarbha* (amber, coral, diamond, or emerald) and *musāragalva* (ammonite, agate, or coral). While the translations of *suvarṇa* (gold), *rūpya* (silver), *vaidūryā* (lapis lazuli), *sphāṭika* (crystal or quartz) and *muktā* (pearl) are certain, others are open to interpretation.

Once the content of *sapta-ratna* was established, it continually appears in works such as the *Mahāvastu*, as a token of valuable decoration and as a symbol of wealth, of happiness or of Buddhist paradises. The palace of the king who claimed Buddhahood by virtue of his donation is made of seven treasures (I 49, p. 41; 52, p. 44; 53, p. 45; 63, p. 52); the monasteries in a Buddha's land shine with the seven treasures (I 112, p. 89; 116, p. 91); and a sage king's royal city is surrounded by the trees with leaves of the seven treasures. In short, the seven treasures symbolize the collection of the best substances in this and other worlds, and thus became a standard formula in Buddhist worship.

The significance of the fixed list of the *sapta-ratna* in the *Mahāvastu* is clear only when referring to archaeological finds in north India. The collections which fall under the designation of the seven treasures must have included gold, silver, blue precious stones, transparent precious stones, red jewels, pearls and coral or similar substances. The stone casket found in a stupa chamber of Kalawan, Taxila, provides a good sample of how the *sapta-ratna* was embodied among Buddhists in the Kushan period. This collection includes gold sheets and disks, silver sheets and disks, a piece of quartz, crystal beads, both transparent materials, a beryl bead which is green, green glass beads, a piece of garnet which is red, pearls, a piece of turquoise, and bones as relics of the Buddha (Marshall 1951: I, 327). The donor was quite successful in fulfilling the requirements of the *sapta-ratna*.

Although the translations of *vaidūrya* (lapis lazuli) and *sphāṭika* (crystal or quartz) are certain, in reality they might have denoted different things, namely anything that looked like lapis lazuli or crystal. Considering that so many glass beads, either green or transparent, are found in Buddhist sites, it is possible that, either, the glass beads were substitutes for lapis lazuli and crystal because glass was cheaper, or that *vaiḍūrya* and *sphāṭika* designated a variety of similar precious materials. As we have already learned, *vaiḍūrya's* Pali form *vaiḷurya* was the origin of the Chinese word for glass, *liu-li*, mainly opaque glass, and the Pali for *sphāṭika*, *phalika*, gave the Chinese the name of transparent glass, *po-li*. This change of meaning when the words were translated into another language might have been related to the actual items in transaction, for the receivers would naturally have identified the words with the goods they received.

Having found that the sacred *sapta-ratna* is composed of important Indian exports to China, one also encounters the main Indian import from China—silk—in the text of the *Mahāvastu*. I discussed earlier the widespread use of silk in court and urban life as shown in the *Mahāvastu*. In the context of worship

he who has placed a festoon of fine silk on a monument of the saviour of the world prospers in all his aims, both among gods and among men, avoids base families and is not reborn among them. He becomes wealthy and affluent, a sovereign in this world (*Jambudvīpa*) (II 365, p. 332).

Decorating Buddhist monuments with silk is one of the many forms of worshipping the Buddha encouraged by the *Mahāvastu*, which explicitly promises worshippers higher status, and even material gain. That the Buddha himself had renounced exactly these secular goals demonstrates just how much the Buddhist theology represented in this work deviates from earlier Buddhist teachings. The appearance of the *Mahāvastu* in the early centuries AD embodied the great influence of commerce-oriented lay worshippers on Buddhism. The promise of these kind of rewards certainly encouraged Buddhist believers to decorate stupas with thousands of silk banners.

In the *Mahāvastu* the purpose of worship and making donations is no longer limited to reaching nirvana. The text promises that worshippers and donors will attain kingdoms, wealth, the status of gods, and many other secular aspirations (II 363–97, pp. 330–54). There are also many Buddhas' lands (*buddhabhumi*) where life is much more pleasant and interesting than in the pure state of nirvana.

Since nirvana could only be achieved after many life cycles' efforts, these rewards were much more appealing to common lay devotees.

Lay devotees did not need to worry about joining the sangha to reach arhatship because, according to the *Mahāvastu*, enlightenment was no longer the result of an individual's effort. Buddhas, such as the Samitavin Buddha, vowed that they would lead others across the sea of suffering to nirvana (I 50, p. 42) and that they were willing to share the merit they had accumulated with devotees. However, the power of sharing merit with lay devotees who worshipped and made donations still remained the privilege of Buddhas. Bodhisattvas in the *Mahāvastu* are religious apprentices who have to undergo four stages of transformation before reaching their goal, nirvana (I 1, p. 1).

The concept of Bodhisattvas as candidates for Buddhahood reaches full maturity in the *Saddharmapuṇḍarika* (The Lotus Sutra). This work was translated into Chinese many times, starting with the third century AD and has enjoyed great influence in both China and Japan.[4] It is virtually a workshop manual rather than a text of Buddhist philosophy. The early part of the book develops the idea that the wisdom of the Buddha is very hard to obtain and that only the Buddha knows all (II 1–21). The text further emphasizes the emptiness of all dharmas and the idea that the true dharma is beyond understanding (V 74–82). This agnosticism pushes the divinity of the Buddha to an extreme; since no one other than He Himself is able to attain true knowledge, no human can attain that knowledge. Thus, memorizing Buddhist teachings and rules is not essential for preaching and converting. Instead supernatural power gains importance. The *Saddharmapuṇḍarika* not only gives examples of conversion through magic power (VII 97, XXV trans. 421–2) it also provides talismanic charms that protect those who recite the sutra (XXI trans. pp. 371, 372, 374).

Once the devotees were deprived of the ability to approach the Buddha through understanding, it followed logically that both the monks in the order and laymen were able to communicate with the Buddha only by worship and donation. In the *Saddharmapuṇḍarika* the Buddha demands that his followers make 84,000 stupas for

---

[4]The first translation was done by Dharmaraksha in the Western Chin (AD 265–316).

him, inside which should be urns containing fragments of his bones, decorated with the seven treasures (xxii-2, trans. pp. 382–3). This precise prescription evokes the stone caskets of the Buddha's relics found in both Kushan India and China in the Northern dynasties. Although it is hard to date the *Saddharmapuṇḍarīka* more precisely than to the second or the third century AD, the text coincides with the practice of burying relic caskets with jewels in north India and pre-dates the same practice in north China. These are clear links between actual Buddhist practices and the text's composition. If the *Saddharmapuṇḍarīka* was the result of a few centuries' votary movement in north India, it also inspired Chinese donors several centuries later.

According to the *Saddharmapuṇḍarīka* the ideal stupa designed for a Buddha land should be one made of the seven treasures which the Buddha showed to his disciples as models of the stupas they should build for him (xi-1, trans. pp. 227–9). Of course, not all devotees were able to build such luxurious stupas, but those who built stupas of wood, brick, or even earth and sand, could reach enlightenment (ii 77–81). This flexibility provided quite a wide range of possible donations from devotees. Both rich and poor could reach nirvana through donations. But the seven treasures nevertheless epitomized the best gift devotees could give to the Buddha.

In the *Saddharmapuṇḍarīka* the Buddha also requires his disciples to decorate the stupas with silk bands. and bells (xxii-2, trans. pp. 382–3). Stupas may also be decorated with canopies or flags (I 45; vi-25, trans. p. 147; vi 37). Donations of canopies or staffs for canopies (*chatrayaṣṭi*) turn up in inscriptions of the Kushan period (e.g. Sircar 1965: 136–8, ii no. 37, 39). Perhaps because flags were too small a donation to record, they do not appear in inscriptions. In worshipping images of Buddhas and bodhisattvas the devotees should contribute flowers, incense, garlands, ointments, powder, clothes, necklaces, gems and jewels, as well as canopies, flags and banners (x-1, trans. p. 215; 15–16; xi 66–7; xvi xx-1, trans. p. 366; xxii 2-trans. p. 389). This list is so similar to that listing the daily necessities of the *nāgaraka* (city residents) in the *Kāmasūtra* (fourth–sixth centuries) that one cannot help thinking the Kushan Buddhas who appreciated such donations were probably the predecessors of these city residents of the Gupta period.

According to the *Saddharmapuṇḍarika*, one can reach nirvana through worship. The symbolic vehicle which carries the worshipper across to enlightenment is a bullock cart made of the seven jewels furnished with additional silk mattresses to make it comfortable (III 38–9; 82). Before reaching nirvana it is possible to choose many other places to stop. Many Buddha fields and other heavens are decorated with the seven treasures and silk bands, and the major material is lapis lazuli (*vaidūrya*; xi-1, trans. p. 234; xxii-1, trans. p. 377; xxv, trans. p. 429; xvi 36–7; 39–40). This blue-green stone represents the highest Buddhist fantasy of purity and bliss.

The donation of luxuries offers even more rewards for the donors than it did in the *Mahāvastu*. Donors expected to obtain vehicles to Buddhahood in exchange for gifts to Buddhas (I 14, 15). By giving a Buddha an invaluable gem a woman changed her sex to gain Buddhahood (xi 51–2). The merits of teaching and hearing *The Lotus Sutra*, the sutra of worship, can cause one to be reborn with six perfect organs (xviii, trans. pp. 336–53), or with a fine body, or with a status which enables one to ride in a horse-drawn carriage, and enjoy many other secular pleasures (xviii, trans. pp. 328–5).

Although donation provides the means to enlightenment, the *Saddharmapuṇḍarika* reminds its readers again and again that there is only one vehicle. Fortunately this vehicle can carry many beings (II 72). In this text it is the fixed vow of all the *Tathāgata* to lead others to enlightenment (II 99; –1, trans. p. 120).[5] Even more compassionate than the Buddhas, the Bodhisattva Avalokiteshvara vows to save all creatures before he reaches Buddhahood. He is the hero who saves people in trouble. He rescues those burning in fires, those drowning in the currents of rivers, those cast on an island by a strong wind when sailing with the seven treasures, and those in endangered caravans (xxiv, trans. pp. 406–8). Worshipping Avalokiteshvara is unfailingly beneficial (xxiv, trans. p. 409). The merit gained equals that of worshipping sixty-two times as many Buddhas as the sands of the Ganges (xxiv, tran. p. 410). Before the *Saddharmapuṇḍarika* , the rewards of a better life could be realized only after the worshipper passed into another world. Here, Buddhist thinking sent Bodhisattvas as saviours to rescue

[5] *Tathāgata* normally was another name for a Buddha. Here it represents clearly the concept of a Bodhisattva.

the sufferers in this world even before their ultimate release from it.

Supplementary to Buddhist cosmology represented in the *Saddharmapuṇḍarīka* , the *Sukhāvatīvyūha* (Land of Bliss) is a description of the land of bliss in the western heaven. The simplicity of its contents gives it little value in terms of historical information. Nevertheless this simplicity strengthened the influence of the work by making it accessible to many uneducated devotees. The Amitabha, who vowed to save all beings, never passed into nirvana but created the land of bliss as a way-station for those who proceed to nirvana. This land is full of trees of the seven jewels (Larger §16), adorned with lotus lakes of the seven jewels (Smaller §4). More important, it is very easy to reach this country. Even those who commit the five *ānantarya* sins, i.e. the sins bringing immediate retribution, can reach this land by repeating ten times the thought of reaching that land (Larger §8, 19). The happy results and easy approach are so alluring in comparison to earlier thought that more conservative theorists feared Buddhists would lose sight of the final goal of nirvana and opt to stay in this land of bliss.

The theories of utopian lands often drew their inspiration from long-distance trade and travel. Anecdotes of foreign countries and exotic alien goods provided the best food for the imagination. The *Sukhāvatīvyūha*, developed in the commercial atmosphere of north India during the first few centuries AD, became one of the most influential statements of Buddhist doctrine in China. Its promise may be too simple to appeal to modern readers, but it did not seem so to many sophisticated Buddhist monks who had already accepted the enlarged Buddhist pantheon and cosmos, and who felt that worship and donation were alternate routes to the final goal of nirvana. The text depicts the extreme success one could achieve through worship and donation. Enlightenment is good, but it is remote and vague, often beyond human understanding; it can be achieved only after effort in many life cycles. Emphasis on worship and donation shortens and simplifies the process of accumulating merit. And a rest-station provides benefits in the near future.

These documents reveal a series of developments in north India in Buddhism during the first two or three centuries AD. Changes began in Buddhist cosmology. The Buddhist pantheon expanded from one that included practically only the divinized Buddha to one that encompassed countless Buddhas and bodhisattvas. The

Buddhist cosmos expanded to incorporate many heavens and Buddhas' lands as both the abodes of Buddhas and bodhisattvas and rest-stations for their worshippers on the way to nirvana. All the new deities were willing to share with their worshippers the merit they accumulated. Consequently, Buddhist literature increasingly stressed worship and donation, which ultimately became the major route to enlightenment. Although at the time the earlier Pali Buddhist texts were composed patrons had provided only food and lodging to the Buddha and his sangha, now these Sanskrit Buddhist documents show that the major items of donation were immovables, such as monumental stupas, monastery buildings, plus luxury goods popular in contemporary commerce.

The concept of the *sapta-ratna* attained maturity in the movement emphasizing worship and donation. The standardization of the *sapta-ratna* paralleled the development of the Eurasian trade from the Mediterranean to East Asia. Most of the components of the seven treasures were items either brought to north and north-west India by the trade, or highly popular in markets of other countries. Gold and silver coins were commonly used in the Roman trade. Lapis lazuli was available only from Badakshan in Afghanistan. In order to export lapis lazuli to the Roman empire in western Indian ports, it had to be transported through north-west India. The Roman citizens' preference for Indian crystal (Pliny xxxvii, 9, 10) must have increased its price in India. As substitutes for lapis lazuli and crystal, coloured and transparent glass were transported from the Mediterranean or north India to China. Coral, treasured by both Indians and Chinese, was a major export from the Mediterranean to western Indian ports. Although pearls were indigenous to India, Roman desire for the commodity facilitated their transport to north India and north China.

These Buddhist texts reveal a deep connection between Eurasian trade and the development of the pattern of Buddhist worship and donation: the circulation of luxury commodities stimulated the standardization of the concept of the *sapta-ratna*, and the ritual meaning the Buddhist movement brought to these goods increased their value and enlarged their market. The items most valued as property in the society changed, as did items of donation. In the *Milindapañha*, where the seven treasures had not yet been standardized as a formula of worship and donation, a rich man's property consisted of gold, silver, grains, milk products, honey, sugar and other agricultural produce (IV 1, 27). Even in the *Mahāvastu*, where the concept of the *sapta-ratna* was fixed, the seven treasures do not seem to be the major forms of wealth: a country Brahman owned treasures, granaries, elephants, horses, cattle, sheep, slaves and servants (I 198, p. 156; II 2, p. 2); a guild leader owned money, treasuries, granaries, gold, silver, elephants, horses, goats, sheep, slaves and servants (III 389, p. 389; 402, p. 402). But in the *Saddharmapuṇḍarīka* the jewels with which we are familiar in the trade gain special value as forms of wealth. The property lists include gold, granaries, silver, gems, pearls, lapis lazuli, conch shells, coral, slaves and money invested in business, lending, agriculture and commerce (IV-1, trans. p. 100; XI 41–2; XIII 44–5; XVII-1, trans. p. 329). The transport of pearls, coral, glass objects and precious stones from India to China and Chinese silk to India and the West stimulated the standardization of the *sapta-ratna* concept and of other necessities for Buddhist ceremonies. Simultaneously, the identification of the concept of the seven treasures as symbols of the Buddhist ideal world increased the demand for luxury goods not related to daily life.

As we have seen in Chapter II, the international trade from the Mediterranean to China was essential to the Kushan economy, and even to the very existence of the Kushan empire, which controlled a large territory encompassing people of widely diverse cultures. At the same time, Buddhism's dominance—at least in the urban phase of the Kushan state—suggests that Buddhism functioned as a culturally unifying factor. The link between Buddhist ritual practices and the trade in luxury goods shaped the relationship between the Buddhist monasteries and laity. Buddhism in the Kushan period, as shown in the Sanskrit documents, was more responsive to the devotees' religious aspirations than it had been earlier. The scope of rewards for devotion to the Buddha shifted from reaching nirvana to better birth in future lifecycles, and then to efficacy in this world. The appearance of the bodhisattvas as future Buddhas, especially Avalokitesvara, was a turning point. That the Bodhisattva could save other people through the merit he accumulated implied that merit, like goods, could be transferred and exchanged. Merit was no longer restricted to what an individual could achieve through his own efforts. The commercial features that penetrated Buddhist ideology developed in conjunction with the highly flourishing urban culture and mercantile economy of the Kushan period. This penetration may have prompted, or resulted from, some institutional changes in Buddhist monasteries. The change in ideology created a new dimension in the relationship among the sovereigns, commercial laity and Buddhist monasteries.

CHAPTER V: MONASTERIES AND THE LAITY IN KUSHAN INDIA

By the first few centuries AD Buddhist institutions in north India differed markedly from those of the early Buddhist sangha in the middle Ganges. The early Buddhist sangha was a congregation of monks who aspired to lead a different mode of life than that possible under the dominant Brahman caste system. Under the original sangha regulations the monk's personal belongings were limited to a few pieces of clothing and a begging bowl. Buddhist monks distinguished themselves from Brahman priests by not accumulating property (*Tevijasutta*: II ii 2, Davids 1881: 192). However, a few centuries before the Christian era, as a consequence of its growing membership and social influence, the sangha was gradually institutionalized. These developments changed the internal constitution of the Buddhist sangha and affected its relations with the laity.

How exactly was the Buddhist sangha institutionalized? While most scholars assume institutionalization was an inevitable phenomenon in the process of the growth of a religion, others suggest simplistic causes which barely explain the complex nature of Buddhist institutions in different economic and ecological environments.[1] A recent article by Ivan Strenski (1983) provides the best explanation of the institutionalization, or, in his words, the domestication of the Buddhist sangha. He points out that 'the sangha's status as gift-receiver which in turn called forth certain social obligations' was responsible for this process (470). The transactions between the Buddhist sangha and its laity took the form of reciprocity—donors

[1] For example, the monsoon season in South Asia required the wandering monks to gradually settle down. Strenski refutes these simplistic explanations in detail (1983: 467–8).

gained merit through donations. Materially, this restricted trans-action between two parties actually extended to larger circles; the sangha returned the gifts to the donors in the form of religious ceremonies and monumental structures. The generalized exchanges precluded accurate calculation of direct returns but did not expunge the concept of a more general return. Where the gifts were durable property, such as land and recruits, the Buddhist sangha came under increasing pressure to put its property at the disposal of the society or to participate in economic activities for the benefit of the society. In cases when the sangha refused to do so, the rulers often confiscated the property in the name of purification, as ex-emplified in numerous incidents in the history of China and South East Asia (475–6.)

Strenski's argument sheds light on the institutionalization of Buddhist monasteries under the Kushans. The practice of donation, which reached a high tide during the Kushan period, incidentally provided the basic documentation for the study of the institutional changes of the Buddhist sangha. The frequent transactions between the sangha and its laity, in the form of donations, monumental construction and other exchanges, involved the sangha in the social economy. These economic activities contributed to the process of institutionalization. An examination of the relationship between monasteries and donors as well as the process of institutionalization reveals the role of the Buddhist sangha in the Kushan economy.

MONASTERIES AND VOTIVE DONATIONS

Once Buddhism had become an influential religion in a given region, many people with other than religious motivations entered the sangha. In the *Milindapañha*, Nagasena admits to King Milinda that, of the people

who joined the order, some did so for the Buddhist goal of reaching nirvana, but some have left the world in terror at the tyranny of kings. Some have joined us to be safe from being robbed, some were harassed by debt, and some perhaps to gain a livelihood (*MP*: II 1, 6).

By the early centuries AD Buddhist monasteries had thus become social institutions receiving those who wanted to join and were free to escape social oppression.[2]

The monks, regardless of their reasons for joining the monasteries, seemed to have owned private property. Even before the Kushan period votive inscriptions in north and central India suggest that monks owned more property than allowed by the monastic rules of the *Vinaya* texts. For example, of the 827 inscriptions of the stupas 1, 2 and 3, temple 40 and other monuments dated to about the first century BC in Sanchi, over 200 of them record donations by monks and nuns for the construction of stupas (Marshall 1940: I, 297). The pre-Kushan votive inscriptions are very short and simple, normally including only the names, and sometimes the titles, of the donors. Since the monks and nuns used *bhikkhu* and *bhikkunī* as their titles, they probably had taken the second ordination (*upasaṁpadā*) and had become full members of the sangha. Moreover, a few joint donations by nuns indicate that the donations did not just take place on the occasion when individual nuns took the ordination, be it the first or the second. For example, a certain Balika donated in conjunction with all nuns from a nunnery (I, 334, no. 341). It is unlikely that all the nuns in one nunnery underwent ordination and made donations at the same time. Their donations did not symbolize their giving up secular property on becoming monks or nuns, but rather the continuing contributions of monks or nuns who owned some property.

The inscriptions of the Kushan period contain a little more information than those of Sanchi. Some monks or nuns made donations for the welfare of their parents, relatives and teachers (e.g. *EI* VIII: 176–7; Sircar 1965: 157–8, II no. 54; Lüders 1961: 79–80, §44, K174). Some donated together with lay devotees (Lüders 1961: 86–7, §52, K15; 87, §53, K176; Konow 1929: 147, LXXIV), or with fellow monks (Sircar 1965: 144–5, II no. 44). These links in donations reveal that monks mentioned the names of joint donors when resources other than their own were involved. It seems likely that the donations under only their own names came entirely from their own resources.

The jewellery and coins which Marshall found in the monks'

---

[2] The *Vinaya* ruled that slaves should not be ordained into the sangha (*Mahavagga*: I 47, *Vinaya Texts*: I p. 199).

cells of the Jaulian monastery in Taxila confirm the information from inscriptions (Marshall 1951: I, 385). He also noticed hoards of silver coins and jewellery buried under the debris of stupas in Taxila and suggests that monks hid some of the cachés in the stupas, such as the Dharmarajika stupa or the stupas of Giri (347). Of the ninety-four silver coins recovered from the stupa at Kunala, forty-one are from the debris around the stupa and fifty-three from the monastery area, more specifically from the cells that the monks lived in or the veranda in front of the cells. These coins were either offerings to the stupa or monks' property. The collection of coins from Kunala includes punch-marked, local Taxilan, Greek, Parthian and Kushan coins. Only one coin is dated after the Kushan period (352–3). Coins could circulate centuries after they were issued, and Kunala and many other Taxila monasteries collapsed in the violence of the fifth century AD, so one cannot exclude the possibility that these coins circulated until then. But the conspicuous absence of coins later than those of the Kushan period in many monastery sites of Taxila suggests that some of these coins were hidden in the stupas and their living cells in the later Kushan period. Monks at that time probably owned some property in the form of currency or jewellery.

In the Kushan period, like individual monks, monasteries also accumulated property. At the time of the Buddha halls (*vihāra*) and gardens belonged to the whole sangha. But inscriptions of the Kushan period show many donations made for specific groups of Buddhist teachers, mostly to *Mahāsānghika* and *Sarvāstivādin* (e.g. *EI* viii: 181; xxx: 184; Lüders 1961: 114, §79, K115; 191–2, §157, K86; 165, §125, K208; 31–2, §2, K165). The practice of making donations to different schools reflects the fact that these donations became the property of individual schools. *Prātimokṣa Sūtra* (*c.* 100 BC–AD 100), a monastic code of the *Mahāsānghika* school, mentions the wealth accumulated in the sangha and that distributed among monks (Prebish 1975: 74). At this stage, however, the property of Buddhist monasteries seems to have been limited to the monks' residences (*vihāra*), monumental buildings such as stupas and images, and maybe to some currency and jewellery. There is no indication that the monasteries owned land.

Where did the monks and monasteries obtain their wealth? In Sri Lanka Buddhist monasteries received land grants as early as

MAP 7. Archaeological Sites in South Asia, First-Third Centuries (Heitzman 1984: Fig. 3; Dupree 1973: 288–95, 303–11. See Appendix v).

LEGEND.　● 　Buddhist Monastic Site
　　　　　○ 　Non-Monastic Site
　　　　　▲ 　Buddhist Monastic Site associated with Non-Monastic Sites

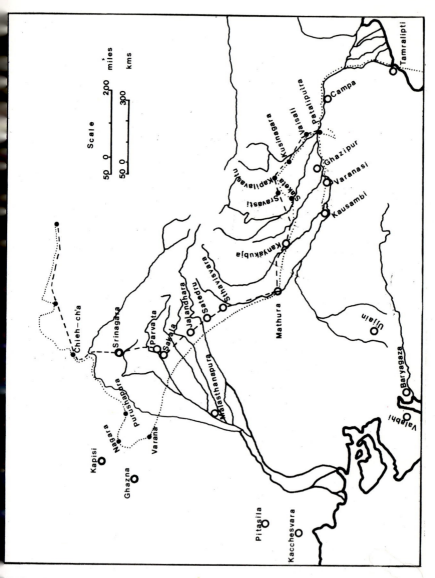

MAP 6. Routes in North India during the Gupta Age (based on Schwartzberg 1978: 28).

LEGEND.
● Cities
○ Flourishing Cities (according to Hsüan-tsang AD 630–44)
--- Routes Followed by Chih-meng (AD 404–24)
... Routes Followed by Fa-hsien (AD 404–14)

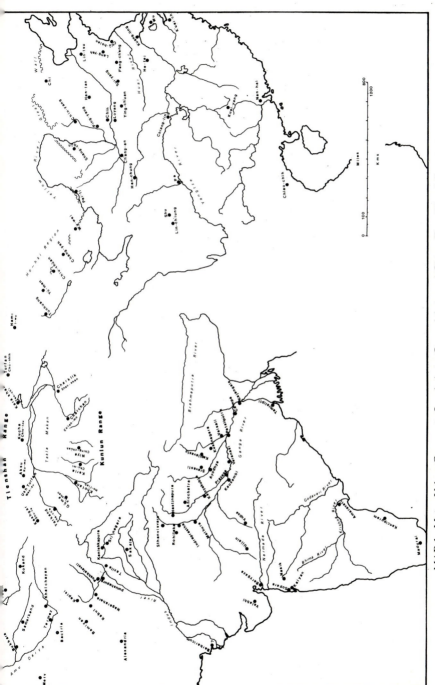

MAP 1. Major Urban Centres in South Asia, Central Asia and China, First-Third Centuries.

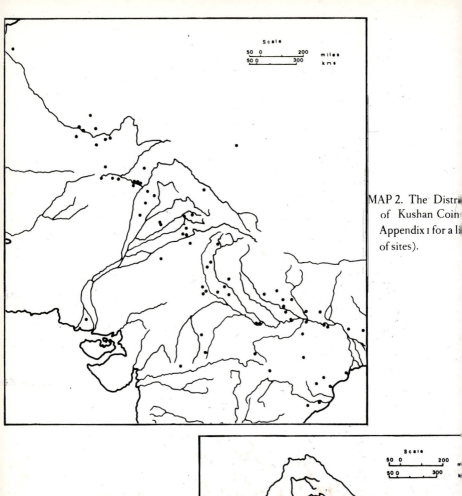

MAP 2. The Distri
of Kushan Coin
Appendix I for a li
of sites).

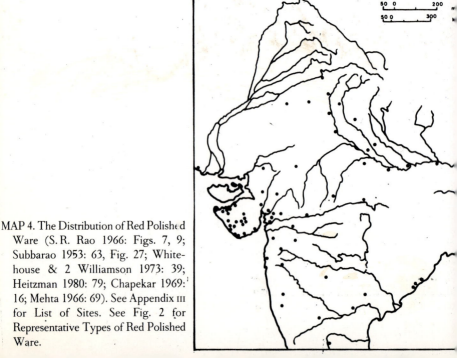

MAP 4. The Distribution of Red Polished
Ware (S. R. Rao 1966: Figs. 7, 9;
Subbarao 1953: 63, Fig. 27; White-
house & 2 Williamson 1973: 39;
Heitzman 1980: 79; Chapekar 1969:
16; Mehta 1966: 69). See Appendix III
for List of Sites. See Fig. 2 for
Representative Types of Red Polished
Ware.

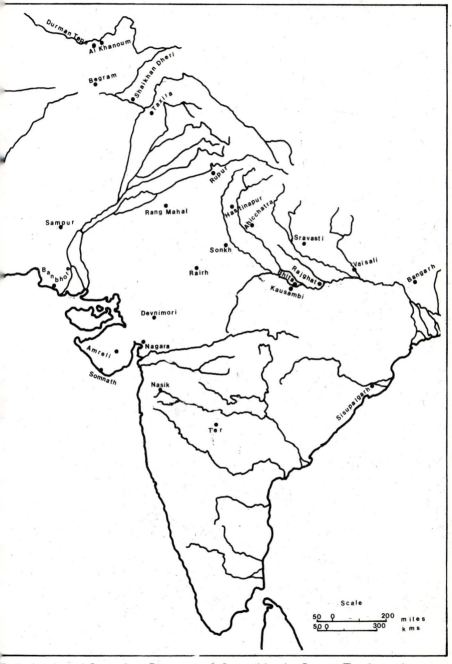

3. Archaeological Sites where Pottery was Influenced by the Ceramic Typology of
rth-West India in the First–Third Centuries (see Fig. 1 for Representative Types of
tery from North-West India. See Appendix II for Sources of Information).

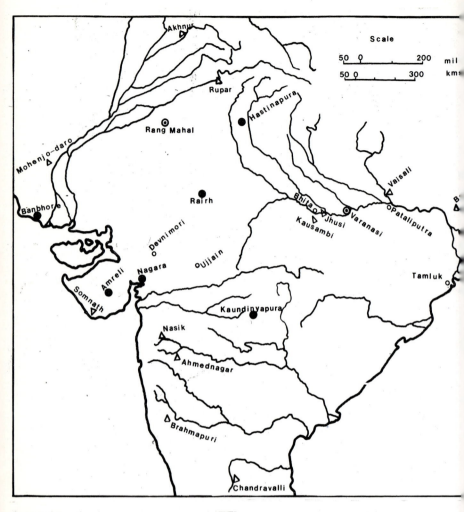

MAP 5. The Distribution of Sprinklers (see Appendix IV).

LEGEND.
● Red Polished Ware
○ Other Kinds of Fabric
⊙ Red Polished Ware and Other Kinds of Fabric
△ Fabric Uncertain

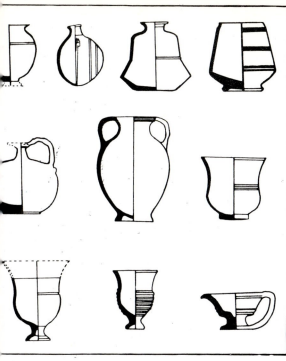

FIGURE 1. Representative Ceramic Types of North-West India, First-Third Centuries (Marshall 1951 III: Pottery nos. 41, 44, 60, 61, 72, 81, 87, 90, 99, 134).

URE 2. Representative ypes of Red Polished Ware not in proportion). According to Y.D. Sharma 1953: 59; G.R. Sharma 1969: 78.

FIGURE 3. Silk Sample found in Central Asia: Bodhi Tree on Strips, Fifth or Sixth Century (Museum of Sinkiang Uighur Autonomous Region: 1972, Plate 23).

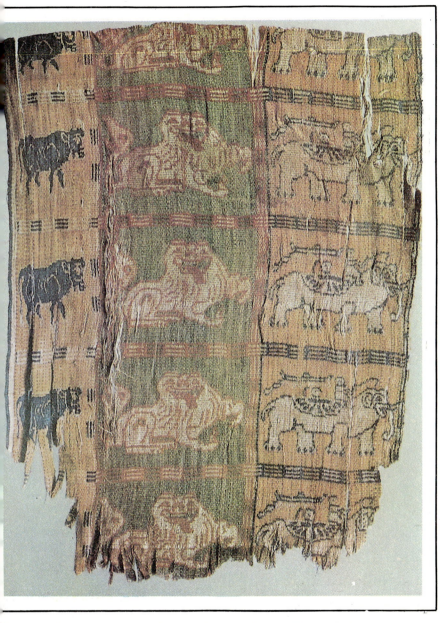

FIGURE 4. Silk Sample found in Central Asia: Chess Design, Fifth or Sixth
Century (ibid., Plate 26).

FIGURE 5. Silk Sample found in Central Asia: Confronting Peacocks in Pearl Roundel, Fifth or Sixth Century (ibid., Plate 27).

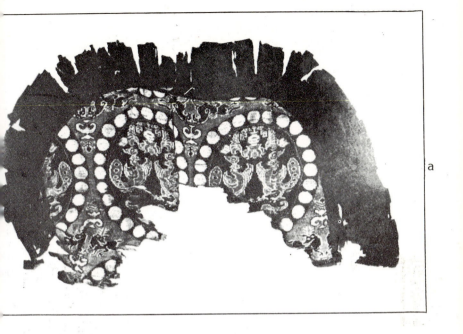

FIGURE 6. (a) A Sample of Confronting Peacocks in Pearl Roundel (Riboud 7: 443); (b) Peacock on a Carving from Begram, Kushan Period (Hackin 1939: e XLII, Fig. 92).

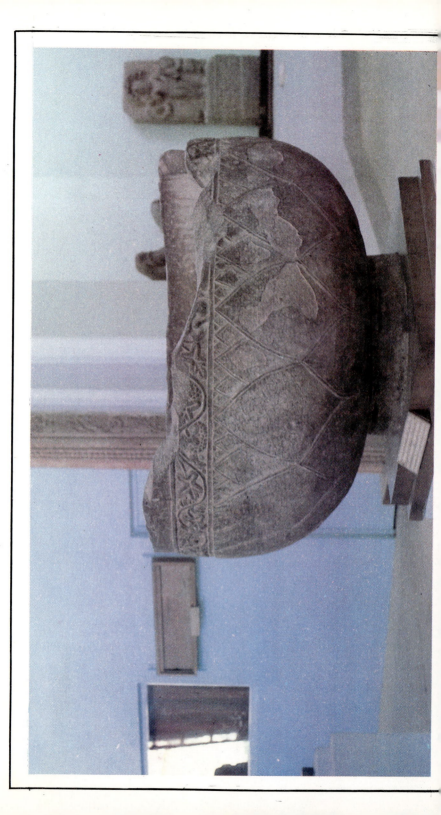

the second century BC (Gunawardana 1979: 53), and in western India around the second century AD (Chapter VI). Monasteries in north India did not seem to receive income from landed property in this early period. Monasteries could gain wealth through the patronage of the commercial community or even by participating in trade. In Mathura several huge symbolic begging bowls represent a new style of patronage during the Kushan period (Figure 7). These stone bowls, probably located in front of monasteries, replaced the begging bowls of individual monks as receivers of donations. It is highly unlikely that donors would have had cooked food poured into these stone carved bowls. The donations might have been money or valuable items.

James Heitzman's study of the spread of Buddhist institutions demonstrates that monastic establishments were intimately connected with urban settlements, trade routes and imperial domains (1984: 131). The distribution of urban centres in the first three centuries AD and that of monastic sites of the same period reveals a clear correlation between urban development and the institutional expansion of Buddhism. Buddhist monasteries also closely follow the trade routes from western India to the north-west and the Ganges plain (see Map 7). Buddhist monastic sites were found in many important urban centres, such as Kapisi (Begram), Taxila, Kausambi, Mathura, Sanchi, Sopara (Appendix IV).

Some Buddhist sites were located along the trade routes, although not near big cities. The clusters of Buddhist sites in the north-west and western coast fall into this category. Himanshu Ray convincingly demonstrates that in the western Deccan the very survival of Buddhist monasteries depended on the trade routes (1983). These monasteries were located on crucial points along the routes. The silting up of the port of Sopara towards the end of the Satavahana period and the resulting disuse of the Nana Ghat routes linking Junnar to Sopara caused the desertion of the large monastic complex at Junnar (Ray 1983: 229). Some monastic sites, such as Hadda and Bamiyan in Afghanistan, were associated with caravanserais (Dupree 1973: 305, 306).

Kushan sculptures reveal the urban setting of Buddhist monasteries. In contrast to the sculptures on the railings around the stupas in Bharhut and Sanchi, where the Yakshis were surrounded by forest and animals, the beautiful girls depicted on the railings of

Mathura and Sanghol (Gupta 1985) are often in street scenes. They are shown looking into mirrors, doing acrobatics, playing musical instruments, and drinking wine, and so vividly recall the urban life described in the *Buddhacarita*, the *Saundarānanda*, and other Buddhist works of this period. Furthermore, in the background of the major figures there is often a veranda or a window where the people looking on take great interest in the street activities. The designers of these works of art might have had the same purpose as that of the Buddhist writers, i.e. to denounce the indulgence of mundane pleasure by comparing it with the pure life of the Buddhist sangha. These works of art, however, like Buddhist literature, betray the proximity of the mundane life to the monasteries.

At the beginning of this chapter I mentioned the reciprocity governing the exchanges between Buddhist monasteries and their laity. Monasteries returned donations in the form of religious merit and ritual ceremonies. As the value of donations to the monasteries escalated, donors came to expect more in return. The inscriptions in the Kushan period no longer contained only the single short phrase indicating who the gift was from, but expressed some specific purpose for the donation. Having honoured all the Buddhas, the donors often wished their deceased religious teachers, parents or other relatives to attain nirvana or wished the living to be healthy and happy. At the end of the inscriptions, they wished the happiness of all creatures. A typical inscription of this period runs:

for the worship of all Buddhas. Through this bestowal of the religious gift, let there be attainment of nirvana by the teacher Saghadasa, for the cessation of all unhappiness of his parents...for the welfare and happiness of all sentient beings (Lüders 1961: 64–5, §29, K49).

Sometimes the donors also wished for the happiness of the king and his relatives. We have seen that, according to the *Mahāvastu* and the *Saddharmapuṇḍarika*, Buddhas and bodhisattvas could share their merit with devotees. Here in the inscriptions of the Kushan period the donations brought much merit to the donors.

The donors not only shared the merit of the Buddhas and Bodhisattvas but were able to transfer them to others. One inscription gives a long list of beneficiaries. The King of Kings, Huvishka, received the principal portion of the merit, followed by the donor's parents; having given a share of the merit to his brother, relatives, friends and associates, the donor retained a share for himself. Then he granted some share of merit to all beings, from the egg-born to those of formless existence, his own descendants, and those who 'are not heretics'. Even men of false belief received a substantial share (Konow 1929: 170, LXXXVI). Beyond expressing the extreme altruism of sharing merit with even one's religious opponents, this inscription clearly reflects the contemporary Buddhist view of social structure and human relationships. Both material trans-actions and transactions of religious merit were carried out in this matrix.

The inscriptions also indicate that the donors believed that donations could bring immediate benefits in this world. They often asked for the gift of health to themselves and their loved ones. A female donor made it very clear that she—

installs this image for the veneration of her favourite deity, the *Bhagavata* (the Buddha), the *pitāmaha*,[3] who is truly and completely enlightened (*bhagavato pitāmahasya sammyasambuddhasya svamatasyadevasya*), for the cessation of all misery (*sarva-dukkha-prahāṇārttham*) (*EI* XIX: 97).

Here the donor bypassed all the doctrinal quandaries a Buddhist priest might have faced in trying to explain the incompatibility of the Buddha's human behaviour with his divine nature by simply placing the Buddha besides other Indian deities, although admit-tedly as her favourite one.

The transformation following first the divinization of the Buddha and then the development of the conception of sharing merit that we have seen in the Sanskrit Buddhist literature composed around the first two or three centuries AD reflects actual changes in Buddhist institutions and their relationship with the laity during that period. As lay devotees expected more in return for their religious dona-tions, Buddhist monasteries also came to respond more actively to their religious aspirations. Monasteries were no longer the abode of the congregation of monks living outside the pale of normal society. A group of special cloisters appeared in the Kushan period. They were associated with the names of individuals, families, or other social groups. The Kushan kings Kanishka and

---

[3] Probably a designation for the Buddha.

Huvishka had their own monasteries (*vihāra*) (Konow 1929: 137, LXXII; *IA* XXXIII: 101, no. 11). The genitive form of the names of the kings does not reveal whether these viharas were donated by the kings or built for their benefit by other people, but no doubt the kings had some special interest in these viharas. Less important people also owned viharas. In these cases it is clear they donated the buildings. For example, one woman set up a bodhisattva image in her own vihara (*svake vihāre*) (Lüders 1961: 172, §136, K25). A survey of the monastic site of Kara-tepe, old Termez, suggests that in the Kushan period an individual vihara included a complex of buildings housing a hierarchical community of monks. Vertogradova also thinks that the personal name attached to the vihara was the name of the donor (Vertogradova 1983: 70). If the whole monastic complex was the donation of one person, there must have been a strong personal connection between the donor and the monastery. Some donors gave only a portion of a vihara. A wife of a goldsmith (*sovaṇikasa kūṭubiniye*) donated an image of a bodhisattva in her own worshipping hall (*svakāyā cetiyākaṭiyā*) (Lüders 1961: 187–8, §150, K14).

Some inscriptions indicate that minor donors could donate to other's viharas. For example, a monk donated the base of a pillar in the vihara of the king Huvishka (*IA* XXXIII: 101, no. 11). There were private enclosures where others could donate viharas. The vihara of Kanishka was located in the *samghārāma* (grove of the community) of a certain Mahasena. Some donated a gift in this vihara Konow 1929: 137, LXXII). A monk erected a bodhisattva image in his own hall of worship in a vihara of timber merchants (Lüders 1961: 191–2, §157, K86). On another occasion, a donor placed the Buddha's relics in a stupa in the king's grove (*rajaraṁñammi*) (Konow 1929: 158, LXXII). If donors could donate in the viharas under the names of other devotees, the latter did not necessarily consider the viharas their own private property. They might have just been the first and the major donors. Those donors sometimes called themselves 'master of the vihara' (*vihārasvāmi*). Since they donated the main part of the buildings it follows that they might have enjoyed some privilege of worship in the viharas, perhaps even some type of special religious service, although no information is available about the benefits of having one's own cloister. It is possible that the lesser donors who donated to other viharas were somehow subordinate to the master of the vihara.

There were also viharas linked with specific social groups. A vihara of timber merchants (*Kaṣṭikiya vihāra*) (Lüders 1961: 191–2, §157, K86) and a vihara of cloak-makers (*pravarikavihāra*)(Lüders 1961: 110, §74, K24) seem connected with artisan or merchant guilds. Collective donations appeared in the first century BC in the inscriptions of Sanchi. There are several inscriptions describing collective donations by ivory workers (*daṁtukāras*) of Vidisha, blacksmith (*dhamakas*) and other professional groups from Ujjain[4] (Marshall 1940: I, 298), by Buddhist assemblies (*bodhagoṭhī*) (nos. 96–8, 178), by nuns of a place (no. 341), and by a village (*gāma*) (no. 308, 345, 359, 635, 642). But there is no indication that these groups formed special organizations connected with Buddhist monasteries.

A series of Kushan inscriptions in Mathura reveal the emergence of a type of lay association (Lüders 1961: 83–4, §47, K181; 84, §48, K182; 84–5, §49, K183; 85, §50, K185; 85–6, §51, K184). These organizations might have been based on secular organizations, such as guilds. But in the context of donation they formed a religious organization directly related to the Buddhist sangha. A *saṅghaprakṛta*, literally 'employed by the sangha', translated by Lüders as 'commissioner of community', was probably the organizer of the community. The community was headed by one of its members (*pramukhānaṁ*) Lüders 1961: 85, §50, K185). The term 'elders of the community' (*saṅghastavira*) which appears in another inscription (Lüders 1961: §59, K191), may refer to an elder of a monastery. Judging from a later Chinese translation (*i-lao*) the word might have denoted senior members of the lay associations.

Lay associations sprang from the development of guild-caste organizations in urban centres. The increasing responsiveness of the Buddhist sangha towards the laity facilitated their birth. The lay associations intensified contact between Buddhist monasteries and lay devotees. As the Buddhist texts promised more rewards to donors, so too monks become more active in attracting converts and soliciting donations.

It is likely that monks initiated collective donations. The purpose of making substantial donations motivated lay devotees to organize

---

[4] *Magalkatiya, sāphineyaka, tāpasiya, vākiliya.* The translations are not certain.

themselves according to the model of their own guilds and that of sangha administration. Although there is no direct evidence that monks encouraged lay associations to make donations, some inscriptions show that monks were active in encouraging donations by 'masters of the vihara'. Following a monk who raised a monumental pillar, a mistress of a vihara (*viharasvāmini*) donated the base of the pillar and an enclosure (*parivaram*) (Konow 1929: 141, LXXIV). Some inscriptions give the monk's name in the genitive form, but that of other donors in the instrumental form. For example, one inscription is translated as: 'A Bodhisattva [image] of the monk Bala, who is versed in Tripitaka, is established by the great governor (*mahākṣatrapa*)...' (Sircar 1965: 136–7, II no. 38). So the image was donated under the name of the monk Bala. The most likely explanation for this arrangement is that the monk initiated the donation but the lay devotees financed it.

The practices where monks donated jointly with lay devotees, where masters of a vihara donated jointly with minor donors, or where lay associations donated collectively were all new forms that developed in the Kushan period and reveal the increasing connection between Buddhist monasteries and the laity. They made possible the movement emphasizing worship and donation which produced the brilliant Kushan Buddhist art. Having promised more merit and provided more religious services to the donors, and having partially returned the donations to the society in the form of monuments, were Buddhist monasteries still pressurized to contribute to the economy? Would the increasing accumulation of wealth in the monasteries invoke the envy of the rulers and the masses, thus causing either the persecution or 'purification' of Buddhism? A discussion of the relationship between monasteries and the laity, including both royal patrons and urban residents, reveals further links between the spread of Buddhism and the prosperity of the Kushan commercial economy.

LAITY: COMMERCIAL COMMUNITY AND THE STATE

Buddhist Sanskrit texts indicate that the traditionally close relationship between the Buddhist sangha and the commercial community, which dated to the time of the Buddha, continued in the first two or three centuries AD. The major audience for Buddhist teaching in the Kushan period still consisted of different types of traders. In the Sanskrit texts, Buddha addresses his audience as *kulaputra* (sons of good families). For example, those *kulaputra* who worship a Buddha called Dharmaparyaya with flowers, incense and other consuming goods could achieve enlightenment (*SP*: x-1, trans. p. 215; 15–16). *Kulaputra* is the Sanskrit form of *Kulaputta*, which in turn is the Pali designation of 'son of a good family'. In Buddhist literature these good families were either Kshatriyas or the numerous castes engaged in trade (Anderson 1917: II, 79). *Kulaputta* were the main patrons of Buddhism in its early years on the Ganges plain; *kulaputra* played the major role in encouraging donations in north India in the Kushan period.

The activities of rich merchant patrons of Buddhism was a favourite topic in Buddhist literature. The story of the first two lay followers who gave alms to the Buddha soon after his enlightenment appears many times in Pali literature. Its repetition in the *Buddhacarita* stays close to the version in the Pali texts (xv 60–4). The *Mahāvastu* retells this story. Many gods participate in the dramatic scene of the Buddha receiving food from the two traders. In early Pali texts two merchants, Tapussa and Bhallika, pass by the tree where the Buddha is fasting (*Mahāvagga*: I 4, *Vinaya Texts*: I, 81–4). In the *Mahāvastu* the author depicts Trapusa and Bhallika as the heads of a caravan. Where in the Pali text the Buddha received four stone bowls to place the alms of rice and honey from the four guardians of the heaven, in the Sanskrit text the four deities first give the Buddha the choice of bowls made of gold, silver, pearls and other materials of the seven treasures (*MV* III 303–11, pp. 290–8). This elaboration on the tradition may suggest an increase in the material prosperity of the merchants from the earlier to the later period, and these richer merchants continued to patronize Buddhism when the new text was composed. It could also reflect an increase in the prosperity of the sangha, when it received those precious items as donations from the traders.

Sanskrit texts also record some stories telling of frequent interactions between Buddhist monks and merchants which are unknown in the earlier Pali texts. In the *Milindapañha* Nagasena receives the patronage of a merchant on his way to Pataliputra to improve his knowledge of Buddhism (I 33). The author of *Mahāvastu* relates the story that a monk Abhiya slandered his fellow monk Nanda and a rich merchant's daughter because the merchant did not accord him the same respect as he did to Nanda. When Abhiya worshipped the Buddha Sarvabhibhu with some *kesara* perfume, he obtained the promise of buddhahood from the Buddha Sarvabhibhu as a reward. The perfume dealers who donated the *kesara* to Nanda assumed that they would share the merit of Abhiya and become the future Buddha's disciples. The story ends as the merchant's daughter vows to take revenge on Abhiya by making false accusations against him in all his lives until he achieves enlightenment (I 35–45, pp. 30–9). The complicated plots of the stories, which were based on the working out of karma and the idea of sharing merit, reflect frequent contact between merchants and monks.

In another story a princess, Malini, offends the Brahmans by serving a former Buddha Kasyapa. In a time when the Brahmans were numerous and powerful the king, in order to prevent an uprising, gives Malini up to the Brahmans who want to kill her. But the king's soldiers, ministers and the townspeople, who have all converted to Buddhism, decide to protect Malini. The Brahmans, frightened by the big crowd which supports Malini, turn their anger against the Buddha Kasyapa who unsuccessfully tries to preach to them. When the goddess of the earth comes to help she declares that the Brahmans are 'earth bound' slaves and destroys them (*MV*: I 301–17, pp. 249–65). This story reveals a clear-cut confrontation between the Brahmans on the one hand, and an alliance of the royal court and the townspeople on the other, with the Buddha as their leader.

The Buddhist Sanskrit literature of the Kushan period also reflects new developments in urban economy. Figures of speech about the Buddhas often employ the caravan imagery. In the *Milindapañha* the Buddha 'is like a caravan owner to men in that he brings them beyond the sand desert of rebirth' (IV 4, 14); in the *Buddhacarita* the Buddha, like a guide of a caravan, should not be disturbed (XIII 62); in the *Mahāvastu* the Buddha is a caravan-leader in the world, to be honoured by deities with infinite splendour (II 393, p. 351); and in the *Saddharmapuṇḍarika* the Buddha creates an illusion of a city to encourage believers to proceed in the search for the Buddha's knowledge, for they, like the travelling merchants, need a place to rest (XIII, 45–53; VII 92–102). Abundant experience of long-distance trade provided the inspiration for these images of the Buddha as a guide for travellers and merchants.

The landscape of the Buddhist texts expanded with the development of long-distance trade. The lands of the Shakas and Greeks, China, Vitata, Alexandria,[5] Nikumba, Benares, Koshala, Kashmir, Gandhara, all appear (*MP*: IV 8, 88). People skilful in many urban professions from the countries of Shaka, Bactria, China, Vitata, Ujjeni (Ujjain), Bharukaccha (Barygaza), Benares, Koshala and border lands; from Magadha, Saketa, Surattha and the West; from Kotumbara, Madhura, Alexandria, Kashmir, and Gandhara; all came to the ideal Buddhist city (*MP*: V 4).

There are many descriptions of sea trips in the Buddhist Sanskrit texts. Nagasena uses a series of similes related to ships to explain Buddhist doctrines (*MP*: VII 2). Rich merchants were either caravan leaders or ship-owners, such as the sea-faring merchants in 'The Story of Dharmalabdha' (*MV*: III, 286–300, pp. 274–87), and 'The Story of Ājñāta Kauṇḍinya' (III 350–3, pp. 346–50). It was said the Buddha protected merchants on the sea in his former lives: he carried 500 merchants away from sirens in the form of the heavenly horse *Keśin* (III 67–90, pp. 70–93), and he sacrificed his own life to save fellow merchants in a shipwreck (III 354–6, pp. 351–4). Calling the Buddha's name could save ships trapped on the high sea. Five hundred merchants in a storm on the sea, after vainly invoking many gods' names, saved their lives only by invoking the Buddha's name (I 245, pp. 200–1). Both the merchants trading with China through Central Asia and those trading with the Roman empire must have sought protection from the Buddha.

Buddhism, as a cosmopolitan religion in the Kushan period, attracted devotees from other countries outside north India. Inscriptions record donors with Iranian names (Lüders 1961: 91–2, §60, K189; 92–3, §61, K204; 93–4, §62, K190; 103–4, §68, K196; 171–2, §135) and with Greek names (Konow 1929: 98, XXXVII, no. 2). A Bactrian (*bahaliena*, ins.) placed the Buddha's relics in his own Bodhisattva chapel (*taṇuvae bosisatvagahami*) in the monastery Dharmarajika of Taxila (Konow 1929: 77, XXVII). No extant evidence

---

[5] There were many Alexandrias on the borders of India. For example, the one on the Oxus, perhaps the Greek city Ai-Khanoum; the one in Afghanistan, perhaps Kandahar. It could even refer to Alexandria in Egypt, with which north India had trade connections.

exists concerning the circumstances of these foreigners' conversion to Buddhism, but it is unlikely that they came to north India only for the purpose of religious devotion. They were probably merchants trading in the land and converted to Buddhism either because they wanted to facilitate their contacts with Indian merchants, or simply because Buddhist doctrine appealed to them. For strangers who came to India, sacred places such as Buddhist monasteries were suitable places to make contacts and build trust. Whereas Indian merchants must have frequented the monasteries they made donations to, Buddhist ideology opened the sangha to patrons from various regions, regardless of their social status and ethnic origins.

Although only a few of the donors left titles indicating their occupations, the limited information from inscriptions confirms that merchants still avidly supported Buddhism in the early Christian era. In the Sanchi inscriptions dated to *circa* the first century BC, nineteen donors called themselves 'banker' or 'chief merchant' (*setthi*), five 'merchant' (*vanija*), one 'householder' (*gahapati*); some other urban residents were 'cloak-maker' (*pāvārika*), 'weaver' (*sotika*), 'foremen of artisans' (*āvesani*), and 'mason' (*vadhaki*) (Marshall 1940: I, 297). In the succeeding Kushan period, donations were made by the wife of a caravan merchant (*sārthavahāsa kutubiniye*) (Lüders 1961: 199–200, §172, K88) and by a merchant's daughter (*vahārisya masyagu [tta]sya dhitā*) (Sircar 1961: 146, II no. 45A).[6] There are also inscriptions linked to artisans, such as goldsmiths (Lüders 1961: 187, §150, K14) and builders (*navakarmega, karavakasa*) (Konow 1929: 150, LXXVI; 151, LXXVIII).

More characteristic than donations made by individuals were donations made by lay associations. The Kushan inscriptions by the 'commissioners of community' (*sanghaprakrta*) do not give information about the members' occupations, but a similar inscription in the Gupta period makes it clear that they were merchants (*vyavahārī*) (Lüders 1961: 100–2, §65, G5). Since the Gupta and Kushan inscriptions all came from the Mathura region, and supposing the Gupta example represents a tradition dating back to the Kushan lay communities, these organizations in the Kushan period

---

[6] Sircar reconstructs *vahāri* as Sanskrit *vyavahārinah*, which he translates as 'of the magistrate' (Sircar 1965: 146). I prefer to translate this as 'merchant', because if it meant 'magistrate there sould be some other words defining the title.

may well have been merchants' associations founded for the purpose of organizing donations. No evidence indicates that lay associations later developed into institutions active in Indian society, but their successors and counterparts in China played an important role in succeeding periods (see Chapter VIII). Because Buddhist monasteries in the Kushan period did not own sizeable amounts of landed property or other permanent property which provided a constant income, and because they conducted many expensive religious activities, they may well have relied on continuous donations from the urban laity. Here, the significance of the lay associations is that by organizing many moderate-income donors into groups, and by enlarging the contacts of Buddhist monasteries with minor traders, they enabled monasteries to receive many donations which facilitated large-scale construction.

During the same period that commercial groups extended their support to Buddhist monasteries, the relationship between the Kushan government and Buddhists was quite stable. According to Hsüan-tsang, the Kushan king Kanishka sponsored the fourth conference of Buddhism held in Kashmir (Beal 1906: I, 151–2). Although, as with the case of Ashoka, no inscriptions indicating that this event actually occurred have been found, many votive inscriptions made during Kanishka's reign indicate that he favoured Buddhism. Some of the donors mentioned in the inscriptions were related to Kushan officials or their subordinates. A bronze casket that contained a gold box, a gold coin of Huvishka and other small items, was a gift of a Kapisi Kshatrapa (*Kviśiakṣatrapasa*) who might have been a governor under the Kushan kings (Konow 1929: 150–1, LXXVII). An inscription found in the Jamalpur Mound of Mathura gives the donor's title as 'the great general (*mahā-dandanāyaka*) under the king Vasudeva' (Lüders 1961: 65–7, §30, K58). I have already mentioned the monk Bala who initiated a donation which was actually funded by Governor (*kṣatrapa*) Vanaspara, and Great Governor (*mahākṣatrapa*) Kharapallana (Sircar 1965: 137, II no. 38). A monk, Pushyavudhi, initiated a similar donation to which the same two governors also contributed (Sircar 1965: 136–7, II no. 37). Clearly Kushan officials were personally active in the donations to monasteries.

Because it is impossible to tell whether the kings built the so-called 'viharas of the kings' or whether others built them and then named them for the kings, the personal role of Kushan kings in organizing donation remains unclear. In addition to Kanishka's vihara and Huvishka's vihara there were also royal viharas and Buddhist enclosures (*rajaramñaṁ*) that did not bear the name of any specific king (Konow 1929: 158, LXXXII; Lüders 1961: 64, §29, K49). They may have been the property or a religious service institution for the whole royal family.

Although the exact nature of the kings' viharas is unclear, the very existence of this type of vihara nevertheless shows a subtle change in the relationship between the Buddhist sangha and its royal patrons. In the five centuries before the Christian era some monarchs patronized Buddhism and some did not. Buddhism developed and prospered in spite of the periodically negative attitudes of some rulers. There is no evidence to suggest that Buddhists made efforts, such as keeping special viharas for kings, to attract royal patronage. However, during the Kushan period, even if one cannot ascertain whether or not monasteries bearing the name of a king actually provided him with special religious services, Buddhist literature reveals the efforts made to claim affiliation with the rulers. For example, when the author of the *Mahāvastu* tells the Buddha's birth story he declares that bodhisattvas are born into either *Kshatriya* or Brahman families. When Kshatriyas are in power a bodhisattva is born into a Kshatriya family. When Brahmans are more powerful he is born into a Brahman family (I 197, p. 156; II 1, p. 1). The main concerns are that the bodhisattvas must be born into a high caste, and into a ruling family.[7] The author takes pains to identify Buddhist deities with secular rulers. He is not satisfied with Shakya's Kshatriya status but deliberately tries to connect Shakya with the solar lineage, Ikshvaku.[8]

The Buddhists' eager quest for royal patronage reflected the fact that the Buddhist sangha was no longer a social group which defied the norms of society. Even though it continued to absorb some social outcasts, it acted as a social institution that accommodated both secular authority and social conventions.

However, the dependence of Buddhist monasteries on royal

[7] Here the bodhisattva means religious figures in their last incarnation before reaching buddhahood.

[8] In Pali the Shakya's ancestor is *Okkāka*. The *Mahāvastu* sanskritized the name as *Ikṣvāku* (Malalasckera 1937; *MV*: I 348, p. 293).

patronage was still limited in the Kushan period. There are no records of land grants to monasteries by the Kushan kings, although in the western Deccan land had been granted to monasteries in the contemporary Satavahana period. Kushan kings patronized Buddhism just as they did other religions; inscriptions show that Kushan officials made contributions to Jaina and Brahmana institutions as well. A certain Kushan subordinate, the scion of Kanasarukamana, the Lord of Kharasalera and Vakana,[9] made an endowment of 550 *purāṇas* to an unidentified guild (*rākaśreṇīye*) and 550 *purāṇas* to a guild of flour-makers or millers (*samitakaraśreṇī*), from which the interest was to be used to feed 100 Brahmans daily (*EI* xxi: 60–1). Here we cannot exclude the possibility that Kushan rulers did the same thing for Buddhists, but this inscription definitely shows that even though Buddhism was the dominant religion, other religions competed with it. The Kushan kings recognized other religions and did not claim legitimacy on the basis of Buddhist support. They were the first to carve royal statues in India and also the first to call themselves 'son(s) of heaven' (*devaputra*). They built shrines of *devakula* (family of gods), which contained statues of Kushan kings and princes.[10] Divinizing themselves may have been a means for Kushan kings to claim the legitimacy to rule a vast, culturally diverse country.

In spite of competition from other religions and the efforts of Kushan kings to claim divinity, the relationship between the Kushan rulers and the Buddhist monasteries seems to have been harmonious. The personal beliefs of the Kushan kings may have varied, but there are no Buddhist records of persecution or destruction as during the reigns of earlier and later monarchs. Kushan kings surely encouraged, or at least tolerated, the great expansion of Buddhist institutions, and the vigorous proselytizing activities of that period. If Kushans did not depend on Buddhists to support their political claims and their personal devotions were not exclusively Buddhist, what motivated them to patronize Buddhism?

Indian kings patronized religion to win prestige from their subjects. As King Milinda said when persuading the elder Nagasena to accept his gift of a robe worth 100,000 *kahāpaṇas*:

[9] Badakshan according to Sten Konow (*E 1* xxi: 60).

[10] The shrines are found in both Surkh Kotal in Bactria, and Mat near Mathura. (see Rosenfiels 1967: 154ff.)

You should protect both me and protect yourself—yourself from the possibility of a public rumour to the effect that you convinced me but received nothing from me, and me from the possibility of a public rumour that although I was convinced I would give nothing in acknowledgement. (*MP*: III 7, 17)

To be generous to religious orders was a respectable action for a king. Thus when King Milinda's servant argued he should allow only ten of the many followers of Nagasena to visit the court, the king reproaches him: 'Does he suppose we are not capable of feeding so many?' (II 1, 3).

In addition to the pressure to fulfil the moral criteria of a virtuous king, there were few fundamental conflicts of interest between the Kushan rulers and Buddhist institutions. There was no reason why the expansion of Buddhism should have threatened political power and the economy. Because the Kushan state's prosperity was based heavily on an urban economy and a commercial network uniting a large portion of the Eurasian continent, Buddhist contributions to the trade network encouraged the harmonious relationship between the Kushan rulers and Buddhist monasteries. We have learned that the demand for many commodities in the Eurasian trade was prompted by Buddhist rituals, and that merchants were apparently avid supporters of Buddhism. However, with wealth flowing into the Buddhist sangha through donations, did monasteries actively participate and contribute to the economy in order to win the support of merchants?

Even though the market created by the Buddhist rituals for certain goods benefited merchants in the long run, the lengthy cycle of exchanges pushed the rewards far beyond where those traders' vision could reach. Perhaps the donors were never aware that they or their descendants would benefit from the enhanced value which Buddhism brought to the commodities they traded. Even the sangha itself could not know how the enhancement of the concept of the seven treasures would contribute to the growth of trade. Did the monasteries feel the obligation to pay back to the society in a more tangible way? As for the merchants, in addition to the general religious piety their devotion to the sangha was probably based on the more immediate and material contribution of the sangha. The sangha may well have provided banking services and lodging for the merchants that few other institutions in

Kushan society could. However, due to the dearth of information on monastic life in this early age, to prove this is difficult. Before analysing the few clues that exist about the possible monastic involvement in the Kushan commercial economy, I will give examples of ancient religious institutions outside India which provided the infrastructure for trade.

In the Hellenist world, in many cities, temples functioned as banks. Along with city banks and private banks, temples took deposits and made investments. The city temple banks at Delos, Ephesus and Sardis crossed the state borders; they kept deposits of people in other cities and granted loans to cities and private persons. In Ptolemaic Egypt temples in Halicarnassus issued their own currency even when the royal bank worked under a king who cast official coins (Rostovtzeff 1941: 1279–80). Under the Roman empire large and influential temples survived as banking concerns, especially in the eastern provinces. The temple of Jerusalem was the place where both rich and poor Jews deposited money (Rostovtzeff 1926: 541).

The power of temple banks derived from their sanctity. They could create trust among strangers, thus facilitating transactions among different states. The sanctity they provided also enabled temples to give non-military protection to traders and to serve as witnesses to transactions, as in the ports of trade. In Alexandria traders from various parts of the Hellenistic world swore before the altar of the guardian god Hephaestion (Polanyi *et al.* 1957: 61).

Here I should remind the reader that the Roman traders who went to the Indian coast were mostly from the eastern provinces— Egyptian Greeks. In west India the Greeks made donations to Buddhist caves. One of them even had a sphinx made in Karle (Kosambi 1955: 58). Similarly, foreign traders made donations in Mathura and Taxila. For foreigners who came to India to trade, Buddhist monasteries were appealing as sacred places to carry out their transactions. Kosambi argues that the structure of some western Indian viharas indicates that certain cells were used as treasuries (1955: 52). Even if the monasteries could not provide the same kind of banking facilities as the Hellenistic temples did, the sanctity they offered guaranteed trust for the trading parties.

In China, Buddhist monks in Tunhuang often signed their names on treaties as arbiters of property disputes and witnesses of deals (Giles 1957). Four kinds of financial practices in China, i.e. the pawn shop, the mutual financing association, the auction and the sale of lottery tickets, originated in Buddhist monasteries whose financial functions appear in historical records as early as the fifth century AD (Yang Lien-sheng 1961: 199). Unless Chinese monks invented all the practices, they may well have learned from their colleagues from India, Central Asia or Iran.

While evidence outside India suggests that Buddhist monasteries in Kushan India may have participated in trade by providing the necessary facilities, conclusive proof has yet to come from within India itself. The institutional changes during the Kushan period made monasteries act as financial agents, at least for their own holdings. The huge stone symbolic begging bowls indicated not only that the sangha had more wealth but also that they somehow had to convert the money and other valuables they received into provisions, clothes and monuments. Converting small donations into the integrated art works of the Sanchi stupas was a complicated managerial process. While the donors of Sanchi came mostly from the Malwa region, patrons in Mathura and Taxila gathered from many different areas. Only the core role of monasteries made the large-scale monuments possible.

The close correlation between trade routes and the distribution of monasteries also suggests that the Buddhist sangha provided valuable services for the traders. As the monasteries depended on the donations of the passing merchants, they should have been willing to help their patrons. Two remarkable archaeological discoveries suggest that monks actively participated in trade. At the monastic site Devnimori in Gujarat some Roman amphora shards were found along with the Red Polished Ware and some less fine ware. A black residue on the amphora shards attracted the excavator's attention. Chemical analysis suggests that the resinous material was the sedimentation of wine (Mehta 1966: 77). Monks in that monastery either enjoyed or handled expensive imported wine.[11] Up in the north-west, at Shaikhan Dheri, the Kushan site of the city Pushkalavati, a workshop or storeroom of distillation apparatus was found in a Buddhist shrine (Allchin 1979: 776–7).

[11] However, one cannot exclude the possibility that the resinous material on the amphora shards is the residue of some kind of medicine, which is still evidence of trading.

Having carefully identified the pottery for making and storing liquor, Allchin cannot help suggesting that this Buddhist shrine was associated with the consumption of liquor for a long period of time (779). The two finds coincidentally reveal that Buddhist monasteries were enagaged in a liquor trade. If monasteries could purchase and sell this commodity, which was banned for the monks, they probably also traded in other items. For example, trading in incense and precious stones for use in Buddhist rituals would be a much less serious violation of Buddhist rules than trafficking in wine.

Finally, the strong links of certain monasteries with special groups, be it a family or a trade guild, also increased their obligation to their patrons. Here the transaction was restricted to only two parties, the pressure for the receiver to return was higher than in the case of a monastery open to the public.

Up to this point little hard evidence proves the hypothesis that Buddhist monasteries provided infrastructure—facilities for transactions and travel—for Eurasian trade in the Kushan domain. But evidence within and without India indicates that the monasteries were ready for the role and that their relationship with the laity required them to do so.

Chapter vi: Further Changes in Indian Buddhist Institutions

Western India: Signal of Transition

Before discussing certain fundamental changes in Buddhist institutions during the Gupta period I would like to mention some developments concerning Buddhism in western India. These developments, which were contemporary with the Kushan state but took place outside the region of the Kushan political domain, provide important links for an understanding of the changes and continuity from the Kushan to the Gupta period. The strategic significance of this region made it vulnerable to both northern and southern invaders. Both the Western Kshatrapas and Satavahanas controlled it for different times *circa* the second century AD. But the real reason for its inclusion here is its close contacts with north-west India, the core region of the Kushans.

From the post-Mauryan period on, numerous cave-temples appeared in the Western Ghats. Among the 915 caves in western India surveyed by archaeologists before 1880, 720 were Buddhist, mostly built before the Gupta period (Fergusson and Burgess 1880: 170). As we will see in the next chapter, the early large-scale Buddhist construction in Central Asia and China were mainly cave excavations. However, in north and north-west India, the core region of the Kushan empire, the main forms of Buddhist buildings were stupas and viharas, with the caves of Bamiyan providing the major exception. In order to trace the model for the Buddhist caves in China one can easily follow the trade routes linking western India with Central Asia and China. Many *yavana*, i.e. Greeks or other foreigners, and people from the north-west, probably traders, left their names in the cave inscriptions (e.g. *EI* vii: 52, Karle no. 4; 53, no. 6; 53–4, no. 7). Two brothers who came from Bharukaccha (Barygaza) (Burgess 1881: 49 Junnar no. 20) connected the Buddhist cave in Junnar to the famous seaport which linked north-west India to the Roman trade.

With the huge influx of northerners in western India, certain developments in the relationship of the monasteries with the laity in north India occurred. Many monks and nuns made donations under their own names (e.g. *EI* vii: 51, Karle no. 3; 54–5, no. 8; 56–7, no. 12; 63, no. 15; 63, no. 16; 64, no. 19) or together with laymen (e.g. Burgess 1881: 50–1, Junnar no. 22). There are traces of collective donations or lay organizations. The Nasik people collectively donated a village (*EI* viii: 92, Nasik no. 18); a man from the lay community of *chetika* (*chetika upāsakiyasa*) donated a cave (*EI* viii: 77, Nasik no. 9); and a guild of bamboo workers (*seniye vasakarasa*) and a guild of braziers (*kāsakāresu seniye*) shared the expenses of making a donation (Burgess 1881: 47, Junnar no. 16). Similarly, the gifts of many individual donors demonstrate the strong ties between the urban communities and the monasteries. Many householders and merchants made substantial donations to the cave excavations (e.g. *EI* viii: 95, Nasik no. 25; Burgess 1881: 40, Junnar no. 8; 51, no. 23; 60–1, Kanheri; 68, Ajanta no. 2). One donor called himself householder (*gahapati*) and merchant (*nyegama*) (*EI* viii: 75, Nasik no. 6). Another called himself chief householder (*gahapatipamugha*) and upright merchant (*dhamanima*) (Burgess 1881: 42, Junnar no. 4). A banker (*setthi*) built a rock-cut hall (*caitya*) (*EI* vii: 48–9, Karle no. 1), a perfume dealer (*gamdhika*) from north-west India left an inscription in a cave doorway (*EI* vii: 52, Karle no. 4). Householders' wives (Burgess 1881: 38–9), mothers (*EI* vii: 52, Karle no. 5) and other female relatives also made contributions.

More evidence of merchant support for monasteries survives from the western Indian caves than it does from those of the north. A Saka woman in the ninth year of the king Isvarasena (*c.* AD 259) gave an endowment to three different guilds and designated the interest to provide medicine for monks in a sangha (*EI* viii: 88–9, Nasik no. 15). A merchant named Ramanaka gave an endowment directly to a sangha and specified that the interest should be used to supply clothes to monks who spent the rainy seasons there (*EI* viii: 90, Nasik no. 17). If the Saka woman's financial arrangement represents a monastery's transactions with urban institutions, the endowment in the monastery hints that the sangha itself functioned as a financial institution—in that it could invest money as it wished.

The interdependence of merchants and monasteries moulded the Saka kings' attitudes towards Buddhism. Members of the royal family (e.g. *EI* VIII: 81–2, Nasik no. 11), ministers (e.g. Burgess 1881: 51–2, Junnar no. 25) and their relatives (e.g. *EI* VIII: 91, Nasik no. 19) patronized Buddhism by donating caves. The most active among them was Ushavadata, son-in-law of the Shaka king, and Mahakshatrapa Nahapana. When he made donations to Buddhists he did not forget to boast about his contributions to Brahmans. He gave rest-houses in four towns, including Barygaza (*EI* VII: 78ff, Nasik no. 10; 85ff, no. 14a), and made an endowment of 3000 *kāhāpaṇa* to two guilds of weavers in the town of Govadhana to support the monks who lived in a cave. These endowments were registered in the *nigamasabhāya* (*EI* VIII: 82ff, no. 12).[1]

Whether or not the Western Kshatrapas were politically subordinate to Kushans is hard to determine. But they certainly shared similar attitudes towards religion; they patronized both Buddhism and Brahmanism, especially Buddhism, perhaps because of the sangha's close links with commercial society. The urban economy provided the primary means of patronage: constructing monumental or residential buildings and making endowments through urban institutions.

The southern rulers who governed western India during part of the second and the third centuries AD also patronized Buddhist institutions there, but in a quite different way. In addition to cave excavations, such as those funded by a queen (*EI* VIII: 60ff, Nasik no. 2), the Satavahanas granted whole villages to the monasteries, and, unlike the Shaka kings, did not make endowments through guilds. The Satavahana king Sadakani Gotamiputa ordered the officer at Govadhana to donate a village (*EI* VIII: 71–3, Nasik no. 4) and because the first one had been deserted, exchanged it for another a few years later (73–74, Nasik no. 5). His son and successor Pulumavi Vasithiputa also donated a village to a sangha in Nasik (*EI* VIII: 65ff, no. 3). A prince and a king donated villages to Karle monasteries (*EI* VII: 61–2, Karle no. 14). These possessions of the monasteries were exempt from many kinds of tax, not subject to official inspections and protected from unofficial intruders.

Some individuals followed suit and donated land to monasteries

[1] City hall or assembly, either an administrative unit or an autonomous organization.

(Burgess 1881: 44, Junnar no. 9; 45–6, no. 13; 46, no. 14; 47, no. 15; 48, no. 17, 48–9, no. 18). Even a Shaka prince, the son-in-law of Nahapana, donated a village to supply provisions to monks who spent the rainy season in the monastery (*EI* VII: 57ff, Karle no. 13).

Both endowments and landed property supplied Buddhist monasteries with a regular income. This independence from constant donations further facilitated the expansion of the monasteries and their preaching activities. We have seen that some donations were designated to support wandering monks. Those who spent only rainy seasons in the monastery were mostly missionaries and pilgrims who travelled to propagate knowledge of Buddhism. On the other hand land grants recorded and fixed the monasteries' subordinate relationship to the government. One inscription indicates that the Satavahanas actually sent an official to take charge of the monks at Nasik (*EI* VIII: 93, no. 22).

Early in the second century in western India—an area where northern and southern polities confronted each other—the succession of totally different patterns of patronage towards Buddhism signalled a change in the social system that would take place on a larger scale and over a vast landscape in succeeding periods. The granting of land to religious institutions became popular in north India with the Gupta period. The significance of this change in Indian history has neen recognized by historians only gradually. Its contribution to the development of the Buddhist sangha in north India and to the establishment of the Buddhist sangha in north China will be discussed in the following pages.

LANDED PROPERTY AND RITUALS IN THE MONASTERIES OF GUPTA INDIA

After the disintegration of the Kushan state in the third century, Buddhism in north India underwent further transformations. It suffered increasingly severe competition from Vaishnavism and Shaivism. These new sects of Brahmanism, which encouraged more the worship of gods than sacrifices to them, gradually became the dominant form of religious practice. Buddhists nevertheless took advantage of the new political and economic conditions of the Gupta period (from the fourth to the sixth century) to fortify their monasteries, which survived as important institutions in parts of

India, mainly in the eastern Ganges and Kashmir, as well as in a few spots in western India, the Deccan and the north-west for another five or six centuries.

As Buddhisrr in Gupta India was losing out to Brahmanism, the Buddhist influence in China increased. Although the Gupta rulers did not take the same interest in Central Asian affairs as did the Kushans, communication between India and China via Central Asia intensified. For the Chinese Buddhists India was still the holy motherland of their sacred religion. Sanskrit canonical literature supplied fresh inspiration for their doctrine, and practices in north Indian monasteries provided models for their own institutions. Consequently, changes in monastic practices in Gupta India directly affected the young and undeveloped Buddhist monasteries in China. Although Buddhists in Gupta India no longer attracted as many donations as they had under the Kushans, the monasteries' efforts to further embellish ceremonies created more texts elaborating the concept of the seven treasures. The message of these practices and literature came to reach Chinese Buddhists and lay worshippers, and so helped to enhance the market value of the items required to perform rituals. In spite of the changes in markets and routes of supply taking place in the Eurasian trade network from China to the Mediterranean world, traders, accompanying pilgrims and preachers, transported certain luxury commodities between the two countries.

Because Buddhism lost its predominant position in many parts of Gupta India, information about Gupta Buddhism is even scarcer than that concerning the Kushan period. Even in the eastern Ganges, where Buddhism continued to thrive, inscriptions diminished as the fashion for donation lost its momentum. All we have are a few inscriptions, and the pilgrim Fa-hsien's accounts. However, given its important influence on Chinese Buddhism and the Sino-Indian trade, it is necessary to draw a sketch, no matter how faint or tentative, of Buddhism in the Gupta period.

In addition to competing with each other, Buddhism and Brahmanism also compromised and complemented each other. When Fa-hsien recounts the hostility of 'heretic religions' towards Buddhism he is also puzzled by the similarity of different religions in India:

In the middle country,[2] there are ninety-six different religions. They all

___
[2] The west and middle Gangés plain.

know the conception of rebirth. Each of them has its own disciples and followers. They all beg for food, only they do not carry begging bowls [as the Buddhist monks do] (861a).

For a Chinese monk the concept of rebirth and the practice of begging pertained only to Buddhism. Fa-hsien did not expect to see other religions, described as 'heretic religions' in Buddhist canons, which also accepted similar ideas and practices.

When Fa-hsien notices that other religions follow what he considers uniquely Buddhist concepts and practices, he also accidentally records some practices that he thinks Buddhist but which actually reflected Buddhist compromises with Brahmanism and other religions. The best example is of a Buddhist priest who lived in Pataliputra. This monk was from a Brahman family and enjoyed great prestige in the country. Only because of him, says Fa-hsien, followers of 'heretic religions' dare not insult Buddhist monks. This monk of Brahman origin maintained such a high standard that even after the king had held the monk's hands in respect, the monk washed himself afterwards (Fa-hsien: 862b). This Buddhist priest had obviously adopted the Brahmanist conception of purity. A votive inscription in Sanchi also reveals that Buddhists accepted Brahmanical values. The Buddhist donor cursed those who later altered the terms of the donation as committing the same order of sin as killing a cow or a Brahman (Sircar 1965: 281–2; Fleet 1888: 29ff, no. 5).

In general, Buddhists highly respected Brahmanism. Even in ceremonial parades it was the Brahmans of the city of Pataliputra who walked to receive the images of the Buddha (Fa-hsien: 862b). On the other hand these incidents also demonstrate that Brahmans, at least some of them, respected Buddhism too. When the orthodox Brahmans tolerated Buddhism by including the Buddha in the Hindu pantheon, as shown in the *Viṣṇupurāṇa* (III, XVIII–XVIII), others positively supported Buddhism by joining in its activities. Their support helped Buddhism to strengthen its institutions and to function in society.

When losing ground to the revived Brahmanism, Buddhism in Gupta India sustained its institutions by augmenting its economic power, mainly by acquiring landed property. With the Gupta period more and more land-granting inscriptions on copper plates appear in north India. The grantees were religious figures, religious institutions, or individuals who were obliged to maintain temples with the proceeds of the grants. While in north India the over-whelming majority of these recipients were Brahmans or people guarding Hindu temples, Buddhist monasteries also received a portion of the donations. Actually, monasteries in the western and eastern Deccan had received land grants as early as the second and the third centuries. Thus, granting land to Buddhist monasteries was partly the continuation of an established practice and partly an attempt to match the granting of land to Brahmans, as Buddhist monasteries were still important institutions.

In Saurashtra the Valabhi kings granted a number of villages to a Buddhist monastery starting from the early sixth century (*IA* IV: 104ff; *JRAS* 1885: 382ff; *IA* VII: 67ff; IV: 174ff; XIV: 329ff). This monastery, founded by the niece of the king Dhruvasena I, Dudda, was probably a royal cloister. The last inscription recording a royal grant of land was dated in the Valabhi year 286 (AD 605) (*IA* XIV: 327ff). This monastery thus regularly received patronage from the royal family over the course of a century. To the east of Saurashtra, at the boundary of modern Madhya Pradesh, a copper plate found in the debris of a Buddhist cave in Bagh records that the local king Subandha, of the early fifth century AD, granted a vil-lage to a monastery. Revenue from this village provided perfume, frankincense, flowers and other offerings; maintained an alms-house; and supplied all the monastery's necessities (Mirashi 1955: 19–21, no. 7).

To the east of Bagh in Sanchi, a military officer of Chandra-gupta III of the Gupta empire granted a village to a monastery (Fleet 1888: 29ff, no. 5; Marshall 1940: I, 388–9). Fa-hsien's accounts from this part of India, the 'middle country', also testify that kings, elders (*chang-che*) and householders (*chüshih*)[3] built houses for the monasteries, provided the monasteries with land, gardens, tenants and cattle, and recorded those grants on 'iron plates' (*t'ieh-chüan* 859b-c). 'Iron' here perhaps just means 'metal'. Had Fa-hsien specified the material used as copper, his account

---

[3] The Sanskrit origin of *Chang-che*, the elder, might be *sreṣṭhi*, meaning banker; literally the best, or the eldest; or *jyeṣṭha*, head of a guild, also meaning senior, eldest. The Sanskrit origin for *chü-shih*, the householder, is either *gṛhapati* or *kulapati*. In Chinese Buddhist literature, as in Sanskrit or Pali Buddhist literature, the two titles for Buddhist patrons are often mentioned together.

would have coincided perfectly with archaeological finds. In Bengal and Bihar, the core region of Gupta polity and the centre of Buddhist activities in north India, there are also records of land grants to Buddhist monasteries (Niyogi 1972–3: 161–2). The few extant inscriptions show that monasteries which received grants of landed property existed in most regions in Gupta India.

In addition to landed property, monasteries controlled the currency. Two inscriptions from Sanchi dated to the early fifth century reveal that donors deposited money directly in a monastery. The military officer, who granted a village to the great monastery of Kakanadabota in Sanchi in the year AD 412–13, deposited twenty-five gold coins (*dīnāra*) in the monastery. This custom, like that of granting land, had antecedents in the practices of the western Deccan (*EI* VIII: 90, Nasik no. 17). According to the inscription the interest from these coins was to be used to feed ten monks and keep two lamps burning in the jewel-house of the monastery (Fleet 1888: 29ff, No. 5; Marshall 1940: I, 388–9).[4] A female worshipper made a donation of sixteen gold coins in the year AD 450–1 to the Great Monastery of Kakanadabota and stipulated the use of every coin. According to this inscription the interest on twelve gold coins was to be used to feed one monk; the interest on three coins was to keep a lamp burning in the jewel-house; the last coin's interest was to keep a lamp burning in a place where the images of the four Buddhas were seated (Fleet 1888: 261–2, no. 62; Marshall 1940: I, 390). In order to earn interest on the donations the monastery either had to lend the money out or invest it. I have already discussed one example of depositing money in a monastery in west India in the third century AD. From these two Gupta inscriptions it is hard to judge just how far this practice spread in north India during the Gupta period. But the two cases nevertheless provide solid evidence that a monastery in Sanchi, a Buddhist centre along the important trade route from Ujjain to Vidisha, functioned as a financial institution which used its treasury to generate a profit.

Supported by perpetual income from landed property and treasuries, Buddhists in Gupta India maintained institutional stability and visibility. Although great Buddhist centres in north-west

[4] *Ratna-gṛha*, probably a stupa which contained the relics of the Buddha, who was one of the three jewels (*tri-ratna*) of Buddhism.

India, such as Taxila, declined, some monasteries in new centres on the Ganges plain expanded. The best example is the famous Nalanda, which developed into a great educational centre in the north. Fa-hsien and his fellow pilgrim Tao-cheng were deeply impressed by the grandeur and discipline of the Mahayana Sangha in Pataliputra (862b). Lamenting the lack of authentic monastic rules and discipline in Chian, Tao-cheng finally decided to stay in India (864c).

While permanent property facilitated monastic consolidation, relying on this type of support increased the dependence of Buddhist institutions on the patronage of the government and that of a few rich donors. Buddhist monasteries in Sri Lanka, South-East Asia and China all suffered bueaucratic control because they depended on the income from land grants. Unfortunately historical sources in Gupta India do not give much information about governments administering religious institutions under their patronage. Only in the *Mrcchakatika* (c. fifth to eighth centuries AD) does one read of the king appointing a monk as head of all the Buddhist monasteries in the country (*prithivyāh sarvavihāreṣu kulapatiraya kriyatām*) (x 58, pp. 404–5). Given that information about Buddhism is so sketchy in this period of Indian history, this brief snippet suggests that north-Indian kings in the fifth or the sixth century may have set up bureaucratic machinery to control Buddhist monasteries.[5]

Owning permanent property and enjoying constant patronage from royal families relieved Buddhist monasteries of their dependence on steady donations both to maintain buildings and to supply provisions for the sangha. Simultaneously, the trend of donation which had characterized the Kushan period slowed down. The decrease in votive inscriptions signalled a change in the financing of Buddhist institutions. Even in the new Buddhist centres of east India, such as Nalanda, the number of votive inscriptions was tiny when compared to those of the Kushan period from north and north-west India. Actually, land grants and the dependence on

[5] The office of religious minister may have gone back to the Mauryan period, when Ashoka introduced the institution of *dhamma-mahāmattas*, the officer of Dharma. The Mauryan office wielded great power in controlling people's lives (R. Thapar 1961: 156–7). But how this office developed and changed after the Mauryan period is unknown.

income from land shifted the focus of the monasteries to the agricultural areas in the middle and east Ganges, where fertile lands generated more reliable income. Furthermore, of the few Buddhist votive inscriptions left from the Gupta era, most are records of donations by monks and nuns; the monasteries solicited few donations from lay worshippers and had little contact with them. For example, of the nine Mathura donors who indicated their status, seven were monks and nuns (Lüders 1961: 34, §9, G3; 103, §67, G6; 113, §78, G7; 188, §152, G10; 211, §185, G11; 205, §179, G12; 212, §186, G13). Almost all the inscriptions of Ajanta dated to the Gupta period represent donations made by monks, except for a few grants made by the Vakataka royal family and their subordinates (e.g. Burgess 1881: 69ff; 73ff).

While the movement encouraging donations for the construction of monuments provided the major bridge between the Buddhist sangha and its laity during the Kushan period, the monasteries in the Gupta era did not maintain these links. Inscriptions by wives of householders, sons of householders and other lay worshippers appear sporadically (e.g. Lüders 1961: 197, §167, G4; 198–9, §170, G16; Mirashi 1955: 29ff, no. 10; Burgess 1881: 88ff). But these isolated donors do not represent the extent of the activities of the Buddhist monasteries during the Gupta period.

Chinese pilgrims' descriptions of these activities in India suggest that numerous religious ceremonies and other ritual performances superseded donations as the main channels through which monasteries kept in touch with their laity. As he travelled from the Pamir plateau to Pataliputra, Fa-hsien participated in several great ceremonies and encountered many objects of Buddhist worship. In the state of Chieh-ch'a, probably in Kashmir, Fa-hsien witnessed a large congregation of Buddhist monks. This congregation was held once in five years, lasting from one to three months. At the end of the ceremony the king and his ministers granted great quantities of precious items and necessities to the monks. In addition to this big ceremony the king requested that monks congregate annually before the harvesting season. It is said the ceremony could hasten the ripening of wheat, the only crop in the region (857c). Lay devotees might have made donations to fund these services, but this kind of donation was similar to a fee paid for the service and was no longer recorded in inscriptions. The monasteries and monks who received the gifts probably had more freedom to dispose of the income as they wished than they had had under the stipulations in the inscriptions.

According to Fa-hsien Buddhist rituals pervaded the whole society of Nagarahara, a state near Gandhara. A skull bone of the Buddha was the centre of ritual performance, and the king so feared losing the bone that he made the eight big families of the country guard it. Every family held a stamp to seal the container of the bone. Every morning the eight representatives of the families went to the monastery storing the bone, checked their seals on the container and then opened it. They took the bone outside the monastery to a high platform, covered under a round plate made of the seven treasures.

Hearing the music announcing that the bone had been taken out the king went to the monastery to pay homage to the bone with flowers and incense, before conducting any administrative business. The elders and householders of the city also worshipped the bone daily, before conducting their business. After the daily ceremony the bone was taken back into the monastery to its container, which was a small stupa about five feet high and made of the seven treasures. Every morning peddlers met in front of the monastery to sell flowers and incense to worshippers. Kings from other countries also sent envoys to worship the bone. A tooth of the Buddha enjoyed similar veneration in the country, as did a few other objects—such as the Buddhas's stick and cloak. According to local tradition the ceremonies were efficacious for the summoning of rains in the country, which frequently suffered drought (858c–859a).

The most extravagant Buddhist ceremony was the annual parade held in Pataliputra. Big four-wheeled wagons, about twenty in number, carried stupas made of bamboo and white cloth. The stupas were as tall as five storeys, decorated with gold, silver and lapis lazuli or glass, and hung with silk banners. Inside the stupas were images of the Buddha and his attendants. On the day of the parade people of the whole country would get together to enjoy music, dance and other entertainments (862b).

In addition to describing these ceremonies Fa-hsien says that various striking objects attracted many Buddhist worshippers. A big image of Maitreya Buddha in a small state, Darada (T'o-li) in north-west India, attracted the worship of kings (857c–859a). Big stupas near Taxila enjoyed worship from both kings and people (858b). The stupa built by Kanishka in Purushapura (Peshawar) was still the most magnificent and best-decorated in the whole of India (858b). And although the city of Shravasti was desolate, ritual performance in the Jetavana monastery, donated by Anathapindika, never stopped (860b).

Worship as the major form of devotion was popular among all denominations and believers of different statuses, but the objects worshipped differed, depending on the preferences of the worshippers. According to Fa-hsien, in the middle country of India nuns preferred worshipping Ananda because he persuaded the Buddha to allow women to join the sangha. Novices often worshipped Rahula, son of the Buddha. Teachers specializing in *Abhidharma* (Supreme Truth) worshipped the *Abhidharma* texts. Teachers of *Vinaya* (Monastic Rules) worshipped the *Vinaya* texts. Those devoted to the Mahayana school worshipped the text of the *Prajñāpāramita* (Perfection of Wisdom) and the images of Manjusri, Avalokitesvara and other bodhisattvas. These ceremonies were held annually on different dates (859b).

These ritual performances derived and developed on the basis of the practice of giving donations which had characterized the Kushan period; they were also based on the concept of gaining merit by worship and the expectation that the accumulation of merit could culminate in improved future lives. As an inscription from Ajanta (the fifth century AD) vividly puts it: 'A single flower offered to him [the Buddha] yields the fruit known as paradise [and even] final emancipation' (Yazdani 1930–55: IV, 144ff; Burgess 1881: 77ff). Fa-hsien's accounts suggest that ceremonies and worship of objects both provided the main forums for Buddhist preaching activities and constituted the main channels through which the Buddhist sangha maintained contact with its laity in the Gupta period.

According to Fa-hsien rich merchants and big householders played an important role in Buddhist ceremonial activities in major urban centres, although they no longer actively made donations for construction. The elders and householders followed the king of Nagarahara in worshipping the bone of the Buddha (858c). In the middle country they donated lands, houses, gardens, tenants and cattle to the monasteries, and provided cloth and other necessities to monks after their annual ceremonies (895b). In the city of Patali-putra the elders and householders opened charitable houses pro-viding free medical care for poor people. Because Fa-hsien, a Budhist pilgrim, mentioned these merit-earning houses, they were probably attached to Buddhist institutions.

Although landed property provided a steady income for monas-teries, and thus lessened the need for urban patronage—and although the rise of Brahmanism partially directed urban patronage away from Buddhism—the highly ritualized Buddhism of the Gupta period still affected the urban economy and trade, especially the long-distance trade in luxury goods. I have traced in detail in my earlier discussion of commodities (Chapter II) the luxury goods used in the various Buddhist ceremonies and worship, in particular the seven treasures. I have also mentioned that the use of silk banners extended beyond Buddhist ceremonies. Perhaps the most important influence of Buddhism on the Sino-Indian trade was the stress on the importance of the seven treasures trans-mitted to China via translations of Buddhist literature, missionaries and pilgrims. Fa-hsien was only one of several pilgrims who conveyed their impressions of magnificent Indian monastic life to their Chinese colleagues. As for Buddhist translations, following the *Saddharmapuṇḍarīka* (The Lotus Sutra) still more texts carried the message of worshipping stupas with the seven treasures to China. For example, the *Vajracchedikā* (The Diamond-cutter), which was translated into Chinese (*c.* AD 384–417) by Kumarajiva, describes the great merit one may obtain by worshipping the Buddhas with the seven treasures (VIII, XI, in Cowell 1894: 119, 123). The *Amitāyur-Dhyāna-Sūtra* (Meditation on the Buddha Amitayus), which was translated by Kalayashas in AD 424, suggests that worshippers meditate under the trees made of the seven treasures in the Land of Bliss (§12, Cowell 1894: 172). These messages, written in sacred books and carried by devoted monks who suffered all the dangers and difficulties of the long journey, certainly were taken seriously by Chinese Buddhists. By the fifth century, when Buddhist practices dominated religious life in north China and by which time Buddhist values had penetrated many aspects of Chinese social life, the power of these messages would show in the urban economy, especially with regard to the trade in special commodities.

PART III

Chapter VII: The Establishment of Buddhist Institutions in North China

The Early Buddhist Influence in China

When and how Buddhism reached China is a topic of debate for both Buddhists in the past and scholars now. The early Buddhist effort since the sixth century to push back the date of Buddhism's spread to China has evoked skepticism among scholars, prompting them to examine thoroughly the few extant sources on Chinese Buddhism up to the time of the Later Han. E. Zürcher's work (1959) is the most comprehensive in this field. Zürcher concludes that these early tales are all pious apocrypha without any factual basis. He bases his conclusions on an examination of the opinions of T'ang Yung-t'ung and H. Maspero, as well as a series of traditions concerning the earliest Buddhist preaching activities in China, starting from the story of the Sramana Shih-li-fang who went to China in the time of Ch'in Shih-huang (221–209 BC) to the tradition that Emperor Ming of the Later Han (AD 58–75) sent envoys to the Yüeh-chih (Kushans) after dreaming of a golden image of the Buddha (1959: 19–22).

Zürcher argues that Buddhism gradually spread north-west into China between the first half of the first century BC and the middle of the first century AD. At the beginning of the period the Chinese controlled the eastern part of Central Asia; one hundred years later there is concrete evidence of the existence of Buddhism in China. Even in the late first century AD, according to Zürcher, Buddhist communities were largely composed of foreign families dwelling in urban centres. Many Sanskrit texts circulated among them. An Hsüan was a Parthian merchant who arrived in Loyang in 181 AD. Others became Buddhists after their families settled in China (*KSC*: I, 324b-c). Dharmaraksha's (Fa-hu) Yüeh-chih ancestors immigrated to Tunhuang a few generations before him (Zürcher

1959: 23). Despite the presence of these Buddhists the only official Chinese record of Buddhism is a reference about Prince Ying of Ch'u who paid his respects to both Buddhism and Taoism. The first example of a Buddhist temple and large-scale ritual did not occur until over a hundred years later in P'eng Ch'eng, modern Hsü-chou (27–8).

Meanwhile, in the latter half of the second century AD, a group of missionaries began intensive translation activities in Loyang (30–2). The works of the first generation of translators, An Shih-kao, An Hsüan,[1] and Yen Fo-t'iao reflect the coexistence of Hinayana, a school relatively conservative in interpreting early Buddhist doctrine, and Mahayana, a school developed in north India about the beginning of the Christian era which added many new elements to Buddhist doctrine in early Chinese Buddhism (34). The second generation of translators, headed by Lokakshema, a Yüeh-chih or Kushan (Chih Lou-chia-ch'ien), represent the Mahayana school in China.

Zürcher's picture of Buddhism in the Later Han is based on an all-inclusive study of contemporary and later Buddhist and historical records. It demonstrates that preaching activities were largely confined to foreign immigrants. The Parthians, Yüeh-chih and Indians of the second century AD all probably came from the territory of the Kushan state and followed the commercial routes through Central Asia. The fact that the merchant An Hsüan joined An Shih-kao, a monk who was said to have been of noble extraction, in translating Buddhist texts suggests the commercial nature of the immigrant communities and the close contacts between Buddhist missionaries and merchants. Facing the anti-commercial Han government and the treacherous political situation, the traders' diaspora in China naturally rallied around the institution of its home religion. Some Central Asian traditions about early Buddhist missionaries confirm this relationship on the trade routes. The pilgrim Sung Yün in the sixth century recorded a story that the king of Khotan did not believe in Buddhism until a merchant brought a monk to the country. It is said the monk converted the king by creating an illusion of the Buddha (YHC: v, 271). Although this reference is from a late record, it suggests a popular impression in Central Asia that Buddhist missionaries were companions of

[1] Both these two, ostensibly from their surname, were originally from Persia.

traders travelling on the routes between India and China.

Zürcher also demonstrates that Buddhist activities, often mixed with Taoism, enjoyed the patronage of Chinese officials. Even though early Chinese historians usually do not mention foreign religions unless criticizing ostentatious forms of worship, their criticisms reveal that a large temple that could seat more than three thousand people existed, that Buddhism was studied there, and that the 'bathing the Buddha' ceremony was performed there (1959: 28). These records indicate that Buddhist activities were not limited to a few missionary groups in Loyang. Some surveys of early Buddhist sites done by archaeologists, artists and experts on Chinese Buddhism since 1960 support this impression of large-scale participation in Buddhism during the Han dynasty. A survey of the Buddhist cave temples along the Northern Route of Central Asia, from the sites of ancient Kucha to Shan-shan and Turfan, reveals a long history of Buddhist construction. These caves date back to the time of the Later Han (AD 25–220) and continue to prosper until the fourteenth century (Yen Wen-ju 1962: 59). The structure of the earliest big caves, like Kezir no. 47, is similar to those of Bamiyan in Afghanistan (44), but the earliest murals of the caves are stylistically similar to tomb murals in the Later Han (45). It is not surprising to see the eclectic style of Buddhist art in Central Asia, but the early dates of this art suggest that Chinese devotees were active in Buddhist construction campaigns as early as the Later Han.

A recent investigation of a complex of carvings on boulders near Lien-yün-kang, Kiangsu, clearly testifies to the existence of a movement to worship the Buddha in the Later Han (*WW* 1981: no. 7). The motifs of the carvings show obvious Buddhist features. Group no. 2 depicts several images based on the story of the Buddha attaining nirvana. A crowd of mourners surrounds a large supine figure. Group no. 11 portrays the Jataka story of Prince Mahasattva who fed his own body to a hungry tiger. The scenes depicting entertainment and the foreign ethnic apparel also differ markedly from other Later Han sculptures (Lianyungang, Museum of 1981: 6). However, in spite of all the Indian Buddhist charac-teristics, such as the high bun on the head of the Buddha, the halo and the hand posture of the Buddha, the whole complex of sculptures is an unmistakable Later Han Chinese product (Yü Wei-ch'ao and

Hsin Li-hsiang 1981: 8–15). It seems the artists did not have Indian models but based their works on translations of Chinese Buddhist texts. Yü Wei-ch'ao and Hsin Li-hsiang prove that the Buddhist texts which described the motifs appearing on the sculptures had already been translated into Chinese at the time the sculptures were carved (13).

Since the site, K'ung-wang-shan, is located close to the sea there is controversy among the participants of the survey team concerning the route along which Buddhist influence came (Wen-wu Correspondent 1981: 20). Because there is no evidence that Indian Buddhist art penetrated to the Chinese east coast through land routes in this early age, if a stylistic influence from India ever reached K'ung-wang-shan it should have come from the sea routes. However, as I have mentioned above, the artists did not imitate the Gandharan Buddhist sculpture but derived their ideas from Buddhist stories; and they worked with the motivation of accumulating merit for their future lives by worshipping the Buddha. Thus these carvings represent an ideological transmission rather than an influence of art style. The location of the site itself cannot prove this art resulted from direct contact with the statue-building activities in northern and western India through the sea routes.

We know that there was a group of translators active in the capital, Loyang. And moreover, Ch'ü-hsien, the county within which K'ung-wang-shan is located, was not far from the Buddhist centre P'eng-ch'eng, which was connected with Loyang by major trade routes (see Map 1). These facts suggest that the Buddhist sculptures of K'ung-wang-shan belonged to a complex of Buddhist preaching activities of which Loyang was the centre.

K'ung-wang-shan's location is important to the study of early Buddhism because it was an important Taoist region. The sculptures at the site include some Taoist images. Yü We-ch'ao and Hsin Li-hsiang point out K'ung-wang-shan was the site of the famous Taoist Eastern Sea Temple (Tung-hai-miao) (14). This finding confirms the historical account that the Buddha was initially worshipped together with Taoist deities. It is clear that to the indigenous Chinese devotees in the earliest stage of Buddhism in China the Buddha appeared a god. Similar to many other gods in Chinese popular religion, the Buddha was one deity among many, any of whom might demonstrate their efficacy. To enable Chinese devotees to understand Buddhist philosophy would have taken several centuries of translation, interpretation and preaching by learned monks. Instead, Buddhists attracted Chinese converts by encouraging the worship of Buddha and by statue-building activities.

The institutional changes that took place in the monasteries of north-west India, combined with doctrinal shifts, provided the basis for thinking that making donations and worshipping Buddhist deities were the best way to attain Buddhist goals. Merchants in Central Asia carried the idea of worship and the belief that Buddha was a god to China. In the subsequent history of Buddhism in China many philosophical schools developed and much sophisticated discussion of doctrine took place, but the idea that the Buddha was a deity to worship dominated the history of Chinese Buddhism—as it did that of India after the Kushan period.

After the Han dynasty more and more Buddhist preachers travelled to China, accompanied by merchants. The preachers' intimate relationship with traders is often demonstrated in biographies of famous Buddhist monks (*KSC*). For example, Fo-t'u-teng, a preacher who went to China in the early fourth century, frequently sent disciples to purchase incense in Central Asia (*KSC*: IX, 385b). Another monk, Fo-t'o-yeh-she, from a Brahman family in Kashmir, went to China in the later fourth century. After retiring from his preaching in China he entrusted merchants to send Buddhist texts back from his homeland to Liang-chou, the Ho-hsi region (*KSC*: II, 334b).

In the interior of China the situation was somewhat different from that in Central Asia. According to Zürcher, after the disintegration of the Han empire in the late second century AD there occurred the gradual formation of a Chinese-style 'gentry Buddhism'. After the retreat of the Western Chin dynasty to the south the centres of activities of this gentry Buddhism also shifted southwards. The several schools that developed in the south are normally considered to be the mainstream of Chinese Buddhism. The large quantity of literature left by the southerners has attracted the attention of many scholars, including Zürcher. Yet the less sophisticated Buddhism of the north, which Zürcher dubs a 'state church', and which was patronized by rulers of nomadic origin, eventually became the dominant form of Buddhism in all of China. Northern Buddhism produced many 'eminent monks', such as Fo-t'u-teng, who was active in the politics of the Later Chao state (AD 319–50) and who preached benevolence; Kumarajiva, who translated many important Mahayana texts including the *Saddharmapuṇḍarika* (The Lotus Sutra) and the *Sukhāvatīvyūha* (The Land of Bliss); and Fa-hsien, one of the first Chinese pilgrims to reach the Ganges plain.

The cave and statue construction movement in China gained momentum in the third and fourth centuries, reaching its peak during the Northern dynasties. During this period cave temples along the route of the Ho-hsi region were built. There are historical records of cave-cutting around AD 397 in the Nan-shan of Liang-chou (*Chi Shen-chou San-pao Kan-t'ung-lu*: II, 417–18). The Tunhuang caves are known to have been cut in the fourth or the fifth century. But until 1963 no works of art had been identified that pre-dated the Northern Wei unification of the north (AD 439). A survey of the Ping-ling monastery, Kansu, reveals a statue and some frescos of cave no. 169 with inscriptions dating from the Western Chin (AD 420) (Kansu Archaeological Team 1963: 1–2). Another survey conducted by archaeologists of Kansu province on the caves of Ma-t'i monastery, Wen-shu-shan, Ch'ang-ma and other caves in the Ho-hsi region confirms that most constructions of the cave temples in the region started in the Sixteen States period of the fourth or fifth century (Kansu Archaeological Team 1965).

The cave sculptures and paintings of the T'ien-shan range and Ho-hsi region provide important materials for Chinese art history because they represent the early stages of Chinese Buddhist art, bearing the legacy of Gandharan influence. They paved the road for the Yün-kang cave sculptures which developed into a Chinese-style Buddhist art. The cave carving of Yün-kang was done under the instruction of T'an-yao, a monk from Liang-chou, probably one of the monks captured by the Northern Wei army and transferred to the capital, P'ing-cheng (T'ang Yung-t'ung 1927: 496–7; *KSC*: XI, 398b *HKSC*: I, 427c). The achievement of the cave excavation indicates that the Buddhist movement in the north, although of a different form than the more élite style of the south, was just as active and just as important. The quantity and quality of the art are the result of massive preaching activities which must have involved many political and social changes, and which played an important role in the formation of the Chinese Buddhist church.

As we have seen, north China under the nomadic rulers was anything but a desert. Urban culture prospered in spite of the quickly changing political environment. In the following pages I discuss the functions of Buddhism in the north, the legacy from Indian monasteries to north Chinese urban society, the institutional evolution of the Buddhist church under the 'barbarian' northern Chinese regimes, and the correlations between the practice of donation and urban prosperity.

BUDDHIST INSTITUTIONS IN THE NORTHERN WEI

Buddhist institutions developed quickly in north China after the fifth century. A large number of monasteries sprang up, especially in the period of the Northern Wei. There were 6478 officially registered monasteries in north China in the year AD 477 and more than 30,000 in the year AD 534 (T'ang 1927: 512). The expansion of Buddhist institutions in capital cities is even more impressive. Loyang, the capital of the Western Chin dynasty, had only forty-two monasteries by the end of the dynasty (AD 313) (*WS*: CXIV, 3027). There were about 100 monasteries in P'ing-ch'eng, the capital of the Northern Wei, in AD 477. Once the Northern Wei shifted its capital to Loyang the number of monasteries according to official records in the new capital increased from 500 in AD 518 to 1367 in AD 534 (T'ang 1927: 512). This development finally attracted the attention of the official historians who for centuries had kept silent about Buddhism. For the first time in historical writing, Wei Shou included a separate monograph about Buddhism and Taoism in his *History of the Northern Wei* (*Wei-shu* AD 554).

During the same period the practices of cave excavation and statue-building spread throughout all of north China. Inscriptions from cave temples, especially those near the capitals P'ing-ch'eng and Loyang, provide much information on the relation of Buddhist monasteries with the laity. The *Memories of Holy Places in Loyang* (Loyang Ch'ieh-lan Chi) by a petty official of the Northern Wei, Yang Hsüan-chih, gives a unique description of monastic and urban life in the capital city. The three major sources—the official history of the Northern Wei, the inscriptions from cave-temples and the *Memories of Holy Places in Loyang*—provide a good perspective on this short but significant period of the Northern Wei (AD 386–534) in Chinese Buddhist history, particularly around the city of Loyang.

Buddhist institutions and preaching activities of the Northern Wei no doubt developed along Indian models, but they also adjusted to the political and economic environment in north China. From the first to the sixth century, contact between India and China intensified. Table 3, based on the study of Fang Hao (1963: 233–5), summarizes the records of preachers and pilgrims from the Han to the Northern dynasties. These figures represent only the most famous preachers who made special contributions to Chinese Buddhism, and the successful pilgrims who left records of their travels. These numbers nevertheless provide an index to the increase of the Indo-Chinese communication carried out by Buddhists. The total number of preachers was ten during the almost two centuries of the Later Han. During the 169 years of the Southern and Northern dynasties the number reached thirty-two. Three pilgrims started to go westward in the third century; as many as eighty-nine took the trip in the period of the Southern and Northern dynasties.

Most of the famous preachers recorded in Buddhist literature were engaged in translation. While pilgrims paid respect to holy places, they also observed monastic regulations and collected Buddhist texts. After the Han dynasty most texts translated into Chinese were those of the Mahayana school, i.e. the literature developed in India since the beginning of the Christian era. Buddhist literature composed in the Kushan period and the pilgrims' own observations in Gupta India shaped Chinese Buddhist institutions in the Northern Wei far more than the model of the earliest Buddhist sangha. Accordingly, the Northern Wei Buddhist institutions came to resemble those of the Kushan and Gupta periods, not those of the earliest periods of Buddhism. I have indicated in the last chapter that Buddhist monasteries in the Kushan period were urban-based institutions, and that the primary means of maintaining monasteries and links to the laity was through a steady supply of donations. During the Gupta period Buddhist institutions obtained a constant flow of income from land and other property holdings, but the highly ceremonial religion still depended on trade for specific goods used in its ritual performances. In the following pages, I will show how northern Chinese Buddhism reflected both

TABLE 3: BUDDHIST PREACHERS AND PILGRIMS,
FIRST TO SIXTH CENTURIES

	Historical Periods			
	Later Han AD 25–220	Three Kingdoms and Western Chin 220–316	Eastern Chin[2] 317–420	Southern and Northern Dynasties 420–589
Origins of Preachers India	4	4	17	22
An-hsi (Arsaces)	2	3		
Yüeh-chih	2	3	2	
Western Region	2	3	6	6
Others		2	2	4
Total of preachers	10	15	27	32
Chinese pilgrims		3	51	89

the features of Kushan Buddhism and those of Gupta Buddhism.

No matter how hard Chinese Buddhists tried to emulate their Indian counterparts, they could not always determine the nature of their own financial support. Buddhist patrons in China were another factor in shaping Buddhist institutions. In the analysis of Chinese cities I have shown that in spite of the fact that urban residents in the post-Han period often had to migrate following political changes, and that the merchants' livelihood was often subject to the government's whim, there was still a flourishing urban economy. Buddhist monasteries, as new members joining urban life in this politically precarious period, had to depend on the patronage of the government and other social forces to expand. By transplanting a foreign institution to Chinese earth the Buddhists made a special contribution to contemporary political and economic life.

[2] The column 'Eastern Chin' indicates the period in Chinese history, not its territory in the south.

THE STATE AND MONASTERIES IN THE NORTHERN WEI

The Northern Wei dynasty unified north China in AD 439. Liang-chou, the corridor leading to the Western Region, was the last sizable territory brought under the Northern Wei rule in the unification campaign. After this campaign the government forced 300,000 households, plus 3000 Buddhist monks, to migrate from Liang-chou to the capital, P'ing-ch'eng (Fan Wen-lan 1965: 510–11). Buddhism had already begun to flourish in Liang-chou since the early fourth century (*WS*: cxiv, 3032), and by the time of AD 439 a strong monastic tradition was in place. The monks who migrated to P'ing-ch'eng reinforced Buddhist influence in the core region of north China, especially around the capital. Due to their explosive growth, Buddhist institutions posed a constant political problem for the Northern Wei government. Therefore we have detailed information on the government's policies towards Buddhism.

Before the numerous monks from Liang-chou thronged to P'ing-ch'eng the Northern Wei emperors tolerated Buddhism and honoured outstanding Buddhist teachers. Based on the account that, once, Emperor Tao-wu appointed a monk Fa-kuo as the Head of Monks (*Tao-jen-t'ung*), one can surmise that there may have been some kind of bureaucratic system controlling Buddhist monasteries. Fa-kuo responded to the patronage by calling the emperor the modern-day Buddha and saying that monks should pay obeisance to him (*WS*: cxiv, 30–1). The political authorities and the monasteries thus lived harmoniously because the Buddhists submitted to the government.

Soon after the annexation of Liang-chou the Northern Wei government, impatient with the multitude of monks on its territory, ordered all monks under the age of fifty to return to secular life (*WS*: cxiv, 3032). This action heralded the first large-scale perse-cution of Buddhism in Chinese history. In AD 446 the retinue of Emperor T'ai-wu accidentally discovered weapons hidden in a monastery in Ch'ang-an and suspected the monks of conspiring to rebel. The emperor, acting on the counsel of the Taoist prime minister Ts'ui Hao, issued an edict forbidding Buddhist practices in the entire country (3034). The implementation of this edict met strong resistance. Even the crown-prince tried to postpone the enforcement and made it possible for monks to escape and hide texts and icons (3035).

The persecution of Buddhism lasted seven years. As soon as the new emperor, Wen-ch'eng, ascended the throne in AD 452 he issued an edict reviving Buddhism. From then until the end of the Northern Wei dynasty Buddhist institutions experienced unprecedented development. However, this development was subject to government control from the first day of revival. Emperors governed the recruitment of novices and the number and locations of monasteries. The edict of AD 452 allowed every prefecture and county to build a stupa at a heavily populated place. There was no limit on the amount of money that could be spent. Those devoted to Buddhism could join the sangha as long as they came from good families, were highly moral, had no bad habits and were known by the local people. The fixed quota of monks was fifty for a large prefecture, forty for a small one, ten for a remote small one: 'This many is enough to convert bad elements to good people and to spread the influence of Buddhism.' (*WS*: CXIV, 3036). The purpose of reviving Buddhism was to make it a governmental institution. Since the official stupas were located in heavily populated places, namely administrative centres, there must have been official monasteries to conduct religious activities. In the emperor's opinion forty or fifty monks in one of these monasteries were enough to make a positive contribution to society.

However, the number of monks and monasteries soon grew out of control. In AD 477 there were 77,258 registered monks in the Northern Wei territory. The government had to exert restrictions or modify its policies. In AD 486 Emperor Hsiao-wen approved a memorial that eliminated 1327 unqualified monks and nuns following an examination (*WS*: CXIV, 3039). In AD 492 the same emperor issued an edict which stipulated that at two Buddhist festivals every year a large prefecture could recruit 100 novices, a middle-sized prefecture 50 and a small prefecture 20 (3039).[3] Thus the annual recruitment became 200 for a large prefecture, 100 for a middle one and 40 for a small one. These numbers were much larger than the allotment of AD 452.

In AD 517 Empress Dowager Hu further revised the regulations for Buddhist recruitment. The large prefectures with an allotment of 100 novices could send 300 candidates ten days before the festival

[3] The two festivals were the eighth day of the fourth month, the birthday of the Buddha, and the fifteenth of the seventh month, All Souls' Feast or Ullambana.

for selection, while the middle prefectures 200 and small prefectures 100. This edict also threatened with harsh punishment those officials who ignored standards for recruitment (*WS*: CXIV, 3042–3).

This edict did not change the quotas for recruitment but it reflected the fact that the increasing number of candidates for Buddhist novices made restrictions necessary. Considering that there were more than 100 prefectures under the Northern Wei (*WS*: CVI, 2455–2655), and taking the middle sized prefecture as average, i.e. 100 monks were recruited every year, the annual recruitment of the whole country would have exceeded 10,000 monks. Even this number did not reflect the scale of Buddhist recruitment. By the end of the Northern Wei (AD 534) the government no longer had accurate statistics of the registered monastic population. The officially estimated number was more than 2,000,000 in north China (*WS*: CXIV, 3048).[4]

The Northern Wei government's policy of restricting the construction of monasteries in the urban centres, especially the capital, was even less successful than that restricting the number of monks. In the early days of the Buddhist revival the law permitted only the existence of the officially sponsored Yung-ning monastery in the city and a nunnery within the outer wall of the city. Yet by the end of the fifth century this regulation had been broken a number of times. Emperor Hsüan-wu tried in vain to enforce the law. In AD 506 the Head of Monks (*Sha-men-t'ung*) Hui-shen successfully pleaded to the emperor to allow the existing monasteries to stay in the city on the stipulation that new ones would not be built. In AD 509 the government relaxed the restriction to the extent that a congregation of fifty monks or more could build a monastery with the approval of the government (*WS*: CXIV, 3044). In the year 518 the Northern Wei government again tried to eliminate monasteries in Loyang, but to no avail (3044–7).

One of the main factors inhibiting the Northern Wei government's efforts to control the expansion of Buddhist institutions was that rulers of nomadic tribal origins used Buddhism to ensure their claim to power. Before the persecution (AD 446) the Buddhist teacher Fa-kuo secured Emperor Tao-wu's patronage by calling

---

[4] At the same time, the registered households were only about 2,000,000 (Lü 1948: 934). Even though this figure does not include many unregistered households, the comparison with the number of Buddhist staff still indicates the relative strength of the sangha.

him the contemporary Buddha. After the revival (AD 452) the emperors made the Liang-chou monks who held high positions in P'ing-ch'eng use a new approach to claim legitimacy for the Northern Wei regime. When Shih-hsien, a Buddhist teacher from a Kshatriya family in Kashmir, was serving as the Head of Monks (*Tao-jen-t'ung*) the emperor Wen-ch'eng issued an edict ordering a stone image of the Buddha modelled on the emperor to be made. It is said that after it was carved two black spots appeared on the image, resembling the moles on the emperor's body. A few years later, in AD 455, it is said five gold statues of the Buddha were made which imitated the forms of the five Northern Wei emperors (*WS*: CXIV, 3036). In the early 460s T'an-yao, another monk from Liang-chou, succeeded Shih-hsien as the Head of Monks (*Sha-men-t'ung*). He conducted the excavations of the earliest five caves of Yün-kang. The five gigantic statues of the Buddha carved out of the cliff were also probably meant to represent the five emperors of the Northern Wei as incarnations of the Buddha (Tsukamoto 1944: 224–5). Both emperors and Buddhists benefited from these projects. For Buddhists these sculptures, which could survive persecution and natural deterioration, expanded Buddhist influence. Furthermore, to identify benevolent rulers with the Buddha did not contradict the idea that Buddhas who derived from the eternally existent Buddha periodically appear in the world. For the emperors, the Buddhist recognition of them as incarnations of the Buddha gave sanctity to their regimes. The government's policies of controlling and patronizing Buddhism most likely provided opportunities to strengthen Buddhist institutions.

If the government was unable to curb the spread of Buddhist monasteries, what impact did its policies have on these monasteries? Some examples of monk-officials suggest that the Northern Wei government had begun to build a bureaucracy for the purpose of controlling Buddhist institutions even before the first persecution of AD 446. Not only did the monk Fa-kuo hold an official position as Head of Monks—another monk, Fa-ta, also assumed the official title of *Seng-cheng* (*KSC*: XI, 398a). After the revival this system became more comprehensive. The office under the court was called Office of Supervising Merit-creating Affairs (*Chien-fu-ts'ao*, later *Chao-hsüan*). The head of this office was called the Head of Monks (*Tao-jen-t'ung* or *Sha-men-t'ung*). His assistant was called

Tu wei-na. At the local level there was a Head of Monks of the Prefecture whose office was called Office of Monks (*Seng-ts'ao*) and whose assistants were *Wei-na* (Tsukamoto 1944: 141, 192).

Originally the offices of religious affairs were responsible only for monastic matters. But in AD 493 the emperor approved a code of forty-seven items which extended the power of the office of the Head of Monks. According to an edict of AD 508 this code governing monks covered all crimes committed by monks except for 'murder or more severe ones' (*WS*: CXIV, 3040). Thus this office enjoyed some autonomous rights over monasteries and monks.

Our knowledge of the bureaucratic system governing Buddhist institutions in India is too scant to assess how much inspiration the Northern Wei rulers received from the Indian model. The word *Wei-na* was not Chinese in origin. It is commonly accepted that *Wei-na* was an equivalent of the Sanskrit word *karmadāna*, but the etymological link between the two words has not been established. *Karmadāna* denoted a position in the monastery—not an official responsible to the government. *Wei-na* or *Tu-wei-na* (*Wei-na'* Supervisor) were on the one hand government officials assisting the national and local Heads of Monks, and on the other held a position of responsibility within monasteries. The double roles they assumed enabled them to carry out government orders efficiently. For example, *Wei-na*, along with the heads of monasteries, carried out the task of reducing the number of monks in AD 486 (*WS*: CXIV, 3039). *Wei-na* also assisted heads of monasteries in supervising the monks' adherence to monastic rules (3040).

Although the bureaucratic system controlled monastic organization and the governments' code for monks overrode monastic rules, all holders of these positions were Buddhist monks. Administrative power in the hands of these Heads of Monks enhanced their religious influence. They quickly grasped the opportunity to augment the monasteries' economic resources in order to expand Buddhist institutions. In the early 460s, when T'an-yao had just succeeded Shih-hsien as the Head of Monks, he requested permission from Emperor Wen-ch'eng to take captives from the campaign of annexing Ch'i (in modern Shantung) and other captives as tenants for Buddhist monasteries. Those tenants were called 'sangha households' (*seng-chih-hu*). Every household paid sixty *shih* (about 2380 litres) of grain, called 'sangha grain' (*seng-chih-su*), to the local office of monks. T'an-yao also received permission to convert some criminals and official slaves into the so-called 'Buddha households' (*fu-t'u-hu*). These households cleaned or cultivated land for the monasteries (*Wei-shu*: CXIV, 3037).

T'an-yao did not originate the practice of monasteries owning landed property. During the early fifth century Fa-hsien noticed that kings, elders and householders granted land to monasteries in India. On his way back to China Fa-hsien stopped in Sri Lanka where he also noticed that kings gave lands and cultivators to monasteries. He was impressed by the fact no later kings dared to violate the grants which were carved on 'iron plates'. (865b). The *Mahāsaṅghika-vinaya* (Monastic Rules of the Mahasanghika Sect) text he brought back from India mentioned tenants who worked the fields in order to feed monks (*Yüan-min*) and house-cleaners in the monastery (*Ching-jen*) (Tsukamoto 1944: 198–9). About the same period, the owning of landed property was prevalent in Liang-chou (*KSC*: III, 342c) and was also recorded for the interior of China (*KSC*: v, 354b). The *Monastic Rules of the Mahāsaṅghika Sect* (*Seng-chih-lü*) provided the monastic code which Northern Wei monks observed (*WS*: CXIV, 3031). Even though T'an-yao did not have to look to India to find an example of landed property for Chinese monasteries, texts circulating in the fifth century certainly provided legitimation for Buddhists who sought to profit from economic resources.

In theory, these monastic households and the grain they produced belonged to the office of controlling monks, not to the individual monastery or monk. Also, in theory, the office which supervised the grain should have lent it out to needy people during famines. In practice the monk-officials took advantage of this opportunity to make a profit for their monasteries and themselves. Probably because abuses with regard to such sangha grain had reached an intolerable level by AD 511, Emperor Hsüan-wu issued an edict to straighten out the problems involved in the management of grain. The edict pointed out that the office controlling the sangha grain extracted great interest from debtors, with the interest often exceeding the principal; it forced the debtors to pay without considering the amount of the harvest of that year; it sometimes even changed the terms of the loan to cheat poor debtors. Considering the corruption of the office of monastic affairs, the emperor ruled that the

Inspector of a Circuit (*Tz'u-shih*) should supervise the management of the sangha grain (*WS*: CXIV, 3041). About the same time the emperor also approved the prime minister Kao Chao's request to forbid the assignment of sangha households to individual monasteries because of the widespread abuse of the members of these households by the monasteries (3042).

These restrictions on the power of the monk-officials over the management of landed property, including tenants and the sangha grain, had little effect. By the end of the Northern Wei both monasteries and influential monks controlled large amounts of the total economic resources. In the years 528 to 529 the Northern Wei government, under the pressure of a financial deficit, tried to sell official titles for income. The cost of official titles was determined by the amount of grain and the location of governmental granaries the grain was sent to, i.e. whether the granary was in the capital city or in a locality.[5] The prices for purchasing offices of monastic affairs are shown in Table 4.

TABLE 4: PRICES FOR BUDDHIST OFFICES IN THE
NORTHERN WEI, AD 528–9

Price in grain	Granaries paid to	Title granted
4000 *shih* (4500 bu.)	of the capital	*Head of Monks* in home prefecture or a large prefecture
3000 *shih* (3400 bu.)	of a prefecture	*Head of Monks* in a small prefecture
500 *shih* (560 bu.)	of the capital	*Wei-na* in a prefecture
700 *shih* (790 bu.)	of a prefecture	*Wei-na* in a county
300 *shih* (340 bu.)	of the capital	*Wei-na* in a county

(According to *WS*: CX, 2861).

Assuming that the government set the prices after estimating the financial ability of the monasteries and monks to pay, these

[5] Probably due to the difficulties in transport, the locations of granaries were an important component in determining the prices of official titles.

numbers suggest the economic power of Buddhist monasteries. This economic force facilitated the development of Buddhist monasteries in the period from the establishment of the system of the households of the sangha (AD 460s) to the end of the Northern Wei (AD 534). Not only did the total number of registered monasteries increase four or five times, the average size of monasteries also increased from twelve to sixty-eight people, according to calculations based on official records (Tsukamoto 1944: 207).

As the Northern Wei's bureaucratic system for monastic affairs strengthened the finances of the monasteries, its religious patronage also enhanced Buddhist influence. Emperors and empress-dowagers patronized Buddhism mainly by building monasteries and conducting ceremonies. Although we can only speculate about the privileges of Kushan kings or the holdings of special religious services in the monasteries in their names, the interdependence of the Northern Wei regime and Buddhist monasteries is clearly spelled out in Yang Hsüan-chih's *Memories of Holy Places in Loyang*, which provides a wealth of detail about family or dynasty monasteries in Northern Wei China.

The first monastery built by the royal family was the Yung-ning Ssu in P'ing-ch'eng in AD 476. This monastery, with its seven-storey stupa, was the landmark of the capital city (*WS*: CXIV, 3037). The symbol of the Northern Wei state, it embodied the union of political power and Buddhist religion. After the capital moved to Loyang the royal family built another Yung-ning Ssu in the new capital. Tsukamoto argues that the Northern Wei government built this monastery to console the tribal aristocrats who were reluctant to migrate to the heartland of the sedentary agricultural region. The new Yung-ning monastery created some continuity for these élites (1944: 392). Whatever the motivation, the Empress-Dowager Hu decided to make the Yung-ning stupa the main landmark in Loyang. In the period of AD 516–18 she led the entire court in conducting the ceremony to lay the foundation of the monastery. The nine-storey stupa was the tallest building in the city (*WS*: CXIV, 3043).

Located in the centre of the city, near the gate of the palace, the Yung-ning monastery witnessed many political changes. In AD 528 Er-chu Jung led a coup, setting up his headquarters in the monastery (YHC: I, 5). The following year another military

commander who took power, Prince Yüan Hao, also directed his
military actions from there (7). One year later a rebel prince, Er-chu-
Chao, imprisoned Emperor Hsiao-chuang in the monastery (9).
And finally, in 534, the last year of the Northern Wei dynasty, the
stupa accidentally burnt down (12). The Yung-ning monastery
thus faithfully fulfilled its task as the symbol of its patron's power,
collapsing on the ruins of the Northern Wei empire.

Although the Northern Wei government stipulated that only
the Yung-ning monastery could exist within the confines of Loyang
city,[6] the emperors were the first people to build more monasteries
there. Emperor Hsuan-wu built a monastery at the beginning of
his rule (AD 500) (YHC: III, 132), and another one with more than
1000 rooms to receive monks from foreign countries (IV, 235–6).
There were monasteries which served to generate merit for deceased
members of the royal family (II, 94; III, 140; 145). Hu-T'ung
monastery and Yao-kuang monastery were two official nunneries
where members of the royal family and women from other élite
families could spend their widowhood (I, 46; 59). The empress of
Hsüan-wu entered the Yao-kuang monastery built by her husband
after his death (WS: XIII, 337). Many widows followed suit (YHC: I,
46–7).

Following the example of the royal family all sectors of the
Northern Wei court built monasteries in Loyang for themselves.
Princes related to the royal family contributed the largest amount
of money for the construction. Some monasteries were built from
donations made by the princes during their lifetimes (e.g. YHC: I,
52; II, 73; 104; III, 158; IV, 230). Others were their residences
changed posthumously into monasteries, or monasteries built for
the souls of the dead. Political disturbances towards the end of the
Northern Wei dynasty created many such monasteries (e.g. YHC:
I, 38–9; III, 176–7; IV, 185–6; 191; 225). The monasteries built
when the princes were alive automatically became involved in the
business of the afterworld once their patrons died.

---

[6] This rule concerned both the neighbourhoods inside and outside the city
walls. After the AD 528 coup many princes' homes in the neighbourhood of Shou-
ch'iu, west of the city-wall enclosure, became monasteries (YHC: IV, 208). Wei
Shou considered this transaction a violation of the law governing the construction of monasteries in the city (WS: CXIV, 3046).

The political changes resulting in deaths that created many monasteries inevitably also created many widows, not only because emperors kept big harems but also because princes maintained many concubines. The prince Yüan Yung kept 500 concubines in his residence. After his death all the women entered nunneries to preserve the memory of the deceased prince (YHC: III, 176–7). No wonder the rule that there should be only one nunnery in the city was broken.

Next to the princes as founders of monasteries were government ministers. A monastery built in the period AD 504–8 was the collective contribution of all officials of the court (YHC: II, 99). Individual officials from as low as a county administrator (I, 55) to the highest level minister in the court (II, 116–17) competed to build monasteries. Like the princes, these officials also built monasteries to solve their social problems; a high minister, Wang Su, who defected from the southern regime, married into the Northern Wei royal family. His former wife from the Hsieh family in the south escaped to the north, seeking Wang. Wang Su built a nunnery for the Hsieh woman and continued to live with his second wife to resolve this dilemma (III, 146–7).

At times eunuchs wielded great influence in the Northern Wei court. Their political power also expressed itself in monasteries in Loyang. Yang Hsüan-chih mentions six monasteries built by eunuchs (I, 43; 54; II, 87; 88; IV, 195; V, 248) which were all nunneries except for one (IV, 195). Even the imperial guards built a monastery to serve their religious needs (II, 75).

Those members of the royal family, princes, ministers and eunuchs who built monasteries broke the rule made by the early Northern Wei rulers, stimulated the expansion of Buddhist institutions and, most importantly, entered into a deeper and deeper relationship with religion. Since the rulers based their claims to legitimacy on Buddhism, political crises prompted them to invest more and more resources in religious institutions. The concepts of rebirth and transferring merit to one's next life were so deeply implanted in the minds of the élite that religious services for the souls of the dead, as well as for future lives of the living, became increasingly necessary. The intensity of monastic building consequently increased towards the end of the Northern Wei. The northern Buddhism characterized by Zürcher as a 'state church' was not only a religious institution surviving under the tolerance of the rulers but also an ideological and social system assisting and perpetuating their rule. This religious power in the hands of Buddhists enabled the monasteries to expand beyond the control of the government and to communicate with a laity much wider than the few members of the élite in the Northern Wei court.

Chapter VIII: Monasteries and the Laity in the Northern Wei

The Indian Influence

Encouraging donations and conducting rituals were the major forms of preaching activities of Northern Wei Buddhism. These activities derived from Indian models of the Kushan and Gupta periods. While stupas in the Kushan period dominated the landscape in north India and cave excavation formed the major Buddhist construction activities in west India, the Northern Wei Buddhists were busy both constructing monasteries and stupas as well as digging caves and building statues. In Gupta India the pace of donations slowed as the performance of ritual gained significance. Buddhists in north China also enthusiastically organized many festivals.

Information about Buddhist practices was transmitted from India to China along commercial routes. Fa-hsien and other pilgrims such as Chih-meng brought back Buddhist documents, witnessed Buddhist ceremonies performed in fifth-century India, and also paid their respects at many monumental buildings which could be traced back to the period of the Kushan king Kanishka. The messages they carried back prompted their fellow Buddhists in China to persuade their patrons to finance rituals, cave temples and statues. Simultaneously, more and more Indian preachers brought monastic customs to China. In Northern Wei Loyang, 3000 foreign monks resided in the Yung-ming monastery (YHC: IV, 236). The most outstanding ones, such as P'u-t'i-liu-chih, stayed in the royal Yung-ning monastery to translate sutras (*KSC*: I, 428a).

Another source of information encouraging Chinese Buddhists to worship and make donations was the Buddhist canons which were translated continuously into Chinese from the third century AD. Many Buddhist texts composed during the Kushan period had Chinese versions by the fifth century, including the *Milindapañha* (Questions of the King Milinda), the *Buddhacarita* (The Life of the

Table 5: Translations of the Seven Treasures

	The Lotus Sutra			The Land of Bliss	
Trans-lators	Dharma-raksa	Kumara-jiva	Chih Lou-chia-ch'ien	K'ang-Seng-k'ai	Kumara-jiva
Period	265–316	385–417	168–188	220–265	385–417
gold *suvarṇa*	gold *chin*	—[1]	—	—	—
silver *rupya*	silver *yin*	—	—	—	—
lapis lazuli *vaiḍūrya*	lapis lazuli or glass *liu-li*	—	—	—	—
crystal *sphāṭika*	crystal or glass *shui-ching*		—	po-li	—
coral *lohitikā*	coral *shan-hu*	? *mei-kui*	coral *shan-hu*	—	red-pearl *ch'ihi-chu*
? *musāra-galva*	*ch'e-ch'ü*	—	—	—	—
agate *aśma-garbha*	agate *ma-nao*	—	—	—	—
?	amber *hu-p'o*	—			
pearl *muktā*	pearl *chen-chu*				

Buddha), the *Saddharmapuṇḍarika* (The Lotus Sutra) and the *Sukhāvatīvyūha* (The Land of Bliss). Some were translated more than once. For instance, *The Lotus Sutra* was translated by Dharma-raksha (Chu Fa-hu) in the Western Chin (AD 265–316) Tripitaka (vol. 9: 63–134) and by Kumarajiva during the Western Ch'in (AD 385–417) (Tripitaka vol. 9: 1–63). This was also true for *The Land of Bliss*. There is a difference of opinion over who the trans-lators of the few versions of the text were: Tsukamoto's study suggests that most of the early versions of the sutra were done by

[1] A dash means the translation is the same as the one to the left.

preachers from Yüeh-chih (probably Kushan) (1944: 620).

By the time of the Northern Wei *The Land of Bliss* and, especially, *The Lotus Sutra*, were among the most popular texts in the Buddhist canon. As early as the P'ing-ch'eng period (AD 398–494) Emperor Hsiao-wen (AD 472–99) sent an envoy to the south to invite the teacher T'an-tu to lecture in the capital. T'an-tu, specialist in *The Lotus Sutra* as well as other Mahayana texts, attracted a large audience in P'ing-ch'eng (*KSC*: VIII, 375b). Motifs from *The Lotus Sutra* appear in the caves of both Yün-kang near P'ing-ch'eng and Lung-men near Loyang (Tsukamoto 1944: 525).

These translations conveyed to Chinese Buddhists the significance of worship and donation. The concept of the seven treasures as the formula of the Buddhist paradise and the ideal donation for Buddhist deities was a major part of these texts. It seems that the translators were uncertain about what items the Sanskrit names of the seven treasures actually designated. Even translations of the same text give different lists of the seven treasures. Table 5 gives a sample of different lists from the Chinese translations of *The Lotus Sutra* and *The Land of Bliss* before the sixth century AD.

This Table provides some important information. First, the Chinese Buddhists accepted *liu-li* as the translation of the Sanskrit word *vaiḍūrya* (lapis lazuli). Since the Chinese word *liu-li* referred to either a kind of semi-transparent or transparent glass, it is clear that the Chinese Buddhists considered glass one of the treasures of the Buddhist world. Secondly, for crystal and glass the Chinese words *shui-ching* and *po-li* were exchangeable items; even if glass was not as precious as crystal it could be used as a substitute for crystal. As for coral, it could be substituted by a kind of red precious stone (*mei-kui*).[2] Because no one knows what was meant by red pearls, I tentatively propose it might have referred to coral beads. Although the translators consistently translated the Sanskrit word *musāragalva* as ch'e-ch'ü, the meaning of the Chinese word is as obscure as that of its Sanskrit counterpart. Chinese dictionaries define it either as a kind of sea-shell or as a kind of precious stone. However, it seems neither the translators nor Chinese Buddhists in the Northern Wei were any clearer about the last few items than we are. Dharmaraksha actually listed eight possible items to play it

[2] In Buddhist literature *Mei-kui* can mean any kind of red precious material (Chang Hung-chao 1921: 57).

safe; this is also true of the stone casket dated in the Northern Wei found under a stupa in Ting-hsien, Ho-pei. The list of finds includes 5657 items made of gold, silver, copper (coins and vessels), glass, jade, agate, crystal, pearl, cowrie, coral etc. (Hopei Bureau 1966: 253). Buddhist translations and the archaeological evidence suggest that the Northern Wei Buddhists' understanding of the seven treasures in the canon is similar to, and as sketchy as, our knowledge from Sanskrit texts and archaeological finds in north India (see Chapter IV).

DONATIONS AND CEREMONIES

Encouraged by the Indian models and examples in the sacred texts, Buddhist monasteries in the Northern Wei launched a large-scale votary movement. A Buddhist monk in the Sui dynasty (AD 581–618) claimed that 1.5 million Buddhist statues made in previous times had been repaired under the Sui regime. This number shows the scale of statue-making in the Northern dynasties (Satō 1977: 2, *Pien-cheng-lun*: iii, 509b).

In spite of the fact that the monasteries themselves enjoyed a stable income from landed property, large-scale construction still depended on the donations of lay worshippers. Donated objects included stone statues in Buddhist caves as well as stone and copper statues and stupas in monasteries. Satō Chisui has done a thorough analysis and statistical study of the movement to donate images based on 1360 dated inscriptions of the Northern dynasties (AD 420–589). Here I will cite Satō's study to look into the relationship between Buddhist monasteries and their laity in the Northern Wei.

In addition to the huge stone statues of the Shakyamuni Buddha there were huge images of the Maitreya Buddha; the copper Avalokitesvara (Kuan-yin); the scene of the Buddha sitting beside the Prabhutaratna (the Buddha of many treasures, To-pao-fo); a few statues of Amitabha; and various Buddhas in Mahayana texts (Satō 1977: 15–17). The wide variety in objects of worship suggests that the Northern Wei donations were inspired by Buddhist literature composed since the Kushan period in India. The bodhisattva Avalokiteshvara and the scene of the Buddha accompanied by the Prabhutaratna were important topics in *The Lotus Sutra*. The appearance of Amitabha shows that donors knew *The Land of Bliss*, which is a description of Amitabha's heaven. Buddhist preachers then must have made an effort to teach the two sutras to lay worshippers.

Like their predecessors in Kushan India, the Northern Wei donors also expected their donations to bring benefits for their future lives and their deceased relatives. Not surprisingly, they seldom wished to reach nirvana through their pious donations, normally wanting to be born in various heavens, Buddhas' lands or pure lands. More specifically, they yearned for the Tushita heaven, or the most popular land, the Western Land of Bliss of Amitabha (Satō 1977: 22). The lower aspirations of the donors included the prosperity of the state and Buddhism, health and longevity, good harvests, wisdom, knowledge, gaining office and purification from sins (46).

Because they could share merit with others, as monks did, the donors often dedicated the benefit from the donations to them. The most numerous beneficiaries were the donor's direct relatives, especially parents. Sixty-eight per cent of the dated inscriptions of the Northern dynasties mention deceased relatives as beneficiaries of the donations, forty-five per cent as the primary beneficiaries. Other relatives often appear in inscriptions (forty-four per cent), but normally in secondary positions. Recipients termed as 'all beings' appear in forty-eight per cent of the inscriptions, often at the end of the name list. The second group of primary beneficiaries were emperors. Twenty-seven per cent of the inscriptions mention them as beneficiaries, twenty-three per cent dedicated to them. Other beneficiaries included the state, in addition to emperors and the empress-dowagers, court officials, local administrators, religious teachers and lay associations the donor belonged to (Satō 1977: 19).

If this list reflects the donors' perception of society, it reveals that the state machinery occupied a significant position. The emperors alone received even more merit from donations than did the donors' parents and ancestors, who were listed as beneficiaries in twenty-three per cent of the inscriptions, only in nine per cent as primary beneficiaries.

Under this state machinery the leading patrons of Buddhism were the royal family and its ministers. The royal family ordered the excavation of the major caves, the carving of the huge statues of the Buddha in Yün-kang and Lung-men, and the building of major stupas and statues in the capital cities. The Northern Wei emperors and empress-dowagers actually initiated the movement of statue-building. Following the royal family were ministers and officials, who also made large donations. However, in terms of the number of statues, the common people came first. They donated about forty-eight per cent of the statues. Next came monks and nuns (19.7 per cent) and donors' collectives (18.9 per cent) (Satō 1977: 43).

While the inscriptions from Kushan and Gupta India only hint at the existence of Buddhist lay organizations the inscriptions of Northern Wei China reveal complex social institutions. The lay associations called *i-i* ranged from a few members to 1000 people (Satō 1977: 47; Fan Shou-ming: 1/14b; Ch'en Ssu: 20/18a). Some members assumed administrative titles similar to that of the monasteries, such as Lord of the Community (*i-chu*) or Superintendent of Works (*wei-na*). Often monks participated in the activities of the associations as religious teachers (*i-shih*). The status of those in the associations ranged from high officials (e.g. Lung-men no. 583, Mizuno 1941: 299) to untitled commoners. Some inscriptions were flowery poems carved in beautiful calligraphy (e.g. Yün-kang no. 4, Mizuno 1951 II, Appendix: 3–7), some poorly written short notes full of non-standard characters (e.g. Lung-men no. 626, Mizuno 1951 II, Appendix: 305). While many associations claimed equality among members by calling each other brothers, a few showed subordinate relationships within the association through extreme variations in the amount of donations (e.g. Lu Tseng-hsiang: 14/6b–7a). Some of the lists of members' names show strong lineage links, i.e. under the same surname, with a character signalling generations within the family (e.g. Lu Tseng-hsiang: 16/3b–5a; Hu P'in-chih: 1/32a–35a), some listing people of different surnames. Possibly the donations made by associations with strong family and territory ties represented the rural-based Buddhist laity, and the other type those made by urban-based groups.

Whatever their compostion, the purpose of these associations was to organize donations. Monks who served as teachers probably initiated many of the associations by organizing donations. As an important means for monasteries to keep in contact with the laity, the lay associations with their heterogeneous features indicate the many social strata Buddhist preachers tried to assimilate.

The inscriptions by commoners, the most numerous group, leave no information for us to determine the donors' status. Because Chinese society never granted titles to merchants and artisans, and because the donors do not describe themselves, the untitled may well have included plenty of untitled urban residents. Of the 598 Northern Wei votive inscriptions collected by Satō, the cave statues from Yün-kang and Lung-men account for 225. When added to the construction carried out in the cities of P'ing-ch'eng and Loyang it seems that urban residents in the capital cities may have contributed more than half of the Northern Wei Buddhist structures. Even in Yün-kang and Lung-men the royal family and other élites only contributed a small number of the statues.[3] The commoners' contributions were on similar levels to those of monks and nuns.[4] The pace of construction in both Yün-kang and Lung-men dropped quickly once the capital shifted from P'ing-ch'eng and Loyang (Satō 1977: 41). As we have learned in the first chapter, given that rulers of the Northern dynasties forced merchants and artisans to migrate when political centres moved, the decline of the cave temples was not only due to the loss of patronage from the court but also to the loss of urban commoners who had made substantial contributions when residing in nearby cities. The pace of construction at the Lung-men caves did not resume until the Sui and T'ang dynasties re-established Loyang as the capital. The destiny of the Lung-men caves depended on the status of Loyang city.

There is no information on whether donors followed the prescriptions contained in *The Lotus Sutra* about decorating statues and stupas in the cave temples, but Yang Hsüan-chih described the brilliance and beauty of the Buddhist structures in Loyang city. The embellishment of the nine-storey stupa in the royal Yung-ning monastery is well known (see Chapter II), and archaeological finds, such as fragments of pearls, agate, crystal and others, verify Yang Hsüan-chih's records. Stupas decorated with similar kinds of luxury goods were plentiful in Loyang, just smaller in size. The golden top of the three-storey stupa in Ch'ang-ch'iu monastery shone brightly (YHC: I, 43). The five-storey stupa in the Yao-kuang nunnery was as well made as that of Yung-ning (I, 46). A

[3] Yün-kang 13.7 per cent, Lung-men 18.5 per cent (Sato 1977: 43).

[4] Yün-kang commoners 37.9 per cent, monks and nuns 37.9 per cent; Lung-men commoners 32.4 per cent, monks and nuns 36.1 per cent (ibid).

stupa of the same size was located in the Hu-t'ung monastery (I, 59). The embellishment of a seven-storey stupa in the Ching-ming monastery rivalled that of Yung-ning (III, 132). The two stupas of five storeys in the two monasteries devoted to the father of Empress-Dowager Hu imitated the style of Ching-ming (III, 140). Although not all the registered 1367 monasteries in Loyang boasted extravagant stupas, the demand for luxury goods to decorate the few outstanding ones was great enough to keep many merchants busy transporting glass, coral, pearls and other precious items from abroad.

Buddhist statues in Loyang also enjoyed opulent ornamentation, especially on festal occasions. The early part of the fourth month every year was the festival season for the celebration of the Buddha's birthday. Starting from the fourth day an image of the Buddha riding on a white elephant with six tusks, decorated with gold and jade, was paraded on the streets (YHC: I, 55). On the seventh day more than 1000 images from various monasteries assembled in the Ching-ning monastery for a great parade held on the eighth day (III, 133). These famous images attracted large crowds and competed with each in splendour. The statues from Chao-i nunnery of one Buddha with two bodhisattvas were famous for their carvings. On their way to assemble in Ching-ning monastery the three major statues in the host monastery often came out to meet the images from the Chao-i nunnery (I, 54). Some monasteries were famous for the luxurious carriages which they used to carry the images (I, 53, II, 88): the golden carriage of Ching-hsing nunnery was covered by a canopy hung with golden bells and beads of seven treasures. This carriage was so valuable that on parade days emperors often sent imperial guards to carry it (II, 88).

As patrons of Buddhism the Northern Wei emperors were leading participants in all important Buddhist ceremonies and festivals.[5] In the great parade of the eighth day of the fourth month 1000 and more images first entered the city gate, then stopped in front of the gate of the palace to receive flowers from the emperors (YHC: III,

[5] As early as in the P'ing-ch'eng period the emperor, Wen-ch'eng, had conducted the ceremony of tonsure for five outstanding monks as a signal of reviving Buddhism. (WS: CXIV, 3036). Later Emperor Hsiao-wen often held feasts, ceremonies of tonsure or amnesty in the royal Yung-ning monastery in P'ing-ch'eng (3039).

133). Even on less important occasions, such as the six feast days every month, the emperors sent officials to special monasteries (140).

All city residents—not just the emperors—participated in these Buddhist ceremonies. Monasteries paid for acrobats and other performers to entertain urban dwellers (YHC: I, 53). Actually, many important images were accompanied by acrobats and dancers when moving on the street. Not only were the royally patronized monasteries able to present impressive images and performances: even a monastery supported by its immediate neighbourhood, Tsung-sheng monastery, could afford a thirty-eight-*ch'ih*-high image. This image was so beautifully decorated that as soon as it was brought out people emptied out of marketplaces in order to see it. These local performances rivalled the most elaborate one in the city (II, 79). Thus, through these ceremonies and festivals, Buddhist monasteries received patronage from the rulers on the one hand, yet preached to and entertained Loyang citizens on the other.

A SPECIAL ROLE OF BUDDHIST MONASTERIES

No matter how much the Chinese rulers claimed they disliked merchants and artisans, they always wanted the commodities and service they supplied. The emperors of the Northern dynasties forcibly moved urban residents with them whenever they established their state machinery. The rulers and ruled invariably formed the core laity for Buddhist monasteries in urban centres. Between the two conflicting but interdependent groups Buddhist monasteries, which were closely connected with both, functioned as mediators.

Here I will examine the relationship of Buddhist monasteries with non-élite urban residents—a little studied group—to seek further insights into the role of Buddhism in Northern Wei politics and economy.

For the commoners of Loyang devotion to Buddhism was as important as it was for the élite. It is said a man in Loyang intended to sell a cow to gild a Buddhist statue but was unable to do so because of some emergency. In a dream his wife heard the image demanding their son as payment for the long-promised gilding. The child thus died as the image magically became gilded (YHC:

IV, 205–6). The circulation of this kind of story in Loyang suggests that people there believed donating to Buddhism was not only merit-gaining but even an obligation. When members of the élite built monasteries, or donated their residences to monasteries, the commoners followed suit. A neighbourhood of 2000 households managed to finance ten monasteries (II, 78). Citizens also donated their residences for various reasons. Four brothers of a butcher family donated their house as a monastery to redeem themselves (II, 120–1). A remarried widow donated her house because she was haunted by the fear of her former husband (IV, 205). A citizen donated his big house when he discovered the site had been a monastery some 200 years earlier (II, 88–9). With these people's donations, no wonder the prime minister Yüan Ch'eng complained: 'Now Buddhist monasteries are everywhere, filling cities and towns, located next to butchers and wineshops.' (*WS*: CXIV, 3045).

In further connecting the monasteries to the laity, two major sutras aimed at laymen were available during the Northern Wei period. One was a translation of the *Vimalakīrti-nirdeśa Sūtra* (Sutra of Vimalakīrti). As popular as *The Lotus Sutra*, this text had been translated seven times since *c.* AD 188 (Ch'en 1964: 382). Although the Sanskrit original is not extant, judging from the earliest date of translation and its Mahayana features it must be a product of Kushan India. The hero of the sutra is a rich householder, Vimala-kīrti, who has an understanding of Buddhist philosophy superior to that of most of the more famous disciples. He is one of the typical affluent, influential, and senior merchants who often appear in Buddhist literature as great patrons. However, soon after the Chinese version of the text appeared in the third and fourth centuries, Chinese literati who converted to Buddhism but preferred to live a lay life took it over as a special doctrine for élite lay devotees (see Tsukamoto 1944: 531, 623). As Kenneth Ch'en puts it:

Incidentally, the layman Vimalakirti is described in such a manner that he might easily be taken as a perfect Confucian gentleman, being pure in self-discipline, obedient to all the precepts, a householder with wife and children yet learned in the Dharma, a rich aristocrat always self-controlled and restrained in his desires. (1964: 208).

This image of Vimalakirti (Chinese name Wei-mo-chieh) greatly resembled the metaphysical scholars of the Chin dynasty (AD

365–426) and the literati in the south during the fifth and sixth centuries. In the north some princely patrons of Buddhism might have been able to assume this role. For example, Yüan I, Prince of Ch'ing-ho, sponsored a lay association to discuss Buddhist philosophy and organize donations (*HKSC* VI: 474b). But the average merchants and artisans of P'ing-ch'eng and Loyang could not act as such big patrons.

Even if Chinese scholar-officials did not consciously associate themselves with Vimalakirti but left this image for merchants to imitate, Chinese merchants never attained as high a status as great patrons of the Buddhist sangha—as did Vimalakirti or other famous elders and householders in India. In dealing with this section of the neglected laity, a monk in the Northern Wei, T'an-ching, forged a text soon after the Buddhist revival in P'ing-ch'eng (AD 452). This text, called, *T'i-wei Po-li Ching*, was based on the tradition that two merchants gave a meal to the Buddha who had just achieved enlightenment.[6] The heroes here were also merchants who acted as the very first patrons of the Buddha and the very first lay disciples to receive the Buddha's teachings. In the version contained in some Buddhist texts the two merchants led a caravan with five hundred wagons. In others the two elder merchants commanded a group of five hundred traders. The *T'i-wei Po-li Ching* adopted the latter version. There were five hundred merchants who received the teachings on the 'five restraints'.[7] (Tsukamoto 1944: 314).

According to the fragments collected by Tsukamoto (1944: 310–18) the sutra explains the basic rules for lay devotees in terms of familiar Chinese concepts. It describes the punishment in future lives for those who break the five restraints and equates them with Confucian moral standards, such as benevolence (*jen*), righteousness (*i*), etiquette (*li*), wisdom (*chih*) and truthfulness (*hsin*). It tries to put these five restraints into the framework of the Chinese cosmology of heaven and earth, negative and positive forces (*yin yang*). This sutra also describes the rewards for worship. The worshippers who walk around a stupa will be endowed with good looks and good voices in future lives and born into heaven or

---

[6] *T'i-wei* and *Po-li* are transliterations of the Sanskrit names Trapusa and Bhallika.

[7] Restraints from killing, stealing, sexual indulgence, liquor, lying.

families of kings and princes. Finally, they will achieve enlightenment. This kind of reward might have pertained to other forms of
worship mentioned in the texts, such as scattering flowers, burning
incense, lighting lamps and prostration in front of Buddhist
images, but the descriptions have been lost. As a whole, this sutra
was a text easy to understand, suitable for poorly-educated readers
who desired clear rules and obligations. Therefore, this obviously
forged text was well studied by the lower strata of Buddhist devotees
until the end of the sixth century (*HKSC*: ɪ, 428a).

The presence in cities of numerous monasteries and their close
connections with the lower social level of urban residents concerned
the Northern Wei rulers. They had good reason to be upset. When
Emperor T'ai-wu (AD 424–52) found weapons concealed in a
monastery in Ch'ang-an he also found a large quantity of property
hidden there by local officials and rich men (*WS*: cxɪv, 3033–4).
This accident provided T'ai-wu with the pretext he needed for his
persecution of Buddhism, and his successor with the excuse to
absolve him of the charge of being a persecutor of Buddhism
(3036). But the possible involvement of Buddhist monasteries in
rebellions continued to plague later emperors who were devoted
to Buddhism. Perpetual rebellions relating to Buddhism reminded
them of the potential danger of Buddhist contacts with its urban
laity.[8] They made several efforts to reduce the channels of communication between the monasteries and the laity. In AD 472 the
pious emperor Hsiao-wen issued an edict which forbade people
giving hospitality to monks unless the latter held certificates
issued by the offices of monks in the capital, or by the offices of
monks in the prefecture centres or the towns (*WS*: CXIV, 3038).
In Loyang the empress-dowager Hu also tried to stop monks lecturing and collecting donations, but encouraged them to recite sutras
and meditate, thus hoping to reduce the monks' contacts with lay
people (YHC: ɪ, 81). In AD 518, when Yüan Ch'eng complained
about the monasteries in Loyang city, he again reminded the ruler
of the dangers of these monasteries by citing previous instances of
rebellions mobilized under the name of Buddhism, or organized by
Buddhist monks.

The information about Buddhist rebellions is too scanty for us

---

[8] For rebellions led by Buddhist monks, or in the name of Buddhism, see
Tsukamoto 1944: 241–92.

to tell whether the connection that Yüan Ch'eng saw between Buddhist monasteries and rebellions was founded in reality or reflected the paranoia of the Northern Wei élites. But Buddhists in Northern Wei Loyang did participate in politics in a special way. While Indian Buddhists, since the Kushan period, had converted their audience by performing magic tricks, the Northern Wei Buddhists' magic often extended beyond proselytizing. Preachers from very early periods going to China had already learned that this was an effective means to deal with the imperious and despotic warlords of north China. Fo-t'u-teng, who advised the Later Chao (AD 319–50) rulers to be benevolent, emphasized skill in magic because he knew his patrons could not understand Buddhist philosophy. He converted the king Shih Le by magically creating a lotus from a pot of water (*KSC*: IX, 383c).

The Northern Wei rulers were sensitive to Buddhist miracles and tried to connect miracles with political incidents. For example, in AD 466 a general of the South surrendered and handed a large territory north of the Huai river over to the Northern Wei. The emperor Hsien-wen traced the cause of this incident to a Buddhist portent that had taken place seven years before in that territory (*WS*: CXIV, 3037). This kind of incident convinced the Northern Wei emperors that Buddhist portents were effective. In AD 472 a Buddhist statue allegedly turned magically into gold. Considering this a good omen for the state the emperor Hsiao-wen ordered the statue to be sent to the capital and shown to people all along the way (3038).

While the Northern Wei rulers believed that miracles could guarantee the prosperity of their state, they were also scared by inauspicious omens. Yang Hsüan-chih recorded quite a few ominous portents that happened in the last few years of Northern Wei rule. In AD 527 a big golden image in Loyang began to shed tears. The monks in that monastery tried in vain to stop this flow of tears: the face of the image continued to be wet for three days. One year later, Yang Hsüan-chih says a coup took place in which many officials were massacred. Because this statue often made predictions like this, in AD 529, when the image shed tears again, both rulers and commoners panicked. The government had no choice but to forbid people from seeing the image (II, 105).

Once a miracle happened the news spread quickly throughout

the whole city. A big crowd would then surround the monastery. It is not clear whether the Northern Wei rulers most feared crowds or the prediction of a miracle. If something else attracted the crowd—even something like a mulberry tree in front of a Buddhist temple—the emperors could just order the item to be disposed of and the crowd dispersed (YHC: I, 55). However, they could hardly damage a Buddhist statue.

Because so many Buddhist portents occurred in the years when many important political incidents took place, and because these portents disturbed both the rulers and the ruled, one cannot help suspecting that the portents were a part of Northern Wei politics. Most of the miracles recorded by Yang Hsüan-chih betray traces of human manipulation. For example, a statue which was said to have walked around its throne at night and left footprints attracted many worshippers. Its sudden disappearance caused much speculation in Loyang (YHC: IV, 237). It is not that difficult to make footprints around a statue and claim the statue walked around at midnight. To declare a statue missing mysteriously is even easier. Buddhists who were skilful in magic were able to make a metal statue look as if it were shedding tears. Yang Hsüan-chih, the author of these interesting anecdotes, was not a Buddhist. He even requested the Eastern Wei ruler to suppress Buddhism (Fan Hsiang-yung 1958: 12; *Kuang-hung-ming-chi*: VI, 123b, 128b). He described the brilliance of Loyang to express his nostalgia. He even hints at some criticism of Buddhism. As a witness of politics in Loyang, he recorded the Buddhist miracles not in order to advocate Buddhism but because they were of great concern to both the emperors and commoners in the city.

Among the most agitated by the bad omens were those who ruled, especially the last few emperors who sat on the throne for only a few months or a couple of years. In AD 534, the last year of the Northern Wei, upon hearing that a stone statue had nodded its head the emperor Hsiao-wu was so frightened that he went to worship it (YHC: II, 108).[9] Buddhist miracles thus wielded extraordinary power over the Northern Wei rulers.

Although there is no way to tell exactly whether or how these portents affected politics, Buddhist rebellions show that rebels

[9] *Kuai-ch'i-kuei-i* means 'wondered at the inauspicious strange phenomenon'.

from the lower social strata often used portents couched in Buddhist terms to appeal to their followers. Considering that Buddhist portents did cause massive disturbances in Loyang, the government's phobia about the close contacts between Buddhist monasteries and their urban laity probably had a sound basis. Consciously or not, Buddhist monasteries involved themselves and their laity with Northern Wei politics.

Enjoying both religious and political influence, Buddhist monasteries in the capitals of the Northern Wei actively participated in politics, economic production and commercial circulation. The construction of more than 1000 monasteries in the city of Loyang, the production of thousands and thousands of statues, and the sponsoring of frequent festivals all created a demand for handicrafts and trade for certain luxury goods, including items that had to be imported from abroad. Followed by a laity composed of both ruling élites and commoners, Buddhist institutions, on the one hand, helped the Northern Wei government to consolidate their rule by divinizing the rulers, and, on the other, provided opportunities for the socially oppressed but not necessarily poor urban residents to participate in politics.

The difference between Buddhism in the Northern Wei and in Gupta India was that Buddhism in fifth-century India had already passed its golden age but was just reaching its maturity in China. Dissatisfied with the model of Buddhism in contemporaneous Gupta society, the Chinese Buddhists learned more from texts and monuments built in the earlier periods when Buddhism in north India was the predominant religion. Further shaped by the changing political situation, Buddhism in post-Han north China developed into an institution capable of surviving numerous disasters through many dynasties and, ultimately, came to survive even longer than its Indian model.

CONCLUSION

The Eurasian trade linking the Mediterranean to East Asia in the early centuries AD opened an era of frequent trade contacts between north India and north China. The commodities involved in the transaction were mainly luxury goods.[1] While coral, pearls, precious stones, glassware, incense and perfume from India found their way to Chinese cities and stupas, Chinese silk continually moved along the Central Asian routes to India. The trade survived warfare, shifts of trade routes and even regional de-urbanization, and continued to flourish at least until the sixth century AD.

The analysis of the structure of the trade reveals that Buddhist ideology and institutions played a considerable role in economic activities. Using the framework of the Polanyi school I have pointed out that all three forms of transaction—reciprocity, redistribution and exchange—co-existed in a complex economic network (Chapter III). Their respective expression in trade—namely gift trade, administered trade and market trade—overlapped. While Substantive anthropologists insist that in ancient societies redistribution is the predominant form of transaction, and that market exchange has only a marginal impact, in the ancient Sino-Indian trade there were individual merchants who made impressive profits. The force of supply and demand perhaps affected even the domain of administered trade. However, we have to concede that this was an imperfect market system. It was imperfect both in comparison to the modern, western market system, and in comparison to the model of a

---

[1] The trade of staple goods existed before the Christian era. When Chang Ch'ien visited Bactria in the second century BC he noticed that sticks made of a special kind of bamboo cane and cloth from south-west China had been transported to Bactria via India (*SC*: cxxiii, 3166). Although no one has discovered the routes along which these commodities were transported, the exchange certainly existed in that period, perhaps also the later period. However, staple goods in the domestic market may become luxury goods in foreign markets because of their rarity. The bamboo cane Chang Ch'ien had seen was a special species (Ch'iung-chu), and the cloth was also a product of one region. Both bamboo and cloth were abundant in India. There was no reason to import them unless they had served some special purpose.

perfect market system. In the first sense there was a lack of infra-structure for a commercial economy to exist between the two ancient civilizations. Unlike the modern market system, banking, efficient transportation and communication did not affect the daily adjustment of prices according to supply and demand. A partial compensation for the absence of modern facilities was the possible involvement of Buddhist monasteries in the trade. Circumstantial evidence suggests that monasteries provided financial services and travel facilities for traders (Chapter VI).

In a second sense the ancient Sino-Indian market differed from the model of a modern market system for the same reason as a practical modern market system does, i.e. the forces of supply and demand were subject to the influences of cultural values. While in modern societies the demand for both luxury goods and staples comes under the influence of cultural preferences, in the early Sino-Indian trade only luxury goods were affected because only luxury goods were carried long distances, no matter what the form of the transaction. More specifically, Buddhist values created and sustained the demand for certain commodities traded between India and China during the first to the fifth centuries AD.

Parallel to the commercial activities, dramatic changes in Buddhist theology and institutions took place in Kushan India. Starting from the divinization of the Buddha, the Buddhist cosmos expanded to include more heavens and lands of Buddhas. Many deities, especially bodhisattvas, joined the Buddhist pantheon. This theological development changed Buddhist institutions and their relationship with the laity. These rituals for worship created and increased the need for donations, which in turn facilitated the possession and accumulation of property by Buddhist monasteries and monks. The emphasis on rituals crystallized in the concept of the seven treasures, which became the symbol of the Buddhist ideal of purity and the best gift that a devotee could give to Buddhist deities in order to partake of their merit. This concept, along with the whole array of Buddhist ideology and institutions that developed in Kushan India, was transported to China along trade routes. When the rulers of the Northern Wei were captivated by Buddhist ideas of karma and reincarnation and Buddhist ideology became essential to the legitimacy of their rule, monasteries became signi-ficant institutions, especially in urban centres. Drawing their laity from both the ruling élite and common urban residents, monasteries actively participated in urban life through preaching activities, the construction of temples, caves and statues, and by the sponsoring of festivals. Monasteries were also involved in politics in this politically confused age.

Religious development and its propagation influenced the long-distance trade. At this point we can evaluate the extent to which Buddhism was involved in motivating commercial activities and ascertain the reasons for the impact of this religion. In other words, in this pre-modern and non-western context did traders, consumers and donors act economically, as the Formalists contend, or did they subordinate material gain to ideology, as the Substantivists argue? Were their cultural values and economic interests mediated by some more fundamental forces in their societies?

The influence of cultural values on the long-distance trade was expressed in fashion and ritual. The Buddhist theological developments in Kushan India provided a new market by creating the ritual need for certain commodities. The concept of sharing merit encouraged lay devotees to worship and donate, therefore increasing the demand for commodities supplied by the Sino-Indian trade. The desire to donate enlarged the market for goods listed as the seven treasures, most of which had to be transported from India. Not only did the élite desire luxury goods such as glassware to demonstrate their status, even commoners wanted them for the worship of the Buddha. Buddhist ritual guided the production of certain handicrafts, mostly silk banners in the case of north China, to suit both domestic and foreign markets.

Buddhism as a predominant religion affected the tastes and fashions of the urban population. The esteem given to the well-to-do traders of low social status and other commoners encouraged them to associate with Buddhist institutions and to follow the fashions advocated by Buddhism. Here, religious institutions and values worked as agents adjusting social differences. Fashion among urban residents, both élite and commoners—traders, artisan, entertainers, servants, clerks, artists, etc.—was essential to this trade. The cultural preferences of urban residents not only shaped their own taste for commodities but often also directed the pattern of consumption of the rural gentry.

In the context of the ancient Sino-Indian trade, cultural values were conducive to economic activities. However, cultural values evolved in association with economic conditions. For a long period Buddhologists have tended to trace the developments in Buddhism, especially early Buddhism in India, only by the lineages of schools. True, not every school's bifurcation can be extrapolated according to economic or social changes because ideological developments took tortuous paths and did not simply follow economic changes. Nevertheless, the development of the concept of the seven treasures constitutes clear and solid evidence for ideological and economic paths drawing close to—even crossing—each other. Without the trade which shipped non-indigenous commodities, such as coral and pearls, to north India, and without the foreign market which raised the value of products controlled by Indians, such as lapis lazuli and crystal, the maturation of the concept of the seven treasures would have been impossible. The commercialism of a highly urbanized Kushan India was also largely responsible for changes in the Buddhist sangha and its relationship with the laity. In short, the Buddhist values of the seven treasures and the emphasis on donating these items developed out of an economic environment where both ruler and urban dweller sought luxury goods.

Historians have tended to overlook the economic strength of the non-staple trade in Asian societies and to treat the trade as a part of a cultural process which brought foreign influences to various countries. This neglect derives from a systematic underestimation of the social and economic significance of the so-called luxury goods, as well as of the urban aspects of Asian civilizations. These historians assume that ancient Asian societies were assemblages of self-sufficient villages that had little demand for material goods. Since the trade of luxury goods was only for the satisfaction of a small ruling élite, they reason, its impact on the economy of such societies was marginal.

Although the existence and exchange of luxury goods do not directly improve human subsistence, many historical facts demonstrate their vital position in organizing production and shaping social structure. In the early stage of economic development ornaments and tools were probably the first products which were exchanged in quantity (Mandel 1962: 53). Colin Renfrew points out the association of raw materials of ornaments, including gold, with high prestige in prehistoric Europe (1984). In many cases, even basic materials for tools were first used for making ornaments and prestigious objects, such as copper in North America and China and iron in Europe (8–9). Luxury goods were thus a means of marking social disparity. Ever since human society has been divided into rulers and the ruled, rulers have constantly sought rare goods within and outside their domain to mark themselves off from the ruled; the ruled too have constantly striven for goods which might improve their status. Numerous sumptuary laws proclaimed by various rulers in history testify to this desire. The drive for status provided the impetus for long-distance trade in luxury goods. The special qualities of certain goods and the cost of transportation determined their rarity and price.

The strength of long-distance trade in non-subsistence goods is sporadically evident in world history. Eurasian trade in the first few centuries AD which did not supply food, daily necessities, or tools for production nevertheless sustained many caravan cities and seaports from the Mediterranean to East Asia. The shift of trade routes caused the rise and fall of these cities as effectively as warfare or other political crises. In north Arabia caravan cities derived their livelihood entirely from long-distance trade. These shifts in trade routes prompted the growth of new cities and left other cities as ghost towns (Rostovtzeff 1941: 866–7). Palmyra, the city in the Syrian desert, developed into a grand Hellenistic city from the trade in slaves, wood, balm, silk, jade, spices, ebony, myrrh, bronze statues and precious stones (Browning 1979: 15–18). In south Arabia ancient kingdoms gradually collapsed because of political, social and economic conditions in the Mediterranean affecting the incense route (Bowen & Albright 1958). The fabulous states in the desert of Yemen once constructed magnificent buildings with imported alabaster, marble and limestone, and built vast irrigation systems. The Roman trade directly with India and Africa from the first century AD struck a blow at this civilization (3–4). The shrinking market for frankincense and myrrh, due to the opposition of the early puritancial Christians to what they saw as pagan fragrances in the third century, abruptly terminated trade with the cities, and thereby the prosperity of the cities as well as the irrigation system which surrounded them (84–5). In this case only the profit from the lucrative trade made agriculture in a desert possible.

Similarly, in the desert of Soviet Central Asia irrigation systems surrounded urban centres growing under the Kushan state. These irrigation systems deteriorated during the third to the fifth centuries when this sector of the trade routes was deserted and cities declined (Frumkin 1970: 51–2). The survival of a few cities along the trade routes in north India and north China despite the general urban decline after the third century probably also depended on the persistent long-distance trade in luxury goods. When monuments and ceremonies in the termini of the trade routes—the state capitals in north China and the cities of north India—were decorated with imported precious stones and silk, a few cities along the routes also prospered and enjoyed the products of many different regions (Chapter 1).

The clear impact of long-distance trade on ancient urban life reveals that the production of luxury goods constituted a substantial part of all economic production. The mining and processing of precious stones and the weaving of poly-chrome silk demanded intensive labour.[2] Many artisans earned their livelihood by producing luxury goods. These people depended on agriculture and the production of staple goods for food, clothing and shelter, and their profit and demand facilitated further agricultural production. In this way the external trade, either in the form of market exchange or gift-exchange, penetrated the internal economy.[3] The peripheral

[2] The archaeological survey of some lapis lazuli mines in Badakshan, the major lapis lazuli mine in the ancient world, shows the labour-value embodied in this commodity: 'The mines can only be reached by precipitous paths along which all materials for mining must be carried. In the past the mining was done by fire-setting. Fuel and water were carried up to the mines, a fire was lit beneath the face to be quarried and the cold water was thrown onto the heated rock to make it crack. The lapis was then extracted by using picks, hammers, and chisels.' (Allchin & Hammond 1978: 35). The value of the precious stone thus derives from both its rarity and the labour involved.

[3] Some Substantive economists, while conceding that there were markets in pre-modern societies, view the external exchanges and internal exchange, and the market and non-market spheres of the economy, as isolated domains. They argue that there was no interaction between the different domains (Dalton 1968: 157; Meillassoux 1971: 67). According to Dalton, external trade in the western market economy works on the 'least-cost principle: things are imported which can be

market of external exchange exerted more than peripheral impact on the entire economy.

In a highly urbanized society the production of luxury goods played a more significant role in the economy than it did in a rural society. The early Christian era was such a period when cities in the Mediterranean, India and China were busy purchasing and producing luxury goods. The 'Buddhist choice of the seven treasures emerged from this economic environment. The luxury items whose prices were raised by the value placed on them through Buddhist literature had the same properties as other luxury goods. On the one hand they bestowed prestige on the owners—the monasteries, the donors, the purchasers influenced by the fashion. On the other hand their production and transaction encouraged substantial economic activities. Thus Buddhist values reinforced and extended trade while sustaining certain economic activities even through a period of urban decline.

Cultural values evolving from social and economic developments do play a role in promoting and maintaining certain social patterns. For example, Vedic ritual, which arose from a pastoral society, helped to stabilize tribal organization. The Kshatriyas consolidated their status and superiority over the *vis* by distributing and destroying wealth on the occasion of sacrifice. The religious ritual kept a balance between the Kshatriyas and *vis* by preventing the Kshatriyas' unlimited accumulation of wealth (Thapar 1984: 58). Although the articulation was hidden, this cultural value both prevented the accumulation of wealth and preserved the tribal structure of society. Similarly, in pre-modern China the prestige attached to land established through an agricultural society encouraged those who had money, including merchants, to invest in land whenever the situation allowed.

produced at home if such imports are cheaper than the domestic equivalence'. In contrast, in a primitive economy, external trade in induced by the non-availability of the imported items at home (1968: 157). However, there are some obvious similarities between the two kinds of economies which suggest they cannot be distinguished so summarily. In pre-modern societies the 'least-cost principle' itself excluded the importation of most items available at home because the cost of transportation for foreign goods was high, and the difference of labour cost, which causes purchasing goods available at home in modern societies, was not significant in ancient times. In modern societies Americans import French perfume and oriental carpets because of their rarity and high price.

Nevertheless, cultural values alone cannot stop fundamental social and economic changes. Vedic tribal society finally gave way to states based on sedentary agriculture; Chinese landlordism also surrendered to a new social system. This is also true for the influence of Buddhist values on the trade in luxury goods. After the Gupta period, when Buddhist monasteries became more dependent on income from landed property, the concept of the seven treasures began to lose its importance. The few votive inscriptions that have survived from that period show that agricultural products, such as lamp-oil and grains, were major forms of donations as well as major forms of wealth in society. A similar transition took place in China in a slightly later period. The seven treasures became less important after the Northern dynasties, when donations were no longer the major source of income for Buddhist monasteries, even though the *Lotus Sutra*, which stressed the concept of the seven treasures, continued to' be copied and recited by monks and lay worshippers; and even though pilgrims and preachers continued to travel between India and China.

The waves of Hephathalites, Turkic tribes, Arabs and other pastoral people entering Central Asia from the fifth century on did not block the prosperous trade in the Silk Route via Persia. Some of the seven treasures were still available through the Silk Route (Schafer 1963). The changing economic and social conditions in India and China nevertheless lessened the significance of the seven treasures and altered the nature of the Sino-Indian trade. In this case, fundamental economic changes took place in spite of long-standing cultural values.

Going back to the controversy among economic anthropologists, this study suggests that the actors in the ancient Sino-Indian trade and the propagators of Buddhism behaved economically, namely kept their own economic interests in mind, regardless of whether the transaction took the form of reciprocity, redistribution or exchange. While in the situation of a restricted transaction the giver expected rewards immediately, his expectations from more generalized transactions were both long-term and wide-ranging. The forms the economic gain took, or the definitions of this gain, however, varied with social structure, economic pattern or modes of production. Other historical contexts show different views of economic gain. For Kshatriyas in the Vedic period the destruction and redistribution of wealth served a purpose because the sacrificial ritual preserved the tribal structure which enabled them to continue their cattle raids. Chinese landlords who used their surplus either to buy land or hoard gold for future purchases of land did not perceive the gains from investing the money in industry or trade. In the ancient Sino-Indian trade the merchants who supplied the luxury goods and the rulers who provided facilities for or encouragement to the trade no doubt made great profit.

The motivation of donors and patrons of Buddhist monasteries was more complex. In a restricted sense they practised reciprocity with the monasteries in order to earn merit·and guarantee their well-being in future lives. In a more generalized sense the Northern Wei rulers, who had just come out of a nomadic background, used Buddhist values to improve their status among the sedentary subjects and to claim legitimacy for their regime. The Kushan kings, who were less enthusiastic in seeking legitimacy from Buddhism, patronized Buddhism probably because monasteries contributed to the commercial economy. The traders, both Indian and Chinese, who lived in cities where social mobility was more feasible, not only improved their status through their association with Buddhism but also benefited from the institutional functions of monasteries, which sponsored feasts and festivals, provided charity, and probably facilities for trade. The different expectations of donors, either in a strictly economic sense or in a more general sense, were dictated by their different positions in their respective societies.

When certain cultural values were positive factors in promoting a social and economic framework, the actors often sacrificed their material wealth for that value. Under this situation the cultural value coincided with the actor's interests—which is to say the actor gained through his giving, according to the definition of gain accepted by that social and economic framework. Buddhist donors gave away their wealth in exchange for merit, legitimacy, religious services, entertainment, status and perhaps facilities to earn more wealth.

Social and economic changes checked the power of a cultural value to conduct or curb economic activity. Once real change occurred, a new set of values gradually replaced the old ones. This explains why after the sixth century the donation of lamp-oil in front of the image was considered more effective in earning merit than the presentation of the seven treasures to the stupas.

APPENDIX 1: LIST OF KUSHAN COIN FINDS

*Indicates that the sites on Map 2 are estimates, due to a lack of precise information about their locations.

NORTHWEST (INCLUDING AFGHANISTAN)

*Jalalabad, in Ahin Posh stupa. *PASB* 1879: 122–35. In Bimaran stupa and Chahar Bagh stupa. Allchin & Hammond 1978: 247.
Begram (Kapisi). *JASB* III: 159–75; V: 266–8.
*Yusufzai county. Chattopadhyay 1967: 232. Peshawar. *JASB* 1881: 184.
*Sahri Bahlol, Peshawar district. *ASIAR* 1909–10: 49–50.
*Mardan tahsil, Peshawar district. *ASIAR* 1925–6: 167.
Surkh Kotal. *Journal Asiatique* 1952: 444.
Charsada (Pushkalavati). *ASIAR* 1921–2: 109.
Shaikhan Dheri (Pushkalavati). *AP* II: 23.
Tordher, Peshawar district. *ASIAR* 1902–3: 189.
Ai Khanoum, along the Oxus. Bernard, Paul *et al.* 1973: 205.
Balkh. Allchin & Hammond 1978: 247.
Kabul, Shevaki tope. Allchin & Hammond 1978: 247.
Durman tepe, near Qunduz. Mizuno 1968: 18.
Lalma, near Hadda. Mizuno 1968: 84.

PUNJAB

*Manikiwala tope no. 1, Rawalpindi district. *ASIAR* 1925–6: 167.
Kutanwala Pind, between Cakrawala to Kalarkahar. *CASR* V: 93.
Pathankot. *CASR* XIV: 116.
Ransia, 25 miles to the west of Lahore. *CASR* XIV: 48.
Kanhiara, 12 miles to the north of Kangra. *CASR* V: 176.
*Kalka-Kasauli road, Patiala. *PASB* 1895: 2.
Padham, between Etah and Shikohabad. *CASR* XI: 38.
Sunit, 4 miles to the west of Ludiana. *CASR* XIV: 65.
*Shakarkot, Shahpur district. *ASIAR* 1934–5: 91.

*Mound near Machrata, Sheikhpur district. *ASIAR* 1930–4: 309.
Taxila. Marshall 1951: II, 785–91.
Rang Mahal. Hanna Rydh 1959: 179.
*Ajaram, Hoshiarpur district. *IAR* 1975–6: 73.
*Sankhol, Sunet and Bhari, Ludhiana district. *IAR* 1972–3: 57; 1971–2: 70.
*Jammu and Kashmir. *IAR* 1967–8: 62.

MIDDLE AND WEST GANGES

Khaira Dih, Ghazipur district, opposite Bhagalpur across the Ghagra river. *CASR* XXII: 108.
Mathura. *CASR* XX: 37.
Sonkh, Mathura district, 8 miles south to Govardhan. Hartel 1974: 106.
Hastinapur. *AI* X–XI: 104.
Kasia, Gorakhpur district. 1904–5: 52.
Bhita, near Allahabad. *ASIAR* 1911–12: 62–5.
Sahet Mahet (Shravasti). *ASIAR* 1907–8: 83; 1908–9: 33.
Sankisa. *CASR* XI: 25.
Ahicchatra. *AI* I: 39.
Atranjikhera. *IAR* 1960–1: 35.
Kausambi. Sharma, G. R. 1969: 19.
*Sohagaura, Gorakhpur district. *IAR* 1961–2: 56.
*Shahdol district, Madhya Predesh. *IAR* 1964–5: 70.
*Govindhagar, Mathura district. *IAR* 1976–7: 72.
*Muni-ki-Reti, Tehri-Garhwal district. *IAR* 1972–3: 57; 1975–6: 74.

WESTERN INDIA

Sanchi. *ASIAR* 1934–5: 84.
Indo-Khera mound (Indor). *CASR* XII: 43–4.
*Khoh, Jaipur, Rajasthan. *IAR* 1970–2: 63.
Saidpur, 6 miles north by west of Tando-Mahammad-khan in Hyderabad district, Sind. *ASIAR* 1914–15: 95.

ORISSA AND EASTERN MAHARASHTRA

Sisupalgarh. *AI* V (1949): 98.
*Sitabhunj, Keonjhar district. *JNSI* XIII: 69.

*Bhanjakia, Mayurbhanj district. *ASIAR* 1924–5: 131–2.
*Viratgadh, Mayurbhanj district. *JNSI* II: 124.
*Old Nayagadh state. *CASR* XIII: 116.
*Banitia, Balasore district. *IAR* 1976–7: 72.
*Katangi, Bhandara district, Maharashtra. *IAR* 1973–4: 48.

NEPAL

*Bua Dih (near the site of Kapilavastu). *CASR* XII: 206.

BIHAR

Lauria Nandangarh (Laurya Nandon), Champaran district. *ASIAR* 1936–7: 50.
Bodh-Gaya. *JNSI* XX: 1–3.
Pataliputra. *JNSI* XIII (1951): 144–7.
Buxar. *JNSI* XIII (1951): 121; *ASIAR* 1907–8: 83; 1908–9: 33.
Vaisali. *JNSI* XIII (1951): 107–8.
*Bilvadag thana & Karra thana, Ranchi district. *ASIAR* 1930–4: 312.
Sultanganj, Bhagalpur district. *Indian Numismatic Chronicle* II, pt 1: 81ff.
Monghyr. *Indian Numismatic Chronicle* II, pt 1: 79ff.
*Vatara, Darbhanga district. *Annual Report of K. P. Jayaswal Research Institute* 1961: 4.
Darbhanga, Darbhanga district. *Indian Numismatic Chronicle* II, pt 1: 82ff.
*Kumharia, Ranchi district. *IAR* 1966–7: 62.

BENGAL

Mahasthan, Bogra district. *PASB* 1882: 113.
Malda. Ibid.
*Murshidabad district. Chattopadhyay 1967: 238.
Tamluk, Midnapur district. *JNSI* XIII (1951): 107–8.

SOVIET CENTRAL ASIA

*Kaikobad Shah, Kafirnigan valley, Tadzhikistan. Frumkin 1970: 67.
*Toprak Kala, site of Khorezm, Uzbekistan. Ibid., 97.
*Kara-tepe, north-west corner of Termez, Uzbekistan. Ibid., 111.

*Khalchayan, upper Surkhan-Darya, in the Denau region, Uzbekistan. Ibid., 113.

Zar-tepe, 4 kms. south of Angor, 26 kms north-west of Termez, Uzbekistan. Ibid., 115.

Merv, 30 kms. from the modern city Mary Turkmenistan. Ibid., 147.

SINKIANG

Khotan. Stein 1921 III: 1340; 1928 III: 988.

Appendix ii: Sources of Information for Map 3

General

Sharma, G. R. & J. Negi: 1968; Thapar, B. K. 1968.

Individual Sites

Ahicchatra. Ghosh & Panigrahi 1946: 40–55.
Ai Khanoum. Bernard *et al.* 1973: pl. 113–43.
Amreli. Rao, S. R. 1966: 51–81, fig. 10–25.
Banbhore. Khan, F. A. 1960: 30–1.
Bangarh. Goswami 1948: 26–9, pp. xxvii–xxx.
Begram. Ghirshman 1946: pl. xxix–liv.
Bhita. Marshall 1911–12: 809–5.
Devnimori. Mehta & Chowdhary 1966: 69–87.
Durman Tepe, near Qunduz. Mizuno 1968: 19–41.
Hastinapura. Lal, B. B. 1954–5: 63–71.
Kausambi. Sharma, G. R. 1960: 57–73; 1969: 157–92.
Nagara. Mehta 1968: 34–85.
Nasik. Sankalia 1955. 69–70.
Rairh. Sharma, Y. D. 1953: 153–6.
Rajghat. Narain 1976–8: vol. ii, 51–100.
Rang Mahal. Rydh 1959: 137–56, pl. 16–69.
Rupar. Sharma, Y. D. 1953: 124–8.
Sampur. Hargreaves 1929: 3–16, pl. iv–v.
Shaikhan Dheri. Dani 1965–6: 134–214.
Sisupalgarh. Lal, B. B. 1949: 78–89.
Somnath. *IAR* 1955–6: 7; personally seen in Central Antiquary collection, section Purana Qila, Delhi.
Sonkh. Hartel 1976: fig. 18.
Sravasti. K. K. Sinha 1967: 47.
Taxila. Marshall 1951: vol. 3, 402–3, pl. 121–31; Ghosh 1947–8: 48–72.
Ter. Chapekar 1969: 22–77.
Vaisali. Krishna & Mishra 1961: 18–49.

Appendix iii: Sources of Information for Stamped Ware

Ahicchatra. Ghosh & Panigrahi 1946: 46.
Ai Khanoum. Bernard *et al.* 1973: pl. 118, 124.
Amreli. S. R. Rao. 1960: 77ff.
Banbore. F. A. Khan 1960: 29.
Begram. Ghirshman 1946: pl. xxxviii, xlix, l, lii.
Devnimori. Mehta & Chowdhary 1966: 79ff.
Durman tepe, near Qunduz. Mizuno 1968: 40.
Hastinapura. B. B. Lal 1954–5: 17.
Kausambi. G. R. Sharma 1969: 188.
Nasik. Sankalia 1955: 80–2.
Rajghat. Narain 1976–8 ii: 95ff.
Rupar. Y. D. Sharma 1953: 125.
Shaikhan Dheri. Dani 1965–6: figs. 45, 57.
Sisupalgarh. B. B. Lal. 1948: 88.
Taxila. Ghosh 1947–8: 71ff.
Ter. Chapekar 1969: 71.
Ujjain. *IAR* 1956–7: 23, 28.
Vaisali. Krishna & Mishra 1950: 48ff.

Appendix IV: List of Sites of Red Polished Ware

*Indicates that the sites do not appear on Map 2.

North India

Rupar	Kakhrakot
Agroha	Delhi
Hastinapura	Ahicchatra
Rang Mahal	Pariar
Bithur	Kaushambi
Rajghat	Patna
Sonkh	

Western India

Bhinmal	Nagari
Vadnagar	Nagara
Baroda	Maheshwar
Timbarwa	Karvan
Prakasha	Kamrej
Bahal	Nasik
Sopara	Junnar
Karad	Kolhapur
Sanchi	Tripuri
Baroach	Banbhore
Devnimori	Somnath

Gujarat

*Mahadev	*Khandia
*Aniali	*Samadhiala
*Vallabhipur	*Hazr-Ali-Bawa
*Kanpur	*Hathab
Talaja	Sana

Machala
Fasaria
Vaniavadar
Junagadh
Somnath
Antroli
*Andodar
*Kuntiana
Khambodar
*Gop
Dwaraka
*Mora
Baid
Hadiana

Amreli
Babra
Khaprakodia
*Muldwaraka
Madhavpur
*Karegi
*Bokhira
*Shrinagar
*Padiadhar
*Vadarpara
*Bharana
Lakhabavjal
Vasai

East Deccan and the South

Tamluk
Salihundam
Ramtirtham
Sankaram
Kondapur

Nagarjunakonda
Maski
Chandravalli
Ter

According to:

Rao, S. R. 1966: fig s. 7, 9;
Subbrao, B. 1953: 63, fig. 27;
Whitehouse & Williamson 1973: 39;
Heitzman 1980: 79;
Chapekar 1969: 16;
Mehta 1966: 69.
Personally seen in Sonkh collection, Mathura Museum.

Appendix v: Sources of Information for Sprinklers

Somnath. Rydh 1959: 148.

Rairh. Red Polished Ware (RPW), pink. Ibid.

Mohenjo Daro. Ibid.

Ahmednagar. Ibid.

Ujjain. Poor finish. *IAR* 1956–7: 28.

Devnimori. Red ware, Kaolin like ware. Mehta 1966: 82, fig. 32, no. 73; 84, fig. 36, no. 111–13.

Amreli. RPW. S. R. Rao 1966: fig. 11.

Nagara. RPW. Mehta 1968: 78, fig. 44, no. 460.

Banbhore. RPW. F. A. Khan: 1960: 30.

Brahmapuri (Kolhapur). Rydh 1959: 148.

Chandravalli. Subbarao 1956: 47

Kaundinyapura. RPW. Dikshit 1968: fig. 24, no. 172.

Rang Mahal. RPW, grey ware. Rydh 1959: 149.

Hastinapura. Bright red slip. Lal 1954–5: 65, type xv.

Kausambi. G. R. Sharma 1969: 177, type 125.

Jhusi. Rydh 1959: 148.

Bhita. Fine buff clay with red paint. Marshall 1911–12: 83, pl. xxx, no. 52.

Vaisali. Y. D. Sharma 1953: 145.

Bangarh. Subbarao 1956: 47.

Tamluk. Rouletted ware. Subbarao 1956: 106.

Pataliputra. Red ware, black ware. Altekar 1959: 76, fig. 31, no. 11; 82, fig. 35, no. 18.

Rajghat. RPW, red ware. Narain 1977: 52.

Rupar. Y. D. Sharma 1953: 125.

Nasik. Sankalia 1955: 7.

Akhnur, Jammu. *IAR* 1961–2: 15.

Appendix vi: List of Archaeological Sites in South Asia, First-Third Centuries

(Heitzman 1984: 129–30; Dupree 1973: 288–95, 303–11; Allchin & Hammond 1978: 271–8)

B: Buddhist monastic site.
N: non-monastic site.
BN: Buddhist monastic site associated with non-monastic site.

Afghanistan

Balkh N
Begram BN
Shotorak B

Bamiyan B
Jalalabad BN
Tapa Maranjan B

Andhra Pradesh

Amaravati B
Dharanikota N
Gudivada B
Guntapalli B
Kesanapalli B
Ramatirtham B
Yellesvaram B

Bhattiprolu B
Ghantasala B
Gummadidurru B
Jaggeyapeta B
Nagarjunakonda B
Salihundam B

Bihar

Antichak N
Bodh Gaya B
Chirand N
Lauriya-Nandangarh B
Rajgir BN
Vaisali BN

Barabar B
Buxar N
Kasia B
Pataliputra BN
Sonpur N

GUJARAT

Devnimori B
Nagara N
Talaja B

Junagadh B
Sana B

HARYANA

Purana Qila N

KASHMIR

Harvan B

MADHYA PRADESH

Bharhut B
Maheswar N
Tripuri N

Eran N
Sanchi BN
Ujjain N

MAHARASHTRA

Ajanta B
Bedsa B
Bhandak (Vijasan) B
Junnar B
Karadh B
Kondane B
Kuda B
Nadsur B
Nevasa N
Pauni B
Prakash N
Sopara BN

Aurangabad B
Bhaja B
Bhokardan N
Kanheri B
Karle B
Kondivte B
Mahad B
Nasik B
Paunar N
Pitalkhora B
Sirwal B
Ter BN

NEPAL

Rummindei B

ORISSA

Jaugada N
Sisupalgarh N

Sankaram B
Udayagiri B

PAKISTAN

Barikot (Swat Valley) B	Charsada N
Jamalgarhi B	Mallot N
Manikyala B	Mohenjo-Daro B
Sahri-Bahlol B	Sudheran-jo-Dharo B
Takht-i-Bahi B	Taxila BN
Udegram-Mingora BN	

PUNJAB

Rupar N	Sanghol N

RAJASTHAN

Bairat B	Nagari N
Noh N	

TAMIL NADU

Arikamedu N	Kanchipuram N
Kaveripattinam N	Uraiyur N

UTTAR PRADESH

Ahicchatra N	Alamgirpur N
Atranjikhera N	Bairat (Vairata) N
Bhita N	Bhuila BN
Hastinapura N	Indor Khera (Indrapura) BN
Kanauj N	Kaushambi BN
Masaon N	Mathura BN
Pakna Bihar N	Piprahwa B
Rajghat N	Saketa (Ayodhya) B
Sankisa BN	Sarnath B
Sonkh N	Shravasti BN
Bangarh N	Candraketugarh N
Mahasthan N	Rajbadidanga N
Tamluk (Tamralipti) N	

Chronology

India	China
B.C.	
321–181 THE MAURYAN EMPIRE	
221–207	THE CH'IN DYNASTY
206–A.D. 8	THE FORMER HAN DYNASTY
A.D.	
c. 1–300 THE SHAKA-KUSHAN AGE	
25–220	THE LATER HAN DYNASTY
48	The Southern Hsiung-nu surrender to the Han
73	Tou Ku *et al.* attack Hsiung-nu in Central Asia. Pan Ch'ao goes to the Western Region as an envoy
c. 78 Accession of Kanishka	
86–114 Gautamiputra Satakarni rules the Satavahana kingdom	
90	Pan Ch'ao defeats the Great Yüeh-chih
119–125 Nahapana, the Shaka king, rules in western India	
127	Pan Yung pacifies Yen-ch'i
148	An Shih-kao, the Parthian preacher, arrives at Loyang
150 Rudradaman, the Shaka king, rules in western India	
220–64	THE THREE KINGDOMS PERIOD
265–316	THE WESTERN CHIN DYNASTY

	India	*China*
c. 300–550		
	THE GUPTA-VAKATAKA AGE	
317–420		THE SIXTEEN KINGDOMS period (north)
319–20	Accession of Chandra Gupta I	
335	Accession of Samudra Gupta	
375–415	Chandra Gupta II	
404–14	Visit of Fa-hsien	
404–24	Visit of Chih-meng	
386–534		THE NORTHERN WEI DYNASTY (north)
420–581		THE NORTHERN AND SOUTHERN DYNASTIES
439		The Northern Wei annex Liang-chou (Ho-hsi region)
446		The Northern Wei anti-Buddhism movement
494		The Northern Wei moves its capital to Loyang
c. 500	Hephthalites (Hun) gain control over north-west India	
630–44	Hsüan-tsang in India	

ABBREVIATIONS

GENERAL

BC: *Buddhacarita.*
CAKP: *Central Asia in the Kushan Period.*
CII: *Corpus Inscriptionum Indicarum.*
CS: *Chin-shu.*
DAFA: Mémoires de le Délégation archéologique française en Afghanistan.
FH: Fa-hsien, *Kao-seng Fa-hsien Chuan.*
HHS: *Hou-han Shu.*
HKSC: *Hsü Kao-seng-chuan.*
Hopei Bureau: The Hopei Bureau of Cultural Archaeological Team.
HS: *Han-shu.*
HTC: *Hsü Tsang-ching.*
KS: *Kāma Sūtra.*
KSA: *Kumārasambhava.*
KSC: *Kao-seng-chuan.*
MA: *Mālavikāgnimitra.*
Manu: *Mānava Dharma-Śāstra.*
MASI: *Memoirs of the Archaeological Survey of India.*
MD: *Meghadūta.*
MK: *Mṛcchakaṭika.*
MP: *Milindapañha.*
MV: *Mahāvastu.*
RA: *Raghuvaṁśa.*
SBE: Sacred Books of the East.
SC: *Shih-chi.*
Sinkiang Museum: Sinkiang Uighur Autonomous Region, Museum of.
SK: *Abhijñānaśakuntala.*
SKC: *San-kuo Chih.*
SN: *Saundarānanda.*
SP: *Saddharmapuṇḍarika.*
SS: *Sui-shu.*

SSTS: *Shih-k'o Shih-liao Ts'ung-shu.*
SV: *Sukhāvatī-vyūha.*
Tripitaka: Taishō Shinshu Daizōkyō.
VU: *Vikramoravaśīya.*
WS: *Wei-shu.*
YHC: Yang Hsüan-chih, *Loyang Ch'ieh-lan Chi.*

PERIODICALS

AI: *Ancient India*, Delhi.
AP: *Ancient Pakistan*, Peshawar.
ASIAR: *Archaeological Survey of India, Annual Reports.*
CASR: Cunningham's *Archaeological Survey of India, Reports.*
EI: *Epigraphia India*, Delhi.
IA: *Indian Antiquary*, Bombay.
IAR: *Indian Archaeology*, New Delhi.
JASB: *Journal of Asiatic Society of Bengal.*
JNSI: *Journal of the Numismatic Society of India*, Varanasi.
JRAS: *Journal of Royal Asiatic Society of Great Britain & Ireland.*
KK: *K'ao-ku*, Peking.
KKHP: *K'ao-ku Hsüeh-pao*, Peking.
KKTH: *K'ao-ku T'ung hsün*, Peking.
PA: *Pakistan Archaeology*, Karachi.
PASB: *Proceedings of the Asiatic Society of Bengal.*
WW: *Wen-wu*, Peking.

BIBLIOGRAPHY

GENERAL

Adams, Robert McCormick. 1966. *The Evolution of Urban Society: Early Mesopotamia and Prehispanic Mexico.* Chicago: Aldine Pub.

Adhya, G. L. 1966. *Early Indian Economics.* Bombay: Asia Publishing House.

Agrawala, V. S. 1951–2. 'Catalogue of the Mathura Museum'. *Journal of the Uttar Pradesh Historical Society*, XXIII (1950), 35–147, XXIV-XXV (1951–2), 1–160.

Allchin, F. R. 1979. 'Evidence of Early Distillation at Shaikhan Dheri', *South Asian Archaeology, 1977*, ed. Maurizio Taddei. Naples: Istituto Universitario Orientale. Seminario di Studi Asiatici, Series Minor VI, 755–97.

Allchin, F. R. & N. Hammond. 1978. *The Archaeology of Afghanistan from Earliest Times to the Timurid Period.* London.

Altekar, A. S. & Vijayakanta Mishra. 1959. *Report on Kumrahar Excavations 1951–1955.* Patna: K. P. Jayaswal Research Institute.

An, Tso-chang. 1979. *Liang-Han yü Hsi-yü Kuan-hsi Shih* (History of the Relationship Between the Two Han dynasties with the Western Region). Shantung: Ch'i-lu Shu-she.

Andersen, Dines. 1917. *A Pali Reader.* Copenhagen: Gyldendalske Boghandel-Nordisk Forlag.

Avalon, A. 1918. *Shakti and Shakta.* Reprint, Madras: Ganesh, 1951.

Banerjee, M. 1976. *A Study of Important Gupta Inscriptions.* Calcutta: Sanskrit Pustak Bhandar.

Barfield, Thomas J. 1981. 'The Hsiung-nu Imperial Confederacy: Organization and Foreign Policy', *The Journal of Asian Studies*, XLI, 1, 45–62.

Barthoux, Jules. 1933. *Les Fouilles de Hadda, stupas et sites.* DAFA t. IV. Paris: Art et d'histoire.

Basham, A. L. (ed). 1968. *Papers on the Date of Kanishka.* Leiden: Brill.

_____. 1975. *A Cultural History of India.* Oxford: Clarendon Press.

_____. 1983. 'The Mandasor Inscription of the Silk-weavers', *Essays on Gupta Culture*, ed. Bardwell L. Smith. Delhi: Motilal Banarsidass.

Beal, Samuel (transl). 1906. *Buddhist Records of the Western World*. London: Kegan Paul, Trench, Trubner & Co.

Beck, H. 1941. 'Beads from Taxila', *Memoirs of the Archaeological Survey of India*, 65.

Belshaw, Cyril. 1965. *Traditional Exchange and Modern Markets*. N. J., U.S.A.: Prentice-Hall Inc.

Bernard, Paul *et al.* 1973. *Fouilles d'Ai-Khanoum*. Mémoires de la Délégation archéologique Française en Afghanistan, tomes XXI, XXII. Paris: Editions Klincksieck.

Bernard, Paul and H. P. Francfort. 1978. *Études de géographie historique sur la plaine d'Khanoum (Afghanistan)*. Paris: Centre National de la Recherche Scientifique.

Bhandarkar, D. R. 1927–8. 'Inscriptions of Northern India, in Brahmi and its Derivative Scripts, from about 200 A.C.', *EI*, XIX-XXIII.

Bhandarkar, Devadatta Ramkrishna. 1977. *The Archaeological Remains and Excavations at Nagari*. New Delhi: Indological Book Corp.

Bhandarkar, R. G. 1913. *Vaishnavism, Shaivism and Minor Religious Sects*. Strassbourg. Reprint Varanasi: Indological Book House, 1965.

Block, T. 1903–4. 'Excavation at Basarh', *ASIAR*, 1903–4, 81ff.

Bohannan, Paul & George Dalton (ed). 1962. *Markets in Africa*. Northwestern University Press.

Boulnois, L. 1966. *The Silk Road*. London: George Allen & Unwin Ltd.

Bowen, R. L. & F. P. Albright (eds). 1958. *Archaeological Discoveries in South Arabia*. Baltimore.

Brown, Percy. 1944. *Indian Architecture—Hindu and Buddhist*. Reprint Bombay: Taraporevala, 1965–8.

Browning, Iain. 1979. *Palmyra*. London: Chatto & Windus.

Buddhist Hybrid Sanskrit Grammar and Dictionary. Vol. II. 1953. Franklin Edgerton. New Haven: Yale University Press.

Buhler, Georg. 1879. *The Sacred Laws of the Aryas*. Clarendon Press. Vol. 2, 14 of SBE. Reprint Delhi: Motilal Banarsidass, 1975.

Burgess, James and Bhagwanlal Indraji. 1881. *Inscriptions from the*

Cave-Temples of Western India. Reprint Delhi: Indian India, 1976.

Burrow, Thomas. 1940. *A Translation of Kharosthi Documents from Chinese Turkestan*. London: The Royal Asiatic Society.

Capon, Edmund. 1976. 'Chinese Tomb Figures of the Sixth Dynasties Period', *Transactions of the Oriental Ceramic Society*, XLI (1975–6, 1976–7), 279–308.

Carswell, John. 1978. 'China and Islam: A Survey of the coast of India and Ceylon', *Transactions of the Oriental Ceramic Society*, XLI (1977–8), 25–69.

Central Asia in the Kushan Period. 1974–5. Proceedings of the international conference on the history, archaeology and culture of Central Asia in the Kushan period (Dushanbe, 1968). 2 vols. Moscow.

Chakraberti, Kanchan. 1981. *Society, Religion and Art of the Kushana India*. Calcutta: K. P. Bagchi & Company.

Chakraborti, Haripada. 1978. *India as Reflected in the Inscriptions of the Gupta Period*. New Delhi: Munshiram Manoharlal.

Chakravarti, H. P. 1974. *Early Brahmi Records in India (c. 300 BC–c. 300 AD)*. Calcutta: Sanskrit Pustak Bhandar.

Chandra, Moti. 1940. 'Cosmetics and Coiffure in Ancient India', *Journal of the Indian Society of Oriental Art*, VIII, 62–145.

_____. 1940a. 'The History of Indian Costume from the First Century AD to the Beginning of the Fourth Century', ibid., 185–224.

_____. 1977. *Trade and Trade Routes in Ancient India*. New Delhi: Abhinav Publications.

Chang, Hsing-lang. 1930. *Chung-hsi Chiao-t'ung Shih-liao Hui-pien* (Historical Sources of Communications between the West and the East). Peking: Library of Fu-jen University. Reprint Taipei: Shih-chieh Shu-chü, 1969.

Chang, Hung-chao. 1921. *Shih-ya* (Lapidarium Sinicum, A Study of the Rocks, Fossils, and Metals as Known in Chinese Literature). Geological Survey of China, Series B, no. 2. Second revised ed. Peking: 1927.

Chapekar, B. N. 1969. *Report on the Excavation at Ter*. Poona: the author.

Charlesworth, Martin P. 1926. *Trade-Routes and Commerce of the Roman Empire*. Cambridge University Press.

_____ 1951. 'Roman Trade with India: a resurvey', *Studies*

in Roman Economic and Social History in Honor of Allen Chester, ed.
P. R. Coleman-Norton, Princeton University Press, 1951, 131–43.

Chattopadhyay, Bhaskar. 1967. *The Age of the Kushanas, a Numismatic Study*. Calcutta: Punthi Pustak.

——————. 1975. *Kushana State and Indian Society*. Calcutta: Punthi Pustak.

Chattopadhyaya, Brajadulal. 1977. *Coins and Currrency System in South India*. New Delhi: Munshiram Manoharlal Publishers.

Chavannes, E. 1922. 'Introduction to the "Documents Chinois Decouverts par Aurel Stein dans les Sables du Turkestan Oriental"', *New China Review*, IV, 341–59, 427–42.

Ch'en, Kenneth. 1954. 'On Some Factors Responsible for the Anti-Buddhist persecution under the Pei-ch'ao', *Harvard Journal of Asiatic Studies*, XVII, 261–73.

——————. 1964. *Buddhism in China*. Princeton: Princeton University Press.

——————. 1973. *The Chinese Transformation of Buddhism*. Princeton: University Press.

Ch'en, Meng-chia. 1963. 'Studies on the Han Dynasty Slips', *KKHP*, 1963, I, 77–110.

Chi, Hsien-lin. 1957. *Chung Yin Wen-hua Kuan-hsi Shih Lun-Ts'ung* (Essays on the History of Cultural Relations between China and India). Peking: Jen-min ch'u-pan-she.

Chu, Min. 1972. 'T'u-lu-fan Hsin-fa-hsien te Ku-tai Ssu-ch'ou' (The Recently Discovered Ancient Silk from Turfan). *KK*, 1972, II, 28–31.

Ch'ü, T'ung-tsu. 1972. *Han Social Structure*. Seattle: University of Washington Press.

Chung-yao Ta-tz'u-tien (Dictionary of Traditional Chinese Medicine). 1977. Compiled by Chiang-su Hsin-i-hsüeh-yüan. Shanghai: K'e-hsueh Chi-shu Ch'u-pah-she.

Cohen, Abner. 1971. 'Cultural Strategies in the Organization of Trading Diasporas', in Meillassoux (ed.) 1971, 266–78.

Cousens, Henry. 1909–10. 'Buddhist Stupa at Mirpur-Khas, Sind', *ASIAR*, 1909–10, 80–90.

Cowell, E. B. (trans.). 1894. *Buddhist Mahāyāna Texts*. Vol. 49 of SBE. London: Oxford University Press. Reprint Delhi: Motilal Banarsidass, 1978.

Cunningham, Alexander. 1891. *Coins of Ancient India, From the Earliest Times Down to the Seventh Century* AD. London. Reprint Varanasi: Indological Book House, 1963.

_____. 1892. *Coins of Indo-Scythians*. London.

Curiel, Raoul. 1954. 'Inscriptions de Surkh Kotal', *Journal Asiatique*, CCXLII, 189–205.

Dales, George F. 1977. *New Excavations at Nad-i Ali (Sorkh Dagh), Afghanistan*. Berkeley: Center of South and Southeast Asia Studies, University of California.

Dalton, George. 1968. 'Economic Theory and Primitive Society', in Le Clair *et al.* 1968, 143–67.

Damon, Frederick H. 1980. 'The Kula and Generalised Exchange: Considering Some Unconsidered Aspects of Elementary Structures of Kinship', *Man*, vol. 15. 267–92.

Dani, Ahmad Hasan. 1965–66. 'Shaikhan Dheri', *AP*, II, 17–214.

_____. 1969. 'Kushan Civilization in Pakistan', *Journal of the Asiatic Society, Pakistan*, XIV, 1–20.

_____. 1981. *Karakorum Highway Unfolds the Romance of the Past*. Islamabad: Barqsons Printers.

_____. 1983. *Chilas*. Islamabad: the author.

Das, Santosh Kumar. 1925. *Economic History of Ancient India*. Calcutta: Vohra.

Dasgupta, Surendra Nath. 1923–49. *History of Indian Philosophy*. 5 vols. Cambridge University Press.

Davids, Rhys (trans). 1881. *Buddhist Sutras*. Vol. 11 of SBE. London: Oxford University Press. Reprint Delhi: Motilal Banarsidass 1980.

Davids, Rhys. 1903. *Buddhist India*. New York: Putnam's Sons. Reprint Delhi: Motilal Banarsidass, 1971.

Dayal, Har. 1932. *The Bodhisattva Doctrine in Buddhist Sanskrit Literature*. London: Kegan Paul, Trench, Trubner & Co.

Deloche, Jean. 1980. *La circulation en Inde avant la revolution des transports*. Paris: Ecole francaise d'Extreme Orient.

Deva, Krishna & Vijayakanta Mishra. 1961. *Vaiśālī Excavations: 1950*. Vaiśālī: Vaiśālī Sangh.

Dikshit, Moreshwar. 1968. *Excavations at Kaudinyapura*. Bombay: Director of Achives and Archaeology, Maharashtra State.

_____. 1969. *History of Indian Glass*. Bombay: University of Bombay.

Dohrenwend, Doris. 1980. 'Glass in China', *Oriental Art*, XXVI, 4 (1980), 426–46.

Dupree, L. 1958. *Shamshire-Ghar: Historic Cave Site in Kandahar Province, Afghanistan*. Anthropological Papers of the American Museum of Natural History, vol. 46, part 2.

_____. 1973. *Afghanistan*. Princeton: Princeton University Press.

Eberhard, Wolfram. 1949. *Das Toba-reich nordchinas: eine soziologische Untersuchung*. Leiden: Brill.

_____. 1954–6. 'The Origin of the Commoners in Ancient Tun-huang', *Sinologica*, IV, 141–55.

_____. 1957. 'The Political Function of Astronomy and Astronomers in Han China', *Chinese Thought and Institutions*, ed. J. K. Fairbank. Chicago: University of Chicago Press, 33–70.

Ebrey, Patricia Buckley. 1978. *The Aristocratic Families of Early Imperial China: a Case Study of the Po-ling Ts'ui Family*. Cambridge: Cambridge University Press.

Eliot, Charles N. E. 1921. *Hinduism and Buddhism*. London: Routledge & Kegan Paul Ltd., reprint 1962.

Ettinghausen, Richard. 1938. 'Parthian and Sassanian Pottery', *A Survey of Persian Art*, ed. A. U. Pope. London: Oxford University Press, I, 646–80.

Fairservise, Walter A. 1956. *Excavations in the Quetta Valley, West Pakistan*. Anthropological Papers of the American Museum of Natural History, vol. 45, part 2.

_____. 1959. *Archaeological Survey in Zhob and Loralai Districts, West Pakistan*. Anthropological Papers of the American Museum of Natural History, vol. 47, part 2.

Fan, Hsiang-yung (ed). 1958. *Loyang Ch'ieh-lan chi Chiao chu* (Memories of Holy Places in Loyang). Reprint Shanghai: Ku-chi Ch'u-pan-she, 1978.

Fan, Wen-lan;. 1965. *Chung-kuo T'ung-shih Chien-pien* (An Outline of Chinese History). Peking: Jen-min Ch'u-pan-she.

Fang, Hao. 1963. *Chung-hsi Chiao-t'ung-shih* (History of Communication between China and the West). Taipei: Chung-hua Wen-hua Ch'u-pan Shih-yeh Wei-yüan-hui.

Feng, Ch'eng-chün. 1955. *Hsi-yü Ti-min* (Place Names of the

Western Region). Peking: Chung-hua Shu-chü. Revised by Lu Chun-ling, Peking: Chung-hua Shu-chü, 1980.

Fergusson, James and James Burgess. 1880. *The Cave Temples of India*. Delhi: Oriental Books Reprint Co., 1969.

Fleet, John F. 1888. *Inscriptions of the Early Gupta Kings and Their Successors*. Vol. III of *CII*. Calcutta: Government Printer. Third revised edition, Varanasi: Indological Book House, 1970.

Frumkin, Gregoire. 1970. *Archaeology in Soviet Central Asia*. Leiden: Brill.

Fussman, G. 1974. 'Ruines de la Vallée de Wardak', *Arts Asiatiques*, vol. 30, 65–130.

Gardner, P. 1886. *The Coins of the Greek and Scythic kings of Bactria and India in the British Museum*. London. Reprint Chicago: Argonaut, 1966.

Garnsey, Peter, Keith Hopkins, C. R. Whittaker. 1983. *Trade in the Ancient Economy*. London: Chatto & Windus, the Hogarth Press.

Gernet, Jacques. 1956. *Les Aspects économiques du Bouddhisme dans la société chinoise du Ve au Xe siécle*.

Ghirshman, R. 1946. Begram; recherches archéologiques et historiques sur les Kouchans. DAFA t. XII. Le Caire: Imprimerie de L'institut Français d'archéologie orientale.

_____. 1957. 'Le Probléme de la chronologie des Kouchans', *Cahiers d'historie mondiale*, III, 3, 689–722.

Ghosh, A. and K. C. Panigrahi. 1946. 'Pottery of Ahichchhatra (U.P.)', *AI*, I, 39–59.

Ghosh, A. 1947–8. 'Taxila (Sirkap), 1944–45', *AI*, IV, 41–84.

_____. 1951. 'Rajgir 1950', *AI*, VII, 66–78.

_____. 1973. *The City in Early Historical India*. Calcutta: Indian Institute of Advanced Study.

_____. 1975. 'The Kushan Levels at Some Excavated Sites in North India', *CAKP*, II, 108–12.

Giles, Lionel. 1957. *Descriptive Catalogue of the Chinese Manuscripts from Tunhuang in the British Museum*. London: British Museum.

Godard, A., Y. Godard, et J. Hackin. 1928. *Les Antiquités boudhiques de Bāmiyān*. DAFA t. II. Paris: G. van Oest.

Gokhale, Balkrishna Govind. 1983. 'Buddhism in the Gupta Age', *Essays on Gupta Culture*, ed. Bardell L. Smith. Delhi: Motilal Banarsidass.

Goshal, Upendra Nath. 1929. *Contributions to the History of the Hindu Revenue System.* Calcutta: The University of Calcutta.

Goswami, Kunja Gobind. 1948. *Excavations at Bangarh (1938–41).* Asutosh Museum Memoir no. 1. Calcutta: University of Calcutta.

_____. 1930. *The Agrarian System in Ancient India.* Calcutta: The University of Calcutta.

Gunawardana, R.A.L.H. 1979. *Robe and Plough, Monasticism and Economic Interest in Early Medieval Sri Lanka.* Tucson: University of Arizona Press.

Gupta, S. P. (ed). 1985. *Kushana Sculptures from Sanghol (1st-2nd century AD), A Recent Discovery.* New Delhi: National Museum.

Hackin, Joseph, in collaboration with J. Carl. 1933. *Nouvelles Recherches archéologiques á Bamiyan.* DAFA t. III. Paris: G. van Oest.

Hackin, Joseph. 1939. *Recherches archéologiques á Begram, chantier no. 2 (1937),* DAFA t. IX. IX. Paris: Les Editions d'art et d'histoire.

_____. 1954. Nouvelles Recherches archéologiques à Begram (ancienne Kāpici) 1939–40), DAFA t. XI. Paris: Imprimerie nationale, presses universitaires.

Hackin, Joseph, J. Carl et J. Menuie. 1959. *Diverses Recherches archéologiques en Afghanistan.* DAFA t. VIII. Paris.

Hamilton, Hans Claude & W. Falconer. 1954–7. *The Geography of Strabo.* London: H. G. Bohn.

Hammond, N. 1970. 'An Archaeological Reconnaissance in the Helmand Valley, South Afghanistan', *East and West*, vol. 20, 437–59.

Han, Hsiang. 1982. 'Reconnaissances of the Ancient City of Bog-daqin', *WW*, 1982, no. 4, 8–12.

Hargreaves, H. 1929. *Excavations in Baluch, Sampur Mound, Mastung and Sohr Damb, Nal.* Memoirs of the Archaeological Survey of India, no. 35. Calcutta: Government of India.

Harle, J. C. 1973. 'Late Kushan, Early Gupta: a Reverse Approach', *South Asian Archaeology*, ed. Norman Hammond. Park Ridge, New Jersey: Noyes Press.

Hartel, H. 1974. 'The Apsidal Temple No. 2 at Sonkh', *South Asian Archaeology 1973*, ed. J. E. van Lohuizen-de Leeuw & J. J. M. Ubaghs. Leiden: Brill.

_____. 1976. 'The Excavations at Sonkh', *German Scholars on India*, II, 69–99. Ed. Cultural Dept. of the Embassy of the Federal

Republic of Germany, New Delhi. Varanasi: Chowkhamba Sanskrit Series Office.

Hattori Katsuhiko. 1962. 'Hokugi Rakuyō ni okeru Bukkyo Jiin to Keizai', *Journal of Indian and Buddhist Studies*, x, 1, 138–40.

He, Tsu-ch'üan. 1958. *Wei Chin Nan-pei Ch'ao Shih-lüeh* (An Outline of the History of the Wei, the Chin, and the Southern and Northern Dynasties). Shanghai: Shanghai Jen-min Ch'u-pan-she.

Heitzman, James. 1980. *The Origin and Spread of Buddhist Monastic Institutions in South Asia 500 BC–300 AD.* Philadelphia: Department of South Asia Regional Studies, University of Pennsylvania.

_____. 1984. 'Early Buddhism, Trade and Empire', *Studies in the Palaeoanthropology of South Asia*, 121–37. Ed. Kenneth Kennedy & Gregory Possehl.

Henning, W. B. 1948. 'The Date of the Sogdian Letters', *Bulletin of the School of Oriental and African Studies*, xii, 601–15.

Hirth, Friedrich. 1885. *China and the Roman Oriental*. Shanghai & Hong Kong: Kelly & Walsh.

Hirth, Friedrich and W. W. Rockhill. 1911. *Chao Ju-kua: His Work on the Twelfth and Thirteenth Centuries, Entitled Chu-fan-chi*. St Petersburg.

The Hopei Bureau of Cultural Archaeological Team. 1966. 'The Northern Wei Stone Coffin Unearthed at Ting-hsien, Hopei Province', *KK*, 1966, v, 252–9.

Houn, Franklin W. 1956. 'The Civil Service Recruitment System of the Han Dynasty', *Tsing Hua Journal of Chinese Studies*, i, 138–64.

Hsia, Nai. 1962. 'Notes on a So-called "Sino-Kharoshtihi" Coin Found at Ak-sipil Khotan, Sinkiang",' *WW*, 1962, vii–viii, 60–3.

_____. 1963. 'New Finds of Ancient Silk Fabrics in Sinkiang', *KKHP*, 1963, i, 45–76.

_____. 1966. 'The Persian Sassanian Silver Coins Found in the Stone Relic-casket Unearthed from under the Foundation of a Pagoda at Tinghsien, Hoper Province', *KK*, 1966, v, 267–70.

_____. 1974. 'A Survey of Sassanian Silver Coins Found in China', *KKHP*, 1974, i, 91–110.

_____. 1977. 'The Byzantine Gold Coins Unearthed from the Tomb of Li Hsi-tsung at Tsan-Huang County, Hopei Province', *KK*, 1977, vi, 403–6.

Hu, Hsiu-ying. 1980. *Enumeration of Chinese Materia Medica*. Hong Kong: The Chinese University Press.

Hulsewé, A. F. P. 1955. *Remnants of Han Law.* Vol. 1. Leiden: E. J. Brill.

Ingholt, Harald. 1957. *Gandharan Art in Pakistan.* New York: Pantheon Books Inc.

Jayaswal, K. P. 1943. *Hindu Polity.* Bangalore: The Bangalore Printing & Publishing Co.

Jenner, W. J. F. (trans). 1981. *Memories of Loyang.* Oxford: Clarendon Press.

Jha, Dwijendra Narayan. 1967. *Revenue System in Post-Maurya and Gupta Times.* Calcutta: Punthi Pustak.

Joshi, N. P. 1967. *Life in Ancient Uttarapatha.* Varanasi: Banaras Hindu University.

The Kansu Archaeological Team. 1963. 'New Finds at the Cave Temples of Ping Ling Ssu Monastery—Brief Report on the Results of the Second Survey', *WW*, 1963, x, 1–4, & 10.

_____. 1965. 'Reconnaissances of the Cave Temples of the Ma T'i Monastery, Wenshu Shan Hill and Ch'ang Ma', *WW*, 1965, III, 13–23.

Kasuga, Reichi. 1942–4. 'Bukkyō Shijō no Ryūmon' (Lung-men in Buddhist History), *Shina Bukkyō Shigaku*, VII, 1, 41–58.

Kawamura, Leslie S. (ed). 1981. *The Bodhisattva Doctrine in Buddhism.* Waterloo, Ontario: Wilfrid Lanrier Press.

Keith, A. Berriedale. 1924. *Sanskrit Drama.* Oxford: Clarendon Press.

Khan, F. A. 1960. *Banbhore.* Department of Archaeology and Museum, Ministry of Education & Information, Government of Pakistan, Revised edition 1963.

Kitzinger, Ernst. 1946. 'The Horse and Lion Tapestry at Dumbarton Oaks', Dumbarton Oaks Papers, III, 1–72.

Konow, Sten. 1929. *Kharoshthi Inscriptions with the Exception of those of Aśoka.* Vol. II, part 1 of *CII.* Calcutta: Government of India, Central Publication Branch.

Kosambi, D. D. 1955. 'Dhenukakata', *Journal of the Asiatic Society of Bombay*, XXX: 50–71.

Kubota, Ryōen. 1940. 'Shina ni okeru Bukkyō Jiinteki Shakai Katsudosei no kekkan', (The Shortcomings of Social Activities of Buddhist Monasteries in China), *Shina Bukkyō Shigaku*, IV, 2, 77–83.

Lal, B. B. 1949. 'Sisupalgarh 1948: an Early Historical Fort in Eastern India', *AI*, V, 62–105.

_____. 1952. 'Examination of Some Ancient Glass Specimens', *AI*, no. 8, 17–27.

_____. 1954–55. 'Excavation at Hastinapura and Other Explorations in the Upper Ganga and Sutlej Basins 1950–52.', *AI*, x-xi, 5–151.

Lamotte, Étienne (trans). 1962. *The Teaching of Vimalakīrti* (vimala-kīrtinirdeśa). Translated into English by Sara Boin. London: The Pali Text Society, 1976.

Lattimore, Owen. 1951. *Inner Asian Frontiers of China.* 2nd ed. New York: American Geographical Society.

Lebra, Takie Sugiyama. 1975. 'An Alternative Approach to Reciprocity', *American Anthropologist*, vol. 77, no. 3, 550–65.

Le Clair, Edward & Harold K. Schneider (eds). 1968. *Economic Anthropology*. New York: Holt, Rinehart and Winston, Inc.

Lewis, Bernard. 1950. *Arabs in History.* London: Hutchinson's University Library.

Li, Chien-nung. 1957. *Hsien-Ch'in Liang-Han Ching-chi Shih-kao* (A Draft of Economic History of the period from the Pre-Ch'in to the Two Han Dynasties). Peking: San-lien Shu-tien.

_____. 1959. *Wei Chin Nan-pei-ch'ao Sui T'ang Cing-chi Shih-kao* (A Draft of Economic History under the Wei, Chin, Southern and Northern Dynasties, Sui, and T'and). Peking: San-lien Shu-tien.

Li, Yao-po. 1973. 'Liaoning Pei-p'iao-hsien Hsi-kuan-ying-tzu Pei-yen Feng Su-fu Mu, (The Grave of Feng Su-fu of Pei-yen Kingdom, Located at Hsi-kuan-ying-tzu, Pei-P'iao County, Liaoning Province), *WW*, 1973, II, 2–19.

Lianyungang, Museum of. 1981. 'A Report on Stone Statues Discovered in Mt. Kongwangshan, Jiangsu Province', *WW*, 1981, VII, 1–7.

Liebenthal, Walter. 1955. 'Chinese Buddhism During the 4th and 5th Centuries', *Monumenta Nipponica*, XI, 44–83.

Liu, Chih-yüan. 1973. 'Han-tai Shih-ching K'ao' (A Study of Marketplaces of the Han Times), *WW*, 1973, III, 52–7.

Lohuizen-de Leeuw, J. E. van. 1949. *The 'Scythian' Period; an Approach to the History, Art, Epigraphy and Palaeography of North India from the First Century to the Third Century* AD. Leiden: Brill.

_____. 1972. 'Gandhara and Mathura: Their Cultural Relationship', *Aspects of Indian Art*, P. Pal ed., Leiden: Brill, 27–43.

The Loyang Archaeological Team of the Institute of Archaeology, Academia Sinica. 1973. 'Preliminary Survey of the Remains of the Han-Wei City of Loyang', *WW*, 1973, IV, 198–208.

_____. 1981. 'Excavation of the Tower-base at the Yong-ning Temple of Northern Wei Dynasty', *KK*, 1981, III, 223–4, 212.

Lu, Hsün. 1939. *Ku-hsiao-shuo Kou-ch'en* (Collection of Ancient Fiction Extant in Other Works). Lu Hsun Hsien-sheng Chinien Wei-yuan-hui.

Lü, Ssu-mien. 1948. *Liang-chin Nan-pei-ch'ao Shih* (History of the Two Chin Dynasties and the Southern and Northern Dynasties). Reprint Hong Kong: T'ai-p'ing Shu-chu, 1962.

Lüders, Heinrich. 1936. *Texilen in Alten Turkistan*. Abhandlungen der Preussischen Akademie der Wissenschaften, philosophisch-historische Klasse, nr. 3 Berlin: Verlag der Academie der sissenschaften.

_____. 1961. *Mathura Inscriptions*. Gottingen: Vandenhoeck & Ruprecht.

_____. 1963. *Bharhut Inscriptions*. Ootacamund: Government Epigraphist for India.

McCrindle, John W. 1901. *Ancient India as Described in Classical Literature*. Westminster. Reprint New Delhi: Oriental Books Reprint, 1979.

McGovern, William Montgomery. 1939. *The Early Empires of Central Asia*. Chapel Hill: University of North Carolina Press.

Maenchen-Helfen, Otto. 1973. *The World of the Huns, Studies in Their History and Culture*. Ed. Max Knight. Berkeley: University of California Press.

Mai-chi-shan Shih-k'u (Caves of the Mount mai-chi). 1954. Wen-hua-pu She-hui-wen-hua-shih-yeh Kuan-li-chu (ed.). Peking.

Maisey, F. C. 1892. *Sanchi and its Remains*. London. Reprint Delhi: Indological Book House, 1972.

Maity, S. K. 1957. *Economic Life of Northern India*. Calcutta: the World Press.

Malalasekere, G. P. 1937. *Dictionary of Pali Proper Names*. London: John Murray.

Malinowski, Bronislaw. 1922. *Argonauts of the Western Pacific*. Reprint New York: E. P. Dutton & Co., Inc., 1961.

Mandel, Ernest. 1962. *Marxist Economic Theory*. Trans. Brain Pearce, London: Merlin Press, 1968.

Marshall, Sir John Hubert. 1911–12. 'Excavations at Bhita', *ASIAR*, 1911–12: 29–94.

_____. 1931. *Mohenjo-daro and the Indus Civilization*. London: Arthur Probsthain.

_____. 1940. *The Monument of Sāñchī*. Calcutta: The Government of India Press.

_____. 1951. *Taxila*. Cambridge University Press.

Mauss, Marcel. 1925. *The Gift*. Trans. Ian Cunnison, New York: Norton Library, 1967.

Mehta, R. N. & S. N. Chowdhary. 1966. *Excavations at Devnimori*. Baroda: Department of Archaeology, Faculty of Arts, M. S. University of Baroda.

Mehta, R. N. 1968. *Excavation at Nagara*. Baroda: Department of Archaeology and Ancient History, Faculty of Arts, University of Baroda.

Meillassoux, Claude. 1971. *The Development of Indigenous Trade and Markets in West Africa*. London: Oxford University Press.

Meister, Michael. 1970. 'The Pearl Roundel in Chinese Textile Design', *Ars Orientalis*, VIII, 255–67.

Menuie, J. 1942. *Shotorak*. DAFA t. x. Paris.

Miller, James Innes. 1969. *The Spice Trade of the Roman Empire, 29 BC to AD 641*. Oxford: Clarendon.

Mirashi, Vasudev Vishnu. 1955. *Inscriptions of the Kalachuri-Chedi Era*. Vol. IV of *CII*. Ootacamund: Government Epigraphist for India.

Mishra, Ram Swarup. 1971. *Inscriptions of the Early Gupta Kings and Their Successors*. Supplement to Fleet's Corpus Inscriptionum Indicarum III. Varanasi, Banaras Hindu University.

Mizuno, Seiichi. 1941. *A Study of the Buddhist Cave Temples at Lungmen, Honan*. Tokyo: Zaubo Press.

_____. 1941a. 'Unkō no Amida-zō ni tsuite' (On the Statues of Amitabha in Yün-kang), *Shina Bukkyō Shigaku*, V, 2, 77–79.

_____. 1951. *Yün-kang, the Buddhist Cave-Temples of the Fifth Century AD in North China*. Kyoto: Jimbunkagak Kenkyosho, Kyoto University.

_____. 1967. *Hazār-Sum and Fīl-Khāna, Caves-Sites in Afghanistan Surveyed in 1962*. Kyoto: Kyoto University.

_____. 1968. *Durman Tepe and Lalma, Buddhist Sites in Afghanistan Surveyed in 1963–65*. Kyoto: Kyoto University.

Mukherjee, B. N. 1970. *The Economic Factors in Kushāṇa History*. Calcutta: Pilgrim Publishers.

_____. 1976–77. 'The Kushaṇa Empire and the Hsiung-nu', *Journal of Ancient Indian History*, x, 160–65.

Nagata, Hidemasa. 1974. 'Kyoen Kankan no Shūsei' (Collection of Chinese Wood-slips from Chü-yen), *Toho Gaho*, XLVI, 161–85.

Narain, A. K. 1957. *The Indo-Greeks*. London: Oxford University Press.

_____. 1967. *From Alexander to Kanishka*. Varanasi: Banaras Hindu University.

_____. (ed.). 1976. *International Conference on the History of Buddhism, University of Wisconsin, 1976*. Delhi: B. R. Pub. Corp.

_____. 1976–78. *Excavations at Rajghāt, 1957–58, 1960–65*. Varanasi: Dept. of Ancient Indian History, Culture and Archaeology, Banaras Hindu University.

_____. 1981. 'The Kushāṇa State: A Preliminary Study', *Study of the State*, ed. Henri Claessen and Peter Skalnik, New York: Mouton Publishers.

Needham, Joseph. 1954–. *Science and Civilization in China*. Cambridge & New York: Cambridge University Press.

Niyogi, Puspa. 1972–3. 'Endowments in Favour of Early Buddhist Monasteries in Bengal and Bihar', *Journal of Ancient Indian History*, VI, 160–5.

Orton, Nancy Pinto. 1983. 'Red Polished Ware in Western Indian and Adjacent Areas', Paper presented at the 'Indo-Roman Trade' seminar, Mid-Atlantic Regional Association of Asian Studies conference, 30 October 1983.

Pathak, H. 1978. *Cultural History of the Gupta Period Based on Epigraphic and Numismatic Records*. Delhi: Bharatiya.

Peripulus Maris Erythraei (The Periplus of the Erythrean Sea). Trans. & annot. W. H. Schoff. New York: Longmans, Green and Co., 1917. Reprint New Delhi: Oriental Book Reprint Corp., 1974.

_____. Trans. & ed. G. W. B. Huntingford. London: Hakluyt Society, 1980.

Ping-ling-ssu Shih-k'u (The Rock Caves of Ping-ling Monastery). 1953. Peking: Wen-hua-pu She hui-wen-hua Kuan-li-chü.

Pliny. *Natural History*. Trans. H. Rackham. Cambridge, Massachuetts: Harvard University Press, 1956–62.

Polanyi, Conrad M. Arensberg & Harry W. Pearson (ed.). 1957. *Trade and Market in the Early Empires*. New York: Free Press.

Prasad, Kameshwar. 1984. *Cities, Crafts and Commerce under the Kusanas*. Delhi: Agam Kala Prakashan.

Prebish, Charles S. 1975. *Buddhist Monastic Discipline, the Sanskrit Prātimoksa Sūtras of Mahāsāmghikas and Mūlasarvāstivādins*. University Park and London: The Pennsylvania State University Press.

Procopius. VI. Trans. H. B. Dewing. Cambridge, Massachusetts: Harvard University Press, 1935.

Ptolemy. *Geography of Claudius Ptolemy*. Trans. & ed. Edward Luther Stevenson. New York: The New York Public Library, 1932.

Puri, Baij Nath. 1968. *India under the Kuṣāṇas*. Bombay: Bharatiya Vidya Bhavan.

_____. 1977. *Kuṣāṇa Bibliography*. Calcutta: Naya Prokash.

Rao, S. R. 1966. *Excavations at Amreli: A Kshatrapa-Gupta Town*. Bulletin, Museum and Picture Gallery of Baroda, XXVIII.

Raschke, M. G. 1978. 'New Studies in Roman Commerce with the East', *Aufstieg und Niedergang der Romischer Welt*, Berlin, New York: Walter de Gruyter. Band II. 9.2, 608–1378.

Ratnagar, Shereen. 1981. *Encounters: The Westerly Trade of the Harappa Civilization*. Delhi: Oxford University Press.

Ray, Himanshu Prabha. 1986. *Monastery and Guild: Commerce under the Satavahanas*. Delhi, OUP.

Reichelt, Hans. 1931. *Die soghdischen Handschriftenrest des britischen Museums*. Heidelberg: Carl Winters Universitatsbuchhandlung.

Renfrew, Colin. 1984. 'Varna and the Emergence of Wealth in Prehistoric Europe', paper presented at 'Symposium on Commodities and Culture', Philadelphia: the Wharton-Sinkler Conference Center, University of Pennsylvania.

Riboud, Krishna. 1977. 'Some Remarks on the Face-covers (fumien) Discovered in the Tombs of Astana', *Oriental Art*, XXIII, 438–54.

Ritchie, Patrick D. 1937. 'Spectrographic Studies on Ancient Glass', *Technical Studies in the Field of the Fine Arts*, V, 4, 209–16.

Rosenfield, John M. 1967. *The Dynastic Arts of the Kushans*. Berkeley & Los Angeles: University of California Press.

Rostovtzeff, M. 1926. *Social and Economic History of the Roman*

Empire. London: Oxford University Press.

_____. 1932. *Caravan Cities*. London: Oxford University Press.

_____. 1934. *Excavations at Dura-Eurapos*. New Haven: Yale University.

_____. 1941. *The Social and Economic History of the Hellenistic World*. Oxford: Clarendon Press.

Rudolph, Richard C. and Wen Yu. 1951. *Han Tomb Art of West China*. Berkeley: University of California Press.

Rydh, Hanna. 1959. *Rang Mahal, the Swedish Archaeological Expedition to India 1952–54*. Lund: CWK Gleerup Publishers

Sankalia, H. D. & S.B. Deo. 1955. *Report on the Excavations at Nasik and Jorwe, 1950–51*. Poona: Deccan College.

Satō, Chisui. 1977. 'Hokuchō Zōzōmei Kō' (Study of Votive Inscriptions on Buddhist Statues in the Northern Dynasties), *Shigaku Zasshi*, LXXXVI, 10, 1–47.

Schafer, Edward H. 1963. *The Golden Peaches of Samarkand*. University of California Press.

Schlumberger, Daniel. 1952. 'Le Temple de Surkh Kotal en Bactriane', *Journal Asiatique*, CCXL, 433–53.

_____. 1954. Ibid. CCXLII, 161–87.

_____. 1955. Ibid. CCXXLIII, 269–79.

_____. 1964. Ibid. CCLII, 301–26.

_____. 1968. 'Sur La Nature des temples de Surkh Kotal', *CAKP*, II 97–102.

Schoff, Wilfred, H. (Trans.). 1912. *The Periplus of the Erythraean Sea*. New York: Longmans Green and Co. Reprint New Delhi: Oriental Books Reprint Corp. 1972.

Schwartzberg, Joseph E. 1978. *A Historical Atlas of South Asia*. Chicago: The University of Chicago Press.

Sharma, G. R. 1960. *The Excavations at Kauśāmbī (1957–59)*. Allahabad: Department of Ancient History, Culture and Archaeology, University of Allahabad.

Sharma, G. R. & J. Negi. 1968. 'The Saka-Kushans in the Central Ganga Valley', *CAKP*, II, 15–41.

Sharma, G. R. 1969. *Excavations at Kauśāmbī 1949–50*. Delhi: Manager of Publications.

Sharma, Ram S. 1959. *Aspects of Political Ideas and Institutions in Ancient India*. Second ed. 1968. Delhi: Motilal Banarsidass.

Sharma, Y. D. 1953. 'Exploration of Historical Sites', *AI*, IX, 116–69.

Shih-chia-chuang Prefecture. 1977. 'Excavation of Tomb Li Hsi-tsung of the Eastern Wei Dynasty in Tsan-huang County, Hopei Province', *KK*, 1977, VI, 382–90.

Shih Shu-ch'ing. 1962. 'Notes on the Remains at Niya, Min Feng, Sinkiang', *WW*, 1962, VII & VIII, 20–7.

_____. 1980. 'Pei-Wei Ts'ao T'ien-tu Tsao Ch'ien-fo-shih-t'a', (The Stone Pagoda of a Thousand Buddhas Donated by Ts'ao T'ien-tu in the Northern Wei Dynasty), *WW*, 1980, I, 68–71.

Shih Wei-hsiang. 1980. 'Ssu-ch'ou-chih-lu shang-te Tunhuang yü Mo-kao-k'u' (Tunhuang and Mo-kao Caves on the Silk Route), The Tunhuang Research Institute, 1980a, 43–121.

Shukla, Mani Shanker. 1972. *A History of Gem Industry in Ancient and Medieval India*. Varanasi: Oriental Publishers & Booksellers.

Sinha, B.P. & Lala Aditya Narain. 1970. *Pataliputra Excavations (1955–56)*. Patna: Directorate of Archaeology and Museums.

Sinha, K. K. 1967. *Excavations at Sravasti—1959*. Varanasi: Banaras Hindu University.

Sinkiang Uighur Autonomous Region, Museum of. 1960. 'Sinkiang Min-feng-hsien pei Ta-sha-mo chung Ku-i-chih Mu-tsang-ch'ü tung-Han Ho-tsang-mu Ch'ing-li Chien-pao' (A Short Report on the Excavation of a Grave of a Couple in the ancient Cemetery Located in the Great Desert North of Min-feng County, Sinkiang), *WW*, 1960, VI, 9–12.

_____. 1961. 'Ancient Remains in the Taklamakan Desert Near Min Feng County (Niya Site), Sinkiang', *KK*, 1961, I, 119–22, 126.

_____. 1972. *Ssu-ch'ou chih Lu (Han T'ang Chih-wu)*. (The Silk Route, Textiles of Han and T'ang Times). Peking: Wen-wu Ch'u-pan-she.

_____. 1972a. 'Ssu-ch'ou chih Lu shang Hsin-fa-hsien te Han-T'ang Chih-wu' (Newly Discovered Textiles Dated to the Han and T'ang Times), *WW*, 1972, III, 14–19, 13.

_____. 1973. 'Excavation of Ancient Tombs at Astana and Karokhoja in Turfan, Sinkiang 1963–65', *WW*, 1973, X, 7–27.

_____. 1977. *Sinkiang Li-shih Wen-wu* (Historical Remains in Sinkiang). Peking: Wen-wu Ch'u-pan-she.

Sinkiang Turfan Ti-ch'ü Wen-kuan-so. 1983. 'Turfan Ch'u-t'u te Shih-liu-kuo Shih-ch'i te Wen-shu' (The Documents Dated in the Period of the Sixteen states Excavated from Turfan Region), *WW*, 1983, I, 19–25.

Sircar, D. C. 1951. Chapters IX, XI-XIV in *The Age of Imperial Unity*, vol. 2 of *The History and Culture of the Indian People*, ed. R. C. Majumdar. Reprint Bombay: Bharatiya Vidya Bhavan, 1980.

_____. 1965. *Select Inscriptions Bearing on Indian History and Civilization*, vol. 1. Calcutta: University of Calcutta.

_____. 1968. 'Eastern India and the Kushans', *CAKP*, II, 7–14.

_____. 1977. *Some Problems Concerning the Kuṣāṇas*. Dharwar: Kannada Research Institute, Karnatak University.

Skinner, George William (ed.). 1977. *The City in Late Imperial China*. Stanford University Press.

Smith, Bardwell L. (ed.). 1983. *Essays on Gupta Culture*. Columbia, Missouri: South Asia Books.

Smith, V. A. 1919. *Catalogue of Coins in the Indian Museum*. Calcutta: Oxford.

Srivastava, B. 1968. *Trade and Commerce in Ancient India*. Varanasi: Chowkhamba Sanskrit Series Office.

Starcky, Jean. 1952. *Palmyre*. Paris: Librie A. Maisonneuve.

Stein, Aruel. 1912. *Remains of Desert Cathay*. London: Macmillan and Co. Ltd.

_____. 1921. *Serindia*. London: Oxford University Press. Reprint Delhi: Motilal Banarsidass, 1980.

_____. 1921a. 'Notes on Ancient Chinese Documents Discovered along the Han Frontier Wall in the Desert of Tun-Huang', *New China Review*, III, 4, 243–53.

_____. 1928. *Innermost Asia*. Oxford: Clarendon Press. Reprint New Delhi: Cosmo Publications, 1980.

_____. 1929. *An Archaeological Tour in Waʐeristan and Northern Baluchistan*. *MASI*, XXXVII. Calcutta: Government of India.

_____. 1931. *An Archaeological Tour in Gedrosia*. *MASI*, XLIII. Calcutta: Government of India.

_____. 1933. *On Ancient Central Asian Tracks*. London: Macmillan & Co. Reprint New York: AMS Press, 1971.

_____. 1937. *Archaeological Reconnaissances in Northwest India and Southeast Iran*. London: Macmillan & Co.

Strenski, Ivan. 1983. 'On Generalized Exchange and the Domestication of the Sangha', *Man*, vol. 18, 463–77.

Su, Ch'eng-chien. 1947. *Hou-Han Shih-huo-chih Ch'ang-pien* (An

Expanded Monograph on Financial Administration of the Later Han). Shanghai: Commercial Press.

Su, Pai. 1977. 'Tung-pei Nei-meng-ku Ti-ch'u te Hsien-pei I-chi' (Remains of Sienpi in the Northeast and Inner Mongolia), *WW*, 1977, v, 42–54.

_____. 1977a. 'Sheng-le P'ing-ch'eng I-tai-te T'o-pa-Hsien-pei—Pei-Wei I-chi' (Remains of T'o-pa Tribe of Sienpi and the Northern Wei State), *WW*, 1977, xi 38–46.

Subbarao, B. 1953. *Baroda Through the Ages*. Baroda: M. S. University of Baroda.

_____. 1956. *The Personality of India*. First and second ed. Baroda: M. S. University of Baroda. Second ed. 1958.

Sullivan, Michael. 1969. *The Cave Temples of Maichishan*. Berkeley: University of California Press.

Sun, E-tu Zen and John de Francis (trans.). 1956. *Chinese Social History*. Washington: American Council of Learned Societies.

Tambiah, S. 1970. *Buddhism and the Spirit Cults in Northeast Thailand*. Cambridge University Press.

T'ang, Yung-t'ung. 1927. *Han Wei Liang-Chin Nan-pei-ch'ao Fo-chiao Shih* (Buddhist History from the Han to the Southern and Northern Dynasties). Changsha: Commercial Press.

T'ao, Yüan-chen. 1935. *San-kuo Shih-huo-chih* (A Monograph on Financial Administration of the Three Kingdoms Period). Shanghai: Commercial Press.

Tarn, W. W. 1938. *The Greeks in Bactria and India*. 2nd. ed. Cambridge University Press, 1951; reprint New York, 1966.

Teggart, Frederick J. 1939. *Rome and China*. Berkely: University of California Press.

Thakur, Vijay Kumar. 1981. *Urbanization in Ancient India*. New Delhi: Abhinav.

Thapar, B. K. 1968. 'The Kushan Civilization in India: An Appraisal of the Component Elements', *CAKP*, i, 90–4.

Thapar, Romila. 1961. *Aśoka and the Decline of the Mauryas*. London: Oxford University Press.

_____ 1966. *A History of India*, vol. 1. Baltimore: Penguin Books.

_____ 1978. *Ancient Indian Social History*. New Delhi: Orient Longman.

_____ 1984. *From Lineage to State*. Delhi, OUP.

Thomas, E. 1876. *Records of the Gupta Dynasty.* Reprint Varanasi: Indological Book House.

T'ien, Kuang-chin. 1983. 'Chin-nien-lai Nei-Meng-ku Ti-ch'ü te Hsiung-nu K'ao-ku' (Recent Archaeological Works on Hsiung-nu in the Inner Mongolia Region), *KKHP*, 1983, I, 7–24.

T'ien-ying. 1957. *Chung-kuo Ku-tai Ke-yao San-lun.* (Discussion on Ancient Chinese Folklore). Shanghai: Ku-tien Wen-hsueh Ch'u-pan-she.

Trigger, B. 1972. 'Determinants of Urban Growth in Pre-Industrial Societies', in *Man, Settlement and Urbanism*, P. J. Ucko, R. Tringham, & G. W. Dimbleby eds., Duckworth, 575–99.

Tsukamoto, Zenryū. 1944. *Shina Bukkyōshi Kenkyu, Hokugihen* (Study on Chinese Buddhist History, Northern Wei Period). Tokyo: Kōbundō Shobō.

_____. 1961. 'Gishū to Bukkyō' (Wei Shou and Buddhism), *Toho Gakuho*, XXXI, 3, 1–34.

The Tunhuang Research Institute. 1974. 'The Tsin Tombs Found at Tunhuang', *KK*, 1974, III, 191–9.

_____. 1975. 'Tunhuang T'ien-shui-ching Han-tai I-chih te Tiao-ch'a' (Investigation at the Han Site in T'ien-shui-ching, Tunhuang), *KK*, 1975, II, 111–15.

_____. (Dunhuang Institute for Cultural Relics). 1980. *Art Treasures of Dunhuang.* Co-published by Joint Publishing Co., Hongkong, and Cultural Objects Press, Beijing.

_____. 1980a. *Collected Works of the Researches on Dunhuang Caves.* Lanchow: Kansu Jen-min Ch'u-pan-she.

Vertogradova, V. V. 1983. 'Indian Inscriptions and Inscriptions in Unknown Lettering from Kara-tepe in Old Termez', USSR Academy of Sciences, Institute of Oriental studies, All-Union Association of Orientalists, presented at section 3, the 31st International Congress of Human Sciences in Asia and Africa, 31 August-7 September, 1983, Tokyo and Kyoto, published by Nauka Publishers, Central department of Oriental Literature.

Vinaya Texts. Translated by Rhys Davids & Hermann Oldenberg. Vol. 13, 17, 20 of SBE. London: Oxford University Press 1882.- Delhi: Motilal Banarsidass, 1974.

Vogel, J. Ph. 1910. *Catalogue of the Archaeological Museum at Mathura.* Allahabad: Government Press.

Waddell, L. A. 1903. *Report on the Excavations at Patliputra.* Calcutta:

Bengal Secretariat Press. Reprint Delhi: Sanskaran Prakashak, 1975.

Waley, Arthur. 1955. 'The Heavenly Horses of Ferghana', *History Today*, v, 95–103.

Wang, Chung-lo. 1979. *Wei Chin Nan-pei-ch'ao Shih* (History of the Wei, the Chin, and the Southern and Northern Dynasties). Shanghai: Jen-min Ch'u-pan-she.

Wang, Chung-shu. 1957. 'Han Ch'ang-an-ch'eng K'ao-ku Kung-tso te Ch'u-pu Shou-huo' (The First Result of the Excavation on the City Wall of Ch'ang-an Built in the Han Dynasty), *KKTH*, 1957, v, 102–10.

_____. 1958. 'Han Ch'ang-an-ch'eng K'ao-ku Kung-tso Shou-huo Hsü-chi' (More Report about the Excavations on the City Wall of Ch'ang-an Built in the Han Dynasty), *KKTH*, 1958, IV, 23–32.

Wang, Kelin. 1979. 'Excavation of the Tomb of Kudihuilo of the Northern Qi Dynasty (AD 550–577),' *KKHP*, 1979, III, 377–401.

Wang, Kuo-wei. 1959. *Kuan-t'ang Chi-lin* (Collection of Wang Kuo-wei). Peking: Chung-hua Shu-chü.

Wang, Ning-sheng. 1977. 'The Western Regions of the Han and Tsin Dynasties and the Chinese Civilization', *KKHP*, 1977, I, 23–42.

Wang, Yi-t'ung. 1953. 'Slaves and Other Comparable Social Groups During the Northern Dynasties (386–618)', *Harvard Journal of Asiatic Studies*, XVI, 293–364.

Warmington, Eric Herbert. 1928. *The Commerce Between the Roman Empire and India*. Cambridge. Second ed. London: Curzon Press, Ltd., 1974.

Warren, Henry Clarke. 1922. *Buddhism in Translations*. Cambridge: Harvard University Press.

Watt, George. 1908. *The Commercial Products of India*. London. Reprint New Delhi: Today and Tomorrow's Printer & Publishers, 1966.

Wen-wu Correspondent. 1981. 'A Symposium on Stone Statues in Mt. Kongwangshan Held in Beijing', *WW*, 1981, VII, 20.

Wheeler, R. E. Mortimer. 1954. *Rome Beyond the Imperial Frontiers*. London: G. Bell and Sons Ltd.

_____.1962. *Charsada*. London: Oxford University Press.

Whitehead, R. B. 1914. *Catalogue of Coins in the Punjab Museum*.

Oxford University Press.

_____. 1968. 'The First Conference on the Date of Kaniska', Basham 1968, 1–3.

Whitehouse, D. & A. Williamson. 1973. 'Sassanian Maritime Trade', *Iran*, II, 29–49.

Whitfield, Roderick. 1982. *The Art of Central Asia, The Stein Collection in the British Museum*. New York: Kodansha International Ltd. in cooperation with the Trustees of the British Museum.

Williams, Joanna Gottfried. 1982. *The Art of Gupta India*. Princeton. N. J.: Princeton University Press.

Wilson, Horace Hayman. 1841. *Ariana Antiqua*. London. Reprint Delhi: Oriental Publishers, 1971.

Winter, H. J. J. 1975. 'Science', in Basham 1975, 141–61.

Winternitz, M. 1920. *A History of Indian Literature*. Vol. II. Prague. Trans. S. Ketkar and H. Kohn, 1933. Reprint New York: Russell & Russell, 1971.

Wittfogel, Karl August. 1957. *Oriental Despotism*. New Haven: Yale University Press.

Woolner, A. C. and Laksman Sarup. 1930–1. *Thirteen Plays of Bhāsa*. 2 vols. London, OUP.

Wright, Arthur. 1959. *Buddhism in Chinese History*. Stanford: Standford University Press.

Wu, Min. 1962. 'Preliminary Notes on the Ancient Silk (Han to T'ang) Unearthed in Sinkiang', *WW*, 1962, VII–VIII, 64–75.

Yang, Lien-sheng. 1956. 'Great Families of Eastern Han', in Sun, E-tu Zen and Francis 1956, 103–34.

_____. 1961. *Studies in Chinese Institutional History*. Cambridge: Harvard University Press.

Yang, Po-ta. 1979. 'Kuan-yü Wo-kuo Ku Po-li Shih Yen-chiu te Chi-ke Wen-t'i' (Several Problems in the Study of Glass-making History in Our Country), *WW*, 1979, V, 76–8.

Yang, Tien-hsün. 1957. *Shih-k'o T'i-pa So-yin* (Index for Inscriptions on Stones and Their Prefaces and Postscripts). Shanghai: Commercial Press.

Yazdani, G. 1930–55. *Ajanta*. Published under the Authority of the Government of Hyderabad. London: Oxford University Press.

Yen, Wen-ju. 1955. 'Loyang Han Wei Sui T'ang Ch'eng-chih K'an-ch'a Chi' Explorations on Sites of Loyang City Dated to the Times of Han, Wei, Sui, and T'ang), *KKHP*, IX, 117–36.

_____. 1962. 'The Art of Cave Temples South of the T'ien-shan Mountains in Sinkiang', *WW*, 1962, vii–viii, 41–59.

_____. 1981. 'K'ung-wang-shan Fo-chiao Tsao-hsiang te T'i-ts'ai' (The Motifs of the Buddhist Rock Statues on K'ung-wang-shan), *WW*, 1981, vii, 16–19.

Young, Rodney. 1955. 'The South Wall of Balkh, Bactria', *American Journal of Archaeology*, lix, 4, 267–76.

Yü, Wei-ch'ao and Hsin, Li-hsiang. 1981. 'K'ung-wang-shan Mo-ya Tsao-Hsiang te Nien-tai K'ao-ch'a' (The Date of the Buddhist Rock Statues on K'ung-wang-shan), *WW*, 1981, vii, 8–15.

Yü, Ying-shih. 1967. *Trade and Expansion in Han China*. Berkeley and Los Angeles: University of California Press.

Zürcher, E. 1959. *The Buddhist Conquest of China*. Leiden: E. J. Brill.

_____. 1967. 'The Yüeh-chi and Kanishka in the Chinese Sources', in Narain 1967: 72–104.

_____. 1976. 'Buddhism in a Pre-modern Bureaucratic Empire, the Chinese Experience', in Narain 1976, 401–11.

SANSKRIT LITERATURE

Aśvaghosa. *Buddhacarita*. Ed. & trans. Edward B. Cowell, 1893. Reprint New Delhi: Cosmo Publications, 1977.

_____. *Saundarānanda*. Ed. & trans. E. H. Johnston, London: Oxford University Press, 1928. Reprint Delhi: Motilal Banarsidass, 1975.

Bhāsa. *Abhiṣekanāṭaka*.

_____. *Avimāraka*.

_____. *Urubhaṅga*.

_____. *Karṇabhāra*.

_____. *Cārudatta*.

_____. *Dūtaghaṭotkaca*.

_____. *Dūtavākya*.

_____. *Pañcarātra*.

_____. *Pratijñāyaugandharāyaṇa*.

_____. *Pratimā*.

_____. *Bālacarita*.

_____. *Madhyamavyāyoga*.

_____. *Svapnavāsavadatta*.

All Bhasa's works are included in *Bhāsanāṭakacakram*. Original

13 texts. ed. C. R. Devadhar, Poona: Oriental Book Agency, 1962. English translation *Thirteen Trivandrum Plays Attributed to Bhāsa*. Trans. A.D. Woolner & Lakshman Sarup. London: Oxford University Press, 1930, 1931.

Bṛhaspatismṛti. Ed. A. V. Rangaswami. Baroda: Oriental Institute, 1941. Trans. J. Jolly. Vol. 33 of SBE. London: Oxford University Press, 1889; reprint Delhi: Motilal Banarsidass, 1979.

Kālidāsa. *Raghuvaṁśa*.

_____. *Kumārasambhava*.

_____. *Meghadūta*.

_____. *Mālavikāgnimitra*.

_____. *Vikramorvaśīya*.

_____. *Abhijñānaśakuntala*.

_____. *Ṛitusaṁhāra*.

All Kālidāsa's works are included in *The Complete Works of Kālidāsa: The Text in Sanskrit and Prakrit*. Ed. V. P. Joshi. Bombay: Lakhani Book Depot. English translations: *The Dramas of Kālidāsa*, trans. Bela Bose, Allahabad: Kitabistan, 1945; *Kumārasambhava* trans. M. R. Kale, Delhi: Motilal Banarsidass, 1967; *Meghadūta* trans. H. H. Wilson, Calcutta: 1913, 4th ed. Varanasi: Chowkhamba, 1973; *Raghuvaṁśa*, trans. Robert Antoine, Calcutta: A Writers Workshop Publication, 1972.

Kāmasūtra. By Vātsyāyana. Benares: the Chowkhamba Sanskrit Series Office, Vidya Vilas Press, 1929. Trans. S. C. Upadhyaya, Bombay: Taraporevala, 1961.

Lankāvatara Sūtra. Ed. Benyiu Zanjio, Kyoto: Otani University Press, 1923. Trans. T. D. Suzuki, London: Routledge and Sons Ltd., 1932.

Mahāvastu. Ed. E. C. M. Senart. Paris: 1882–97. Trans. J. J. Jones. London: Luzac & Company Ltd., 1949.

Mānava Dharma Śāstra. Ed. Julius Jolly. London: Trubner & Co., 1887. Trans. G. Buhler. Vol. 25 of SBE. London: Oxford University Press, 1886; reprint Delhi: Motilal Banarsidass, 1979.

Milindapañha. Ed. V. Trenckner, London: 1880; reprint London; The Royal Asiatic Society, 1928. Trans. Rhys Davids, Vol. 35 & 36 of SBE, London: Oxford University Press, 1890; reprint Delhi: Motilal Banarsidass, 1975.

Mṛcchkaṭika. By Sudraka. Ed. & trans. M. R. Kale, 1924. New ed. Bombay: Bookseller's Publishing Co. 1962.

Nārada Smṛti. Ed. J. J. Jolly, Calcutta, 1885; trans. J. J. Jolly, vol. 33 of SBE, London: Oxford University Press, 1889; reprint Delhi: Motilal Banarsidass, 1979.

Saddharmapuṇḍarika. Ed. Lokesh Chandra, New Delhi: International Academy of Indian Culture, 1976. Trans. H. Kern, vol. 21 SBE, London: Oxford University, 1884; reprint Delhi: Motilal Banarsidass, 1980.

Sukhāvatī-Vyūha. Ed. Max Müller, Oxford: Clarendon Press, 1881–84. Trans. Max Müller, in *Buddhist Mahayana Texts*, vol. 49 of SBE, London: Oxford University Press, 1894, reprint Delhi: Motilal Banarsidass, 1978.

Viṣṇupurāṇa. Srirama Sarma ed. & trans. in Hindi, Bareli: Sanskrti Sansthana, 1967. English trans. H. H. Wilson: London: 1840. 2nd ed. London: 1888, reprint Calcutta: Punthi Pustak, 1961.

CHINESE LITERATURE

Ch'en Ssu. (Sung Dynasty). *Pao-k'e Ts'ung-pien* (Collection of Precious Inscriptions). Included in SSTS.

Cheng-fa-hua-ching (The Lotus Sutra). Trans. into Chinese Chu Fa-hu (Dharmaraksha, AD 266–313 in China). Tripitaka, vol. 9, 63–134.

Chi Shen-chou San-pao Kan-t'ung-lu (Buddhist Miracles in China). Compiled by Tao-hsüan (AD 596–667). Tripitaka, vol. 52, 404–35.

Chin shu (History of the Chin Dynasty). Compiled by Fang Hsüan-ling *et al.* in AD 644–6. Peking: Chung-hua Shu-chü, 1974.

Chü-yen Han-chien (Documents of the Han Dynasty on Wooden Slips from Edsin Gol). Ed. Lao Kan Taipei: The Institute of History and Philology Academia Sinica, 1957–60.

Chü-yen Han-chien chia-pien (Collection A of the Documents of the Han Dynasty of Wooden Slips from Edsin Gol). Ed. Institute of Archaeology, Chinese Academy of Sciences, Peking: K'e-hsueh Ch'u-pan-she, 1959.

Ch'üan Chin Wen (Comprehensive Collection of Essays from the Chin Dynasty). Included in *Ch'üan Shang-ku San-tai Ch'in Han San-kuo Liu-ch'ao Wen* (Comprehensive Collection of Essays from the Most Ancient Times to the Six Dynasties). Ed. Yen K'o-chün (1762–1843). Photolithograph 1930.

Ch'üan Hou-Han Wen (Comprehensive Collection of Essays from the Later Han Dynasty). Ibid.

Fa-hsien (*c.* AD 337–422). *Kao-seng Fa-hsien Chuan* (Autobiography of Fa-hsien). Tripitaka, vol. 51, 857–66. Trans. & ed. James Legge, New York: Paragon Book; trans. H. A. Giles, Cambridge University Press, 1923.

Fa-hua-ching Chuan-chi (Biography of the Lotus Sutra). Hui-hsiang (T'ang Dynasty). HTC, vol. 134, 336–86.

Fan, Shou-ming. *Hsün-yüan Chin-shih-tzu Pa-wei* (Postscripts of Inscriptions on Metal and Stone in Hsun-yuan Collection). Included in SSTS.

Fo-shou A-mi-t'o Ching (Amitabha Sutra). Trans. into Chinese by Kumarajiva (AD 344–413). Tripitaka, vol. 12, 346–8.

Fo-shuo Wu-liang Ch'ing-ching P'ing-teng-chüeh Ching (Amitabha Sutra). Trans. into Chinese by Chih-lou Chia-ch'ien in Loyang (AD 168–88). Tripitaka, vol. 12, 279–300.

Fo-shuo Wu-liang-shou Ching (Amitabha Sutra). Trans. into Chinese by K'ang Seng-kai (Wei Dynasty). Tripitaka, vol. 12, 265–79.

Han-shu (History of the Former Han Dynasty). Compiled by Pan Ku (AD 398–445). Peking: Chug-hua Shu-chü, 1965.

Hsi-ching Tsa-chi (Anecdotes of the West Capital). Compiled by Ke Hung (AD 284–364). Included in *Han-Wei Ts'ung-shu* (Collection of Essays of The Han and the Wei Times), ed. by Ch'eng Jung (Ming Dynasty). Taipei: Hsin-hsing Shu-chü, 1959.

Hsi-ho Chi (Record of Hsi-ho Region). Compiled by Yü Kuei (Eastern Chin Dynasty). Ed. Chang Shu (Ch'ing Dynasty). Vol. 3181 of *Ts'ung-shu Chi-ch'eng Ch'u-pien*, Shanghai: Commercial Press, 1936.

Hsin-T'ang shu (A History of the T'ang Dynasty). Compiled by Ou-yang Hsiu *et al.* in 1058. Peking: Chung-hua Shu-chü, 1975.

Hsü Kao-seng Chuan (Continuation to the Biographies of Famous Buddhist Monks). Compiled by Tao-hsüan (AD 596–667). Tripitaka, vol. 50, 425–707.

Hsü-tsang-ching (Continuation to the Buddhist Tripitaka). Hong Kong: The Hong Kong Committee on the Photographic Publication of a Continuation to the Buddhist Tripitaka, 1970.

Hsüan-tsang (AD 602–64). *Ta-T'ang Hsi-yü Chi* (Buddhist Records of the Western World). Tripitaka vol. 51, 867–974. Trans. into English by Samuel Beal, London: Kegan Paul, Trench, Trubner & Co., 1906.

Hu, P'in-chih. *Shan-yu Shih-k'o Ts'ung-pien* (Collection of Inscriptions from Shansi Province). Included in SSTS.

Kao-seng Chuan (Biographies of Famous Buddhist Monks). Compiled by Hui-chiao, Liang Dynasty (AD 502–57). Tripitaka, vol. 50, 322–423.

Ku-chin Feng-yao (Folklore from Ancient Times to the Present). Compiled by Yang Shen (AD 1488–1559). Vol. 2988 of *Ts'ung-shu Chi-ch'eng Ch'u-pien*. Shanghai: Commercial Press, 1936.

Kuang Hung-ming-chi. Ed. Tao-hsüan (AD 596–667). Tripitaka, vol. 52, 97–361.

Liang-chou Chi (Records of Liang-chou). Compiled by Tuan Kuei-lung (Northern Liang AD 397–439). Ed. Chang Shu (Ch'ing Dynasty). Vol. 3181 of *Ts'ung-shu Chi-ch'eng Ch'u-pien*, Shanghai: Commercial press, 1936.

Liang-tu Fu (On the Two Capitals). Pan Ku (AD 32–92). Included in *Ch'uan Hou-Han Wen*32–92). Included in *Ch'uan Hou-Han Wen*, 24/1b-9a.

Lu Tseng-hsiang (Ch'ing Dynasty). *Pa-ch'iung-shih Chin-shih Pu-cheng* (Supplement of Inscriptions from Pa-ch'iung-shih). Included in *SSTS*.

Miao-fa lien-hua Ching (The Lotus Sutra). Translated into Chinese by Kumarajiva (AD 344–413). Tripitaka, vol. 9, 1–63.

Pao-p'u-tze Nei-p'ien. Compiled by Ko Hung (AD 284–364). Ed. & annot. by Wang Ming. Peking: Chung-hua Shu-chu, 1980.

Pei-Ch'i-shu (History of the Northern Ch'i). Compiled by Li Pai-yao in AD 636. Peking: Chung-hua Shu-chü, 1972.

Pei-shih (History of the Northern Dynasties). Compiled by Li Yen-shou (T'ang Dynasty). Peking: Chung-hua Shu-chü, 1974.

Pien-cheng-lun. Fa-lin (T'ang Dynasty). Tripitaka, vol. 52, 489–550.

San-fu Huang-t'u (A Description of San-fu Region). Anonymous author of the Southern and Northern Dynasties. One of the *Ssu-pu-ts'ung-k'an San-pien*, Shanghai: Commercial Press, 1935.

San-kuo-chih (History of the Three Kingdoms). Ch'en shou (AD 233–97). Commentary by P'ei Sung-chih (AD 372–451). Peking: Chung-hua Shu-chü, 1959.

San-tu-fu (On the Three Capitals). Tso Ssu (*c.* AD 250–305). *Ch'uan-Chin Wen*, 74/11a-17a.

Seng-chih-lü (Monastic Law). Trans. into Chinese by Fa-hsien (AD 337–442). Tripitaka, vol. 22, 227–549.

Shih-chi (The History). Compiled by Ssu-ma Ch'ien in *c.* 104–91

BC. Peking: Chung-hua Shu-chü, 1959.

Shih-i-chi (Anecdotes). Compiled by Wang Chia (*c.* AD ? –390). Included in *Han Wei T'sung-shu*. Ed. Ch'eng Jung. Taipei: Hsin-hsing Shu-chü, 1959.

Shih-k'o Shih-liao Ts'ung-shu (Collection of Inscriptions Bearing on History). Ed. Yen Keng-wang. Taipei: I-wen-yin-shu-kuan, 1966.

Shih-shou Hsin-yü. Compiled by Liu I-ch'ing (AD 403–444). Ed. Yang Yung. Kowloon: Hong Kong Ta-chung Shu-chü, 1969.

Shih-sung-lü (Monastic Law in Ten Chapters). Trans. into Chinese by Fu-jo To-lo & Kumarajiva (AD 344–413). Tripitaka, vol. 23, 1–470.

Shu-i-chi (Record of Strange Things). Compiled by Jen Fang (AD 460–508). Included in *Han Wei Ts'ung-shu*, ed. by Ch'eng Jung, Taipei: Hsin-hsing Shu-chü, 1959.

Sui-shu (History of the Sui Dynasty). Compiled by Wei Cheng in AD 656. Peking: Chung-hua Shu-chü, 1973.

Taishō Shinshu Daizōkyō (Buddhist Tripitaka). Tokyo, 1924–8.

Tuan, Fang (Ch'ing Dynasty). *T'ao-chai Ts'ang-shih Chi* (Inscriptions from T'ao-chai). Included in *SSTS*.

Wang, Ch'ang (1725–1807). *Chin-shih Ts'ui-pien* (Selected Inscriptions). Included in *SSTS*.

Wang, Fu (*c.* AD 85–162). *Ch'ien-fu-lun*. Ssu-pu Ts'ung-k'an Ch'u-pien, vol. 29. Shanghai: Commercial Press, 1933.

Wang, Yün (Ch'ing Dynasty). *Shih-erh-yen-chai Chin-shih Kuo-yen Lu* (Inscriptions from Shih-erh-yen-chai). Included in *SSTS*.

Wei-mo-chi So-shuo Ching (Vimalakīrti Sūtra). Trans. into Chinese by Kumarajiva (AD 344–413). Tripitaka, vol. 14, 537–57.

Wei-shu (History of the Northern Wei). Compiled by Wei Shou in 551–4. Peking: Chung-hua Shu-chü, 1974.

Yang Hsüan-chih. *Loyang ch'ieh-lan Chi* (Memories of Holy Places in Loyang). Ed. Hsiang-yung, Shanghai: Ku-chi Ch'u-pan-she, 1978. Trans. W. J. F. Jenner, Oxford; Clarendon Press, 1981; Wang Yi-t'ung, Princeton: Princeton University Press, 1984.

Yen-t'ieh-lun (On the Government Monopoly of Salt and Iron). Huan K'uan, *c.* 81 BC. Shanghai: Po-ku-chai, 1864.

INDEX